Motorcycling
the
Right Way

Ken Condon

Motorcycling the Right Way

Project Team
Editor: Heather Russell-Revesz
Copy Editor: Joann Woy
Design: Mary Ann Kahn
Index: Judy Gordon

i-5 PUBLISHING, LLC™
Chief Executive Officer: Mark Harris
Chief Financial Officer: Nicole Fabian
Chief Content Officer: June Kikuchi
Chief Digital Officer: Jennifer Black-Glover
Chief Marketing Officer: Beth Freeman Reynolds
General Manager, i-5 Press: Christopher Reggio
Art Director, i-5 Press: Mary Ann Kahn
Senior Editor, i-5 Press: Amy Deputato
Production Director: Laurie Panaggio
Production Manager: Jessica Jaensch

Library of Congress Cataloging-in-Publication Data
Condon, Ken.
  Motorcycling the right way : do this, not that : lessons from behind the
handlebars / Ken Condon.
    pages cm
  Includes index.
  ISBN 978-1-62008-169-3
  1. Motorcycling. 2. Traffic safety. I. Title.
  TL440.5.C66 2015
  628.28'475--dc23
                    2015015221

This book has been published with the intent to provide accurate and authoritative information in regard to the subject matter within. While every precaution has been taken in the preparation of this book, the author and publisher expressly disclaim any responsibility for any errors, omissions, or adverse effects arising from the use or application of the information contained herein.

i-5 Publishing, LLC™
www.facebook.com/i5press
www.i5publishing.com

Printed and bound in China
15 16 17 18   1 3 5 7 9 8 6 4 2

Contents

What Is "Motorcycling the Right Way"?

There is no single "right" way to ride a motorcycle, but there sure are a lot of "wrong" ways to ride a motorcycle.

The title of this book, *Motorcycling the Right Way*, may imply that there is only one right way to ride a motorcycle, but that's not the case. There are many valid methods and philosophies about how to ride a motorcycle.

Riding the right way means using known and proven principles for effectively controlling your motorcycle and managing risk. Riding a motorcycle the right way involves more than simply acquiring a collection of information and skills. It takes a commitment to developing and nurturing the relationship between you, your bike, and the road. And, just like any worthwhile relationship, it takes effort to keep it vital, healthy, and fun. Think of me as your relationship counselor, here to help make that process easier. The rewards are safety, confidence, and enjoyment.

This book is full of information to help you learn to be a better and safer motorcycle rider. You'll find practical tips and techniques, as well as cautionary tales that illustrate ways to minimize the risk of riding. This book addresses all the facets of motorcycle riding … both the pleasant and the ugly, starting with the often-ignored topic of rider attitude and the sobering subject of risk. Are you motivated to take this ride? If so, let's top off our tanks and get rolling.

Who Am I?

It's smart to know who you are about to share a ride with, so let me introduce myself. My name is Ken Condon, and I'm a motorcycling junkie. For more than 40 years, I have been a commuter, tourer, off-road rider, track day instructor, road racer, drag racer, and plain old street rider who enjoys riding with friends and family.

It's embarrassing to admit, but I started riding as a way to enhance my adolescent manhood at a time when my skinny physique and sensitive demeanor did not exactly make me a chick magnet. It didn't take long to realize that riding a motorcycle wasn't going to make me any more interesting to girls. But, by then, the riding bug had bitten hard and there was no turning back.

As parents are known to say: "it's all fun and games until someone gets hurt." Well, I learned that truth after a couple of mishaps in high school brought the reality of the risks into plain view and threatened to spoil the fun. However, I was not to be deterred. I didn't like feeling vulnerable, so I started improving my riding skill and learning strategies for survival to reduce anxiety and prevent any future pain and repair expense.

This began my long journey toward being the best rider I can be. In addition to my 40 years on two wheels, I also have 20 years of experience as a certified Motorcycle Safety Foundation instructor/ coach, 15 years as a track day instructor, and 3 years as owner of "Riding in the Zone Motorcyclist Training," where I offer real-world, on-street, and on-racetrack rider coaching. I am also author of the book *Riding in the Zone: Advanced Techniques for Skillful Motorcycling* and have written more than 250 skills and safety articles for *Motorcycle Consumer News* (MCN). I am currently the author of the "Street Savvy" column for *Motorcyclist Magazine* and creator of the "Riding in the Zone" blog. I told you I'm a motorcycling junkie.

I've spent 15 years as a track day instructor.

Chapter 1

What Kind of Rider Are You?

While I may not know you personally, the fact that you ride a motorcycle means that you have a higher level of risk tolerance than the general public. And, if you're like most people, your loved ones may not be thrilled with your decision to ride a bike. You have to admit that riding a motorcycle is a little crazy. You obviously feel that the reward is worth the risk and that the risk is manageable, otherwise you wouldn't do it, right?

One thing I can't know about you is your risk awareness, risk tolerance, and how much you value skill development. Let's take a moment to consider various attitudes so we can get a better idea of what type of rider you really are.

Take a look at the "Lesson Learned" box on the next page, and consider the following questions: Which rider do you identify with? Are you like Skip who is skeptical about the benefits of advanced riding skill and knowledge? Do you think that seat time is enough and that close calls and anxiety are normal? Do you consider riders like Earl to be "safety geeks" who don't know how to have a good time? Perhaps you're more like Alice who is somewhat neutral about improving her riding skills. Maybe you

LESSON LEARNED

Who Are You?

Adept Al pulls into the crowded parking lot of a motorcycle café, finds a spot to park his bike, and then makes his way into the café to order an espresso. Al turns to find a seat, but all of the tables are full, except one. He walks over to a table with an empty chair that is occupied by three other riders and asks if he can sit. They nod. Al introduces himself and they do the same. Al learns that Skip, Alice, and Earl have just met for the first time today. Alice gets Al up to speed on their conversation, which involves something Earl learned at an advanced riding school the day before. Earl continues explaining what he learned about cornering and how shifting body weight plays only a supporting role in getting a motorcycle to lean and turn. Earl goes into further detail about how countersteering works and how chassis geometry and tire profiles affect direction control.

Al keeps silent as Earl continues. Al has taken several safety classes, including a few track-oriented courses, and has several motorcycle publications in his personal library so none of this information is new to him. He finds it interesting how each participant is reacting to Earl's monologue and his enthusiasm about this new knowledge. Alice is

identify more with Earl or Al who discovered the value of advanced training. If so, then congratulations. You're one of the riders on the road who understand that well-developed skills make motorcycle riding more fun.

No matter the type of rider you are, you surely want riding to include zero pain. But is it really possible to make riding safer without diminishing enjoyment? Thankfully, the answer is "Yes!" But it takes effort. All motorcycle riders need to develop advanced skills, turn them into habits, and then practice to keep these skills sharp. Let's meet two more imaginary riders named Alan and Oliver and see how their differing attitudes affect their commute to work.

Are You a Good Rider?

When asked, most people think they are a good rider. But what is a good rider? Is it

someone who displays impressive control skills on the racetrack or in the canyons or can do a lengthy standup wheelie? Is it someone who can maneuver an 800-pound (363-kg) motorcycle within tight confines? Certainly, these riders deserve to be recognized for their abilities. However, when it comes to describing a "good" motorcyclist, we must place the ability to make it home every day at the top of the list.

No matter how good a rider you think you are, it's likely that you have at least a few bad habits and attitudes. Poor habits and dangerous perceptions can develop over time without you knowing it. A lot of riders think that seat time is the answer to being a better rider. But experience alone does not make you a good rider. It takes knowledge and purposeful practice to become as good as you think you are.

listening and asking questions, but is restless. Skip is also listening, but seems tense with crossed arms and a scowl on his face.

When Earl finishes, Skip asks why he is so interested in the details of riding. Alice perks up to hear Earl's response. Earl explains that he loves learning all about motorcycling and its challenging opportunities. Alice acknowledges that she also enjoys learning about motorcycling, but is often frustrated because she can't seem to apply the information to her everyday riding or tries a new technique that doesn't seem to work right away. Skip shrugs off both their statements and proclaims that he has been riding for years and he never gives his riding much thought. He says that seat time is all someone needs to ride better.

This is when Al chimes in. He asks Skip if he has ever been cut off by a driver in traffic or experienced panic from riding too fast into a curve. Skip admits that both of those things happened to him just last week and then proceeds to rant about the blind jerk who pulled out in front of him and how the corners on twisty roads should be better marked. After Skip is done, Al points out that he used to experience those problems but hasn't for quite some time due in large part to advanced knowledge and training. Skip rebuts by saying that Al is just lucky and that all riders experience those problems. Alice agrees, saying that she has been to the MSF courses and still has anxiety in traffic and with some corners. Al points out to Alice that it takes regular practice to learn a new technique and gain confidence.

Find out what kind of rider you really are.

LESSON LEARNED

Risky Attitudes

Both Alan and Oliver commute to work through a mix of neighborhood streets and busy arterials. Where they differ is in their attitude toward risk. Alan rides with "eyes in the back of his head," scanning for any signs of intruders or road surface hazards. He knows that the best way to avoid a crash is to spot hazards early, which allows abundant time and space for him to respond if a driver were to cross his path.

Oliver is less concerned. He assumes that other drivers are going to see him and follow the rules of the road—and, in most cases, they do. When something unexpected does occur, Oliver deals with the problem with quick reactions and his ability to skillfully maneuver his motorcycle. This casual attitude works most of the time, but it has its cost; Oliver experiences more close calls, which wear on his riding enjoyment.

One day, both riders encounter a similar situation on the way to work where an oncoming driver turns left across their lane. Because Alan has trained himself to spot subtle clues that alert him of danger, he recognizes that the car is about to turn. The clues Alan notices are the driver turning his head and moving his arm to rotate the steering wheel. Because Alan recognized the problem early and then covered the brakes, he avoids a collision with many feet (m) to spare.

Oliver experiences the same scenario, but, unlike Alan, he isn't looking for clues. The first sign Oliver notices that the driver is turning is the car's front bumper entering his lane. Oliver has little time to react, and, because he is not covering his brakes in preparation for such an encounter, his stopping distance is increased. Fortunately, Oliver's excellent braking skill allows him to miss the car by mere inches (cm).

Because of their different approaches to risk management, Alan and Oliver's perception of the commute differs greatly. When both riders finally get to work, they are each greeted by a coworker who asks, "How was the ride this morning?" Alan doesn't even think to mention the invading car and answers, "Fantastic." Oliver's response was quite different: "It would have been great except for the idiot who almost killed me." Oliver continues bending his coworker's ear about the close call and how drivers really have to pay better attention.

WHAT'S THE LESSON?

Even though both riders experienced the same situation, Alan's attitude toward risk management rendered the potentially deadly situation rather mundane, whereas Oliver's lackadaisical attitude and lack of mental preparation led to a near accident. In addition, Alan's attitude toward risk allows him to ride with less anxiety. Oliver, on the other hand, becomes more and more anxious with each close call he experiences.

Riding with "eyes in the back of your head" through busy streets is a sign of a good rider.

Start by opening to the idea that you don't know all you need to know and evaluate your personal strengths and weaknesses. Don't allow yourself to brush off incidents as an insignificant misstep that is quickly forgotten. Even small mistakes can be a sign that you need a bit more work.

Take some time to evaluate your current habits and assess whether the beliefs and unconscious attitudes you have may be increasing your risk and decreasing your enjoyment. Think back on a recent close call involving a vehicle crossing into your right of way. Suspend any blame for the moment and put yourself in the seat of the driver who pulled into your path. The vast majority of drivers do not wish to cause an accident. So what made him or her think it was okay to proceed? The answer is that the driver either didn't see you, or saw you but did not accurately judge your speed and distance. Ask yourself what you could have done to help the situation. I bet there was at least one action you could have taken to reduce the hazard.

We All Make Mistakes

Why is it that even "good" riders make mistakes? The real reason is that humans aren't perfect, and, no matter how hard you try, mistakes will be made. Fortunately, with self-awareness, we can minimize the number of mistakes we make.

Often, mistakes are the result of weak concentration, faulty perception, poor judgment, or lousy execution. Other times, we make mistakes because of a bad decision, which is often followed by immediate regret. When this occurs, the smart riders asks what was the driving force behind the error.

The point is to increase your awareness of the types of mistakes you typically make. Do you space out and allow yourself to tailgate or enter turns too fast? Are you prone to overconfidence that leads to risky behavior? Self-awareness and vigilance can reduce the likelihood of making a mistake that you could regret for the rest of your life.

The Good Rider Pledge

There is a technique some schools and parents use to help manage behavior in youngsters that involves asking their teenage children to sign a pledge to not

Even riders who think they are good probably have a few bad habits.

drink alcohol, do drugs, or text while driving. The idea behind these pledges is to get the signer to check his or her conscience and think before acting in a possibly harmful way. The promise is made to a respected institution or a loved one, which pressures the signer to keep the promise.

I'm not a respected institution, nor am I your parent, but imagine your parent, children, and spouse asking you to sign a pledge to be the best rider possible. Would that be enough for you to seek opportunities that will lead to this goal? Use this pledge as is, or as a template to create your own. Then sign it in front of your loved ones as a promise to be as safe and skilled as possible. Remember, this not only benefits your loved ones who want you safe, it also makes riding more fun for you!

1. I will continually expand my knowledge of motorcycling safety and control through reading and by taking one formal safety/skills course per season.

2. I will resist complacency and never take my safety for granted.

3. I will practice my physical skills that include emergency braking and swerving to keep them sharp.

4. I will learn and practice mental strategies for managing traffic and other hazardous situations.

5. I will never ride while intoxicated or impaired in any way.

6. I will choose not to ride if my ability to manage hazards is compromised.

7. I will choose to only ride with others who share my commitment to safety.

Are You Really Ready to Roll?

Now that I've sobered you up with all this talk about how dangerous riding is, I wonder how many of you are reconsidering whether riding a motorcycle is such a good idea. Truth be told, riding a motorcycle is not a

LESSON LEARNED

Live & Learn

Lisa and Bill are on their way home after a relaxing ride aboard their middleweight cruisers. Lisa is following a few seconds behind Bill as they negotiate their way through an industrial section of town. There are several side streets and parking lot entrances on the right-hand side of the mostly straight road. Lisa notices a white van on the right waiting to enter the roadway. The van driver appears to see Bill because he passes without incident, but apparently doesn't see the second bike. Suddenly, the van darts out in front of Lisa. She instinctively swerves right, to pass behind the van. The bike misses the van's rear bumper by inches (cm), but Lisa can't stop quickly enough to avoid slamming into the curb. The van driver slows after finally seeing Lisa. But with a shrug he simply drives away.

Lisa is unhurt, but her front wheel is bent. Bill arrives moments later to ask if Lisa's okay. Lisa's reply is barely understandable through the shock and growing anger. Lisa begins to feel rage over the carelessness of the van driver.

The incident occupies much of Lisa's thoughts over the next few days. She tells any one who will listen of the idiot driver who almost killed her. Over time, her anger subsides, but other feelings emerge. Lisa realizes that she dreads getting back on her bike for fear of another close call—or worse. She even entertains giving up riding altogether. But motorcycling is an important part of her life. Lisa realizes that she must take the brunt of the responsibility for her safety even though responsibility is shared among all roadway users because the consequences of a crash are higher for motorcyclists. It is for this reason that Lisa finally evaluates her responsibility in the incident.

WHAT'S THE LESSON?

Focusing on blame can distract you from what you need to deal with in the moment so that you aren't prepared for the next hazard. Also, harboring anger sidetracks an opportunity to prevent a future crash if it blocks you from taking responsibility for mishaps and learning from them.

good idea unless you are committed to being the best rider you can be. I am not talking about becoming a professional-level rider—that's not practical and asks too much from most people. I'm talking about being the best rider *you* can be.

You owe it to yourself and your loved ones to learn to ride a motorcycle the "right" way.

Let me repeat that: *You owe it to yourself and your loved ones to learn to ride a motorcycle the "right" way.* This means increasing the repertoire of tools in your safety and skills toolbox and striving to keep these tools sharp through practice. It takes commitment, but it's not that hard…really.

Chapter 2

Risky Business: Accepting and Understanding Risk

We'd all like to believe that motorcycling is less risky than it is, but the fact is that riding is dangerous. Fortunately, you can develop a positive relationship with risk by recognizing your attitudes toward risk and then implementing measures to make riding safer and more fun.

Accepting Risk

I'm pretty sure you don't ride to be "safe." You ride because of the feeling you get from being on a motorcycle: the freedom, adventure, challenge, camaraderie…and FUN. If your primary goal is to be safe, you would find other things to do, like billiards, golf, or hiking.

There is an old saying that there are two types of riders—those who have crashed and those who have yet to crash. Unfortunately, there is some truth to this. I don't know any rider who hasn't experienced a simple tip-over in a parking lot during some point in his or her riding career. I also know several riders who have suffered significant crashes, and, tragically, some resulted in death.

operate their motorcycle in very risky ways, willing to accept more risk in exchange for opportunities to challenge their skills. These riders are more likely to contain their activity to remote roadways or closed courses where they can manage the risk.

Some riders are in denial about the risks and do stupid things that risk not only their own life, but also the lives of others. The most extreme examples of risk denial are those who underestimate the effects of riding under the influence of alcohol or deny the consequences of racing or stunting in traffic. This unrealistic optimism eventually leads to smashed bodywork and broken bones.

Most of us are somewhere in between the range of very cautious and reckless. We tolerate a level of risk that allows us to enjoy the challenge of riding, but self-preservation doesn't allow us to expose ourselves to excessive or unnecessary danger. Self-preservation is what encourages us to wear protective gear, ride slowly through intersections, and improve our riding skills.

Denial

Even though most riders have a hunch that a crash is possible, many riders don't believe it will happen to them. It's rather easy to see what a rider's beliefs are about risk by the type of riding gear they choose, their behavior in traffic, and their ability to ride within their limits. A rider who has a less-

Riders who are in denial about the risks often end up in dangerous—or deadly—situations.

Each rider's perception of risk contributes to the way he or she rides and decisions he or she makes. Some people perceive the risk as high, or are generally risk-adverse, and therefore ride cautiously to limit risk exposure. They might avoid riding at night or in heavy traffic, and they work hard to keep their accident-avoidance skills up-to-date. As a result, they encounter fewer close calls and are usually more relaxed than a rider who is less prepared.

Risk Tolerance

There are many riders who are perfectly aware of the risks but still choose to

than-realistic perception of risk may not wear protective riding gear.

Accept the possibility that a serious fall may be in your future and prepare for it by protecting yourself from injury. You will avoid a lot of pain and suffering if you are wearing protective gear at the moment when your skill or luck runs out. Hope for the best, but prepare for the worst!

The lesson is, if you think you are safe on a motorcycle, you're wrong! You could die on any ride you take. With this sobering knowledge, what are you going to do about it? I suggest you become the most skilled motorcycle rider you can be.

Defining Risk

An accurate measure of risk includes two factors:

- Your risk *exposure* and the *probability* of a mishap
- The *consequences* of being involved in a crash

The *probability* of a particular danger depends on your risk exposure and your attitude toward risk. Risk exposure is closely tied to your riding environment. For example, riding in pouring rain or in dense traffic is much riskier than riding on a dry day on a deserted road.

Your probability of a crash also depends on your willingness to take risks. For example, if you ride while intoxicated or use the public roadways as a racetrack, then you shouldn't be surprised if you're involved in a higher than average number of close calls and crashes.

The *consequences* of a crash vary depending on several factors, including how fast you are going at the time and whether you slide to a stop in an open area or hit a hard object. Some environments have a higher likelihood of injury. For example, a crash on the street often results in a catastrophic collision with a guardrail or curbing, but this terrible fate is much less likely if you crashed on a racetrack. Even

Some environments have a higher likelihood of injury.

Imagine a "Risk Meter" and "Anxiety Meter" to help gauge risk.

though racetrack speeds may be higher, the lack of roadside barriers decreases the likelihood of injury.

Measuring Risk

Risk perception is formed by our attitude, experiences, knowledge, and ability. People also measure risk and determine their risk acceptance by finding a balance between risk and reward. But sometimes it's tough to know how much risk we are exposed to. An imaginary tool you can use to measure risk is the "Risk Meter." Imagine a gauge mounted next to your speedometer that reacts to the amount of risk you are being exposed to. The needle moves toward "more risk" when you approach a busy intersection or when you approach a decreasing radius curve, and then eases back toward "less risk" when danger passes.

Another instrument you should learn to utilize is your "Anxiety Meter." This gauge responds to your subconscious as it tells you when you are entering a high-risk situation or approaching the limits of your

comfort zone. This usually occurs when you cannot process information quickly enough. One easy way to combat this problem is to always ride at speeds that allow you to calmly respond to any change in your traffic or cornering situation.

About Crashing

It doesn't matter how old or young you are, what type of motorcycle you ride, or where you ride, we all agree that one of the worst things that can happen to you on a motorcycle is for you to crash. Notice that I am not using the word "accident" when describing a mishap. Nobody wants to crash, so technically all mishaps are accidents, but the term "accident" suggests that it was an act of God or a random incident that happens for no reason. Thinking that way will just cause you to get into more "accidents" by not taking responsibility for the incident and therefore learning nothing from the experience.

A crash is almost always caused by someone screwing up. Unfortunately, we cannot expect human beings to be perfect all the time. Whether a crash is the result of another driver's poor judgment or from rider error, the fact is that most incidents can been prevented. I know what you're saying —"it was the other guy's fault!" Maybe. But where does that get you? Your job is to prevent the crashes from happening in the first place.

How Crashes Happen

Every Monday morning, I find myself scanning the news for reports of motorcycle accidents from the past weekend. It may be a rather morbid thing to do, but these reports can provide a glimpse into why motorcyclists crash. Many serious crashes I read about involve another driver, but about half of all fatal crashes are single-vehicle incidents where the rider fails to negotiate a curve.

Too often, the primary cause of crashes is the motorcyclist riding beyond his or her skill level and the limits of the environment. One news report I read described a rider who had collided with a car going in the opposite direction on a lightly traveled scenic road. I am familiar with the corner where the incident took place. It isn't a particularly challenging corner, but witnesses said he had been riding at excessive speed before he crossed the centerline and hit the car head on. It also mentioned that he had been riding with some other motorcyclists who came upon the scene moments after it happened. The

rider died instantly, and the innocent driver was seriously injured and flown out by helicopter.

So, what happened? The news report was vague, so we can't know for sure, but we can imagine that the rider was high on adrenaline, riding with fast friends and pushing his limits. I imagine him drifting wide, panic causing him to grab the brakes and stand the bike upright as his eyes lock on the approaching car.

Crashes like this are avoidable. So why do riders get themselves into such serious trouble? It's usually because riders want to enjoy the feeling of cornering fast, but have an optimistic and inaccurate perception of the risks and their own ability. Optimistic riders are more likely to charge into a blind

corner, willing to gamble that they can handle any situation that may occur. They may also trust that all other road users will behave just as they're supposed to, stopping at traffic lights, changing lanes predictably, and yielding to the right of way. But optimism is a fool's friend in this case.

Identifying a potential hazard is a large part of the battle, but to avoid a collision or crash also requires an avoidance action, such as braking, turning, or swerving. Unfortunately, many riders act inappropriately or fail to act at all. The *Motorcycle Accidents in Depth Study* (MAIDS) report shows that 69.8% of riders attempted some form of collision avoidance before the impact, but that a significant number of riders who attempted no avoiding action. This reaction failure may

Most riders facing a hazard will attempt an avoidance maneuver, but many choose the wrong one or fail to perform well enough.

be because of "panic-freeze" or because there simply was no time to complete the action.

Even when riders have the ability and the time to perform an evasive maneuver, it doesn't mean they will perform well. According to MAIDS, about 20% of riders end up crashing because of a loss of control while attempting an evasive maneuver. The most common example is when a rider over-brakes, skids, and collides with a car, even though the rider may have had plenty of time to stop safely if he had applied the brakes properly and avoided skidding. Another example are riders who enter a turn too fast for their ability and instead of leaning more, stand the bike up and run off the road.

Most riders facing a hazard will attempt an avoidance maneuver, but many choose the wrong one or fail to perform well enough. One example is choosing to swerve instead of brake. An unsuccessful swerve without any significant reduction in speed can be disastrous as the rider collides full-speed into the car or obstacle. Slowing before swerving is an option, but this requires more time and there is a significant risk of losing traction if you swerve and brake at the same time.

There are many reasons why crashes occur. I recommend you take a look at the MAIDS findings for yourself (www.maids-study. eu). You will gain an understanding of crash causation so that you can develop strategies that may help you to beat the odds.

Handling the Aftermath

Bummer! You fell down today. Your bike is heavily damaged, and you will soon be getting an emergency department bill in

RIDING TERM

POST-TRAUMATIC STRESS DISORDER

(PTSD)

Survivors of motorcycle crashes often experience this disorder, which includes feelings of lingering anxiety and ongoing memories of the incident.

the mail. You'll be dealing with insurance companies for months trying to sort out the financial mess. The bike can be fixed or replaced, and your body will heal, but what about the condition of your emotions and mind?

Depending on the severity of the mishap, you may have difficulty trying to comprehend what happened. After a crash, many riders question their perception of safety and continue to suffer because they don't know how to repair the mental damage. This trauma can lead to the person choosing to stop riding if it becomes too stressful for both the rider and his or her family.

PTSD

When a person is involved in a serious crash, there can be significant psychological trauma. Many survivors of motor-vehicle crashes suffer post-traumatic stress disorder (PTSD), which can include lingering anxiety that can easily retrigger feelings that occurred at the moment of the crash. We often associate PTSD with exposure to combat conditions, but the National Institutes of Health report that motor vehicle crashes are one of the leading causes of PTSD.

The American Academy of Family Physicians lists several common reactions to being involved in a crash:

- Shock
- Trouble believing the incident really happened
- Anger
- Nervousness or worry
- Feeling uneasy or scared
- Guilt

It's also common to keep going over the incident in your mind.

Not everyone experiences significant emotional trauma, but some people are more vulnerable than others. The Mayo Clinic lists several factors that may make someone susceptible to PTSD:

- Your inherited mental health risks, such as an increased risk of anxiety and depression
- Your life experiences, including the amount and severity of trauma you've gone through since early childhood
- The inherited aspects of your personality—often called your temperament
- The way your brain regulates the chemicals and hormones your body releases in response to stress.

The American Academy of Family Physicians also mentions several reactions that may indicate the need to seek help:

- An ongoing, general feeling of uneasiness
- Problems driving or riding in vehicles
- Not wanting to have medical tests or procedures
- Overreactions or being overly worried or angry
- Nightmares or trouble sleeping

- A feeling like you're not connected to other events or other people
- Ongoing memories of the accident that you can't stop

One technique that some psychologists and therapists use to treat PTSD is called *eye movement desensitization reprocessing* (EMDR). EMDR is a technique whose effectiveness I can attest to after a health scare resulted in anxiety that affected my day-to-day life. EMDR basically reprograms your cognitive mechanisms to reduce the lingering effects of trauma. Consult a professional to see whether EMDR is something that may help you or a loved on to overcome PTSD.

Debrief and Evaluate

Whether you are involved in a tipover, a close call, or a crash, it is important to take the time to evaluate the situation so you might learn from it. A rider who does not ask "what happened?" is at risk of a repeat performance. Asking this basic question will help you understand how to avoid a similar situation in the future, and it might also help you overcome fear and apprehension.

First, determine the cause of the crash. Resist blaming others. Yes, the "other guy" may have played a significant role in the incident, but you can't directly control others' actions. You can, however, influence their behavior and prevent a crash. In a lot of situations, many factors are within your control: your speed, your lane position, how conspicuous your riding gear is, your ability to predict danger before it becomes critical. These are all ways for you to affect the outcome of a situation and feel less helpless.

Small Mishaps Can Feel Big

Sometimes even small incidents can be a big deal. The most common type of mishap in motorcycling is the relatively benign tipover, which rarely causes serious injury but is notorious for wreaking havoc on confidence.

I know several people who dread making tight U-turns, because of the fear of dropping their bike. Previous experience of a motorcycle falling to Earth can engrain anxiety to a point where simple parking lot maneuvers trigger almost paralyzing fear. Riders with low confidence at slow-speed maneuvering are easily spotted as they paddle-walk their bikes around parking lots, instead of maneuvering skillfully with their feet on the pegs.

Unfortunately, slow-speed maneuvers cannot be avoided. The good news is that learning to overcome the fear of slow-speed maneuvers is not too difficult. (Slow-speed maneuvering is discussed later in the book.)

Even a minor tipover can wreak havoc on a rider's confidence.

Chapter 3:

Managing Risk: How to Ride Smart and Dress for Crashes

U p until now, we've discussed the mental and psychological aspects of riding smart. We learned that a rider who has the tools to preempt hazardous situations is less likely to encounter many close calls and is more likely to avoid a crash.

With this foundation poured and hardened, we can now discuss practical methods for avoiding trouble, starting with areas where riders can fall victim to poor judgment and ineffective strategies. We'll then talk in detail about the importance of seeing and being seen.

Ride Smart

We may not ride to be safe, but this doesn't mean we want to end up in a wheelchair or a casket before our time. Here's a short list of consequences that should make you think about the importance of risk management:

1. **Pain**: Who likes pain? Not me. But pain is what you'll feel even with a minor crash. Protective gear can significantly reduce injury, but it's no substitute for riding well so that incidents don't happen in the first place.

2. **Financial Loss:** Lost time from work, medical bills, medications, insurance deductibles, bike repairs, gear replacement … the list of expenditures goes on and on. A simple failure on your part can cost you thousands. And don't even get me started on the costs of risking a DUI.

3. **Family:** Who do you think will be taking care of you when you get hurt? I don't know about you, but my family and friends have more important things to do with their time than to help me drink my dinner through a straw or even drive me back and forth to doctor appointments because I'm in a cast. And if you die, who do you think will suffer most? Not you, you're dead. It's your loved ones.

I point out the ugly truth to spark your motivation to advance your physical and mental skills, use good judgment, and develop keen survival strategies. Your family and wallet will both thank you for the effort made.

Recognize Limits

One of the easiest ways to stay out of trouble is to know your limits and always ride within them. Anxiety can help you discover your limits. It's a clear sign that you're riding over your head if you feel panicked.

Anxiety can help you discover your limits.

You may be saying, "I know my limits." Perhaps, but there are many variables that make it difficult to know exactly where the limits are, including an unfamiliar machine, a changing road surface, or complex riding situations. These can cause us to exceed the limits without knowing it, until it is too late.

For example, environmental conditions constantly change. A road that at one moment offers excellent grip can change suddenly with a light dusting of sand. Mood, fatigue, emotions, and hunger can also alter where the limits lie. Smart riders are continually evaluating the environment and their mental and physical condition so they stay ahead of trouble.

Mind Over Muscles

The first rule of avoiding crashes is to use good judgment and have effective strategies for avoiding hazards. The best riders rarely if ever need to use their finely honed physical skills to save them from a crash. Instead, they rely on accurately perceiving risk and predicting what other drivers are about to do. They spot hazards early, accurately evaluate their significance, and act appropriately to minimize the likelihood of a crash. These strategies minimize—or dare I say eliminate—the need for heroic action.

Often, a street riding crash is the result of a sequence of factors that fall into place like toppling dominoes. The best riders with the strongest mental skills can detect the often-subtle clues that begin the sequence and act quickly to halt the progression.

Someone told me a story of a young man on a sport bike that rammed into the back of a minivan at a stoplight. He careened out of

Managing risk means wearing protective gear.

control at an excessive rate of speed. The intersection was at the base of a hill where the rider couldn't see the van until it was too late. His youthful burst of adrenaline in a totally inappropriate location put him in the hospital with severe injuries.

It's easy to blame recklessness on youth, but bad judgment applies equally to older riders, like the 50-year-old man who didn't make a corner and hit a stone wall. Apparently, he simply made a bad judgment about the curve and didn't have the skills to make the bike turn at the speed he was traveling. The point is that nobody is immune. It takes constant diligence to keep exuberance at bay.

Dress for the Crash

Managing risk includes protecting yourself from injury by wearing protective gear. Many riders who are involved in relatively minor crashes end up with major injuries simply because they chose not to wear protection. Well-designed protective apparel will reduce skin abrasion and impact injury. This can mean riding home under your own

LESSON LEARNED

Wear Your Gear!

It's one of the first moderately warm days of the season, so you decide to go for a ride. You gained weight over the winter, and your riding jacket is a bit too snug for comfort, so you throw on your work jacket to keep away the cold. You live in a state that allows riders to choose whether or not to wear a helmet, and you often go without for the sense of freedom and the sensation of being completely immersed in the environment.

The air is cool, so you put a knit hat on to keep your head warm. You must navigate through a maze of intersections to get to the outskirts of town where the roads are more enjoyable. The intersection where you need to turn is just ahead. As you approach the crossroad, you see the green arrow turn to yellow for the left-hand turning lane, so you accelerate to avoid needing to stop. Just after you begin to lean into the turn, your tires slide out from underneath you and you land hard on the pavement.

You wake up later in a hospital bed with no recollection of what happened. You have a headache that rivals any pain you've felt before. You hit the call button to summon a nurse who comes in a few minutes later. You ask what is happening and she explains that you were in a motorcycle accident.

WHAT'S THE LESSON?

Your plan was to enjoy a leisurely spin out of town, but it soon turned into an expensive and painful event. What could have been a relatively minor incident ended up being a calamity because you chose not to wear a helmet. Your work jacket minimized other injuries, but the lack of head protection is what landed you in the hospital.

Your choice to beat the light caused you to miss seeing the surface hazards. You forgot about the dangers of accumulated fluids and sand left over from treating winter roads. Many months off a motorcycle dulled your ability to recognize hazards that are of little concern when driving a car but can be a big problem when piloting a two-wheeler.

Next time, make sure you are fully prepared for the challenges of operating a motorcycle and always wear full protective gear, just in case.

power after a minor fall rather than being transported in the back of an ambulance.

All The Gear All The Time (ATGATT)

There's an acronym floating around called ATGATT (All The Gear All The Time). The gear we are talking about includes a helmet, sturdy jacket, sturdy long pants, and full-coverage gloves and boots. By wearing ATGATT, you ensure that you are protected at the moment you need it most. Protective riding gear needs to be worn on every ride since you cannot possibly predict when a mishap will occur.

The good news is that motorcycle gear is better than ever in terms of style, comfort, and protection. Innovative features, such as modern waterproof and thermal liner systems and high-tech venting material, provide versatility. Most touring jackets now come with some sort of impact-absorbing armor in the elbows, shoulders, and knees for impact protection.

Another important piece of protection is a back protector. Rigid back protectors can prevent a sharp object, such as a footpeg, handlebar, or tree branch from doing serious damage. Back protectors are effective in shielding the spine and internal organs, as well as in distributing bone-crushing forces over a larger area. This type of force is common when landing on pavement after being flung skyward during a highside crash.

In the racing world, more and more competitors are choosing a higher level of protection not often used before, such as chest protectors, neck braces, and even airbag suits. These protective systems will become the norm as technologies improve and as top professionals begin to use them more often.

Comfort and Style

It may seem silly to don full gear when the thermometer rises above 90°F (32°C), but crashes happen whether it's 40°F (4°C) or 100°F (38°C) outside. You can bet that skin abrasion injuries are greater during the hottest days of the year when t-shirts and lightweight pants are the norm.

Fortunately, there are mesh jackets that provide decent protection while flowing a lot of air, and these jackets also feature sturdy material in vital places. The same manufacturers also offer riding pants for hot weather that can be worn over shorts

RIDING TERM

CE

Protective gear sold in Europe must conform to the "CE" standards for effectiveness in absorbing impact energy and resistance to abrasion.

or jeans while providing decent protection. And consider that sometimes it's just too hot to ride, so it may be best to leave the bike in the garage if the conditions are such that wearing decent protection risks hyperthermia.

The type of protective riding gear people wear is a personal choice that should be based on risk acceptance and awareness, but more often is based on style and peer pressure. It may be tempting to wear only what is fashionably acceptable by your peers even though it offers little protection. Fortunately, several helmet and riding apparel manufacturers sell protective gear that complements all styles.

Get Seen

Choosing a particular style of riding gear can help you be more visible, such as high-viz yellow or wearing a brightly colored reflective vest over your existing jacket. For the most conspicuity, buy gear with small add-on lights that mount either on a helmet or in the middle of a jacket's upper back. Most can be programmed for steady luminescence or strobe.

Don't want to look like a highway worker or a Christmas tree? Then choose a brightly colored jacket, like red. I know that most

In the racing world, competitors wear the highest level of protective gear.

riders will choose black over safety colors. There is no law against that choice, but just know that you won't be as visible to other drivers, especially in low-light environments.

Not Convinced?

Still on the fence about whether you want to spend money on good riding gear? Consider this: our body will succumb if there is an accumulation of several relatively minor injuries. That means that a serious case of road rash might be too much for your body to handle if it also has to deal with broken bones and a concussion. That's why protecting your body from even relatively minor injury can save your life.

And if you think you'll be okay without full protection because you're just riding around town at "slow" speeds, consider how you'd react if I asked you to go out into a parking lot in your shorts and tank top, run as fast as you can, and dive onto the pavement.

You'd likely tell me to get lost. Even if I offered you money, you'd likely walk away. Now, imagine how it would feel to fall while unprotected at 30 mph (48 kph)—not good.

No Panacea

We'd all love to think we can prevent death or serious injury simply by zipping on a sturdy jacket and strapping on the most expensive helmet we can afford. But the reality is that many deaths occur despite a rider wearing all the best gear. After all, elbow, knee, back, and shoulder armor is no match for a truck or tree. And no helmet made can withstand the impact of more than 300 G, which is a problem when a direct impact at normal speeds can easily exceed 500 G.

According to *Academic Emergency Medicine*, a human head will suffer brain damage 15.4% of the time if exposed to as little as 50 G. And neck and spine injuries are another serious problem that a helmet can't do much about. But don't even think about foregoing a helmet. A helmet provides protection to the most important part of your body, minimizes trauma (in most cases) to prevent traumatic brain injury, and prevents the rest of your injuries from killing you.

By all means, increase your visibility and protection. But don't be fooled into thinking that simply wearing bright clothing will save you from poor decisions. You need to be careful not to adopt a false sense of confidence because you feel less vulnerable. It's human nature to let your guard down when you don't feel threatened (that's why drivers in large vehicles seem less safety conscious). Sure, protective gear does make you less vulnerable to injury, but not enough to think that you can increase risk taking. A thinking adult realizes that protective gear is intended to prevent injury, not give permission to ride recklessly.

Learn to Look

Let's discuss the practical aspects of visibility—both yours and that of other drivers. Many riders don't realize the extent to which eyesight affects motorcycle control and rider confidence. The fact is that you can't manage risk and hazards if you can't first see them. Riders who train themselves to look well ahead don't experience anxiety nearly as often as "near-sighted" riders because they spot potential hazards early to avoid conflict. You will be amazed at how much more secure and in control you will feel if you strive to improve your information-gathering skills. Let's see how.

Look for Trouble

Visual acuity is much more complex than simply looking ahead. To determine whether you're headed for trouble, you must actively

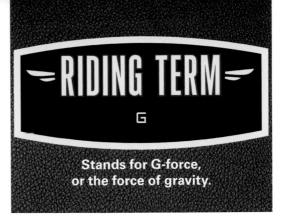

RIDING TERM

G

Stands for G-force, or the force of gravity.

search for hazards by keeping your eyes moving. Quickly scan left, right, and down at the road surface to spot problems. Your eyes should be in constant motion. Avoid fixating on any one object for more than a second. Also, scan your mirrors and check over your shoulder when changing lanes to identify hazards that might be hidden in your blind spots.

It's important to keep your eyes up so you can scan well ahead. Riders who scan only in the near distance are often surprised by obstacles or road characteristics that appear "out of nowhere." In contrast, riders who train themselves to keep their vision "up and out" are able to see hazards much earlier to allow ample time and space to respond. This alone will improve safety and allow a more relaxed and enjoyable ride.

Busy traffic environments or higher speeds require even more aggressive visual scanning. A leisurely rural cruise at the posted speed limit may permit relatively relaxed visual scanning. However, as your rate of speed increases, the time you have to process information becomes condensed as information approaches more rapidly.

Keeping your vision "high" not only helps you spot hazards early, it also positively affects perception of speed. When your eyes scan the distant horizon, the landscape

Busy traffic environments require aggressive visual scanning.

appears to pass by more slowly compared to looking down as the road rushes beneath your tires. A slower perceived rate of speed offers a sense of more time and space to react, therefore minimizing the effects of speed-induced anxiety.

Peripheral vision is as important for spotting hazards. A wide focal field allows you to identify clues about hazards from the side, such as movement that can indicate a car changing lanes or an animal darting from the weeds.

Visual Sense

You must develop a sixth sense about line of sight to ensure that you can see all potential hazards and so that others can see you. Get into the habit of recognizing subtle signs that should alert you to threats. Make a concerted effort to scan the landscape and roadway for anything that can turn into a hazard, such as a reflection on the windshield of a car that is rolling toward you. Ask yourself whether the driver sees you and what the are chances that he will accelerate in front of you. What clues tell you that you are safe, and what clues can you recognize that indicate a threat? Evaluate each clue to determine whether you can reliably read what is being communicated. For instance, direct eye contact with the driver may indicate that he sees you, but don't count on it!

Look well ahead for flashing reflections through vegetation or moving shadows on the road surface that may indicate a nearby vehicle that is on the move. Also, look at the driver's arms and head for movement that could indicate that he or she is about to either accelerate or steer into your lane. Another tip to help detect early movement is to monitor the top of the front tire of a stationary vehicle wanting to enter the road from the side. As soon as the vehicle rolls, you'll know it.

Even though the majority of hazards appear in front, don't forget to frequently scan your mirrors, especially when stopped. And don't forget to use peripheral vision and make quick, efficient head checks over your shoulder to spot trouble. (We will cover blind spots a bit later.)

Looking versus Seeing

We *look* whenever our eyes are open, but that doesn't mean we *see* what's in front of us. It's not unusual for a driver to appear to look directly at a rider just before pulling into his or her path. Perhaps the driver was daydreaming, had poor eyesight, or was focusing on something else behind the rider. Whatever the reason, the driver *looked* but did not *see*.

To understand how the brain processes visual information, it's helpful to understand the difference between *looking*, *seeing*, and *perceiving*. You *look* in the direction where dangers appear, *see* that potential hazards are present, and *perceive* whether the hazard poses enough danger to warrant evasive action. *Looking* is mostly a mechanical activity, and *seeing* is what happens when an object gets your attention. *Visual perception* is what causes your brain to react to keep you safe.

Following Distance

One factor that can prevent you from seeing hazards is riding too close behind other cars and trucks. Riders who follow too closely often find themselves dealing with hazards that appear "suddenly" and often too late to prevent a crash.

Ample following distance provides a wider angle of view to see past the vehicle and allows other drivers to see you. One easy way to determine an appropriate following distance is to use the 2-second method. As soon as the vehicle ahead passes a fixed roadside object, begin counting "one-thousand-one, one-thousand-two." You should complete your count before your front tire reaches the same object. It's important to note that 2 seconds is considered a *minimum* following distance. More space is required if you're a new rider, if the surface is slippery, or if you're riding in a high-risk environment.

Lane Position to See

As motorcyclists, we have the option of riding in the left, center, or right portion of our lane. This gives you the ability to place your bike where you can see farther ahead and where other drivers can see you. Exactly what is the best lane position? In most situations, riding left of the center of your lane makes the most sense. This position allows you to see past the vehicle ahead and gives you a good angle of view of the oncoming lane.

Lane position needs to change continually for optimum visibility. One situation that may require a change in lane position is when you see a waiting driver on a side street to your right who will not see you if you stay in the center or left lane position. In this case, it makes sense to move to the right portion of your lane until you are confident that the driver sees you, and then move away from the car.

Target Fixation

When humans are faced with a threatening situation, we instinctively look at the hazard, which is a response called *target fixation*. The problem is that looking at a hazard tends to direct us toward the danger, which is why it's important to consciously look away from the hazard and focus on a safe escape route. In other words, *focus on the solution, not the problem.*

A common scenario that leads to target fixation is entering a corner too fast. Riders who are anxious about not making a curve will fix their attention on where they are afraid to go. The results are predictable, with the motorcycle veering toward the guardrail or the edge of the road. The solution is to look toward the corner exit and lean the motorcycle as much as necessary to stay in your lane.

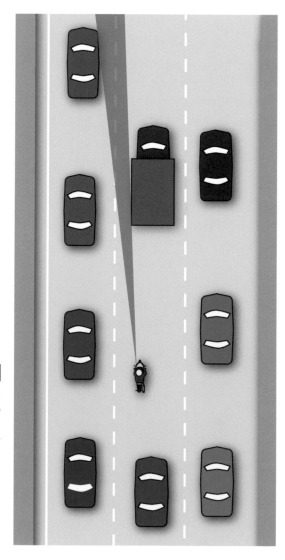

RIDING TERM
TARGET FIXATION

When an individual becomes overly focused on a single object that their ability to avoid it diminishes.

Another common situation that is made worse by target fixation is when a vehicle performs a threatening maneuver. The rider stares at the car and heads right for it even though he or she may have been able to steer around it.

You may not have thought about it, but traffic traveling in the same direction can also present the chance for target fixation. If you fix much of your vision and attention on the car ahead, you risk being lead in a direction you don't want to go. Look past vehicles you are following to maintain your path.

Vision Blockers

Some factors hinder vision, including solar glare, incorrect eye protection, nighttime riding, and impairment caused by aging, alcohol, drugs, or emotional distraction.

Solar glare is caused by the low angle of the sun and occurs in the morning and late afternoon. Sunglasses and tinted shields work to minimize the effects of solar glare but do not completely solve the problem. Some helmets have an integrated pull-down tinted shield that is always available when needed. Open-faced and dual-sport hybrid helmets often include integrated sun visors, which can be a real help in combating solar glare. Full-faced helmets lack the option of a visor for blocking the sun, but I've had some success by simply putting a strip of electrical tape across the top of my shield.

Nighttime visibility is always a challenge. Even with good headlights and clear eye protection, you must accept that you will not be able to see hazards as readily as in the daytime. This means that you must ride at reduced speeds.

There are times when your ability to identify hazards is significantly compromised, such as when riding in rain or fog or when riding impaired. Of particular concern is the use of alcohol or drugs. Not only is this illegal, but it will significantly affect your visual acuity. Impairment from emotional distraction is also a problem because it can cause your mind to fixate on what's bothering you and not on what is right in front of you.

Cornering Vision

The benefits of looking ahead are obvious when it comes to dodging hazards and other roadway users, but your eyes also play a critical role in cornering. Your vision is used for judging proper corner entry speed, as well as in being able to spot hazards around a corner. These hazards include surface debris, such sand, gravel, or diesel fuel, or the road itself if the curve tightens unexpectedly or drops downhill suddenly. The best riders can "read" the characteristics of an upcoming corner.

Visual Timing

Before you decide when to initiate lean, you need to know where you will actually begin your turn and how quickly you must get the bike leaned. This critical information comes from looking at the corner characteristics, such as apparent radius and surface quality. Once you get the information you need,

you can then make those decisions with confidence.

Ideally, you will perform a single steering input to precisely carve into the turn. And you should plan to countersteer only after you've identified your next visual target. So, look first, and then turn. Wait to see where you want the bike to go, and then lean the bike quickly or slowly as needed to achieve your goal.

Corner Positioning

Cornering lines are an important and often underutilized technique for increasing your angle of view to identify mid-corner hazards. The typical cornering line consists of an entry that is near the outside of the lane, heads toward the inside near the middle of the turn, and drifts outside at the exit. This "outside-inside-outside" path gives a better look into the curve.

There are many hazards that can appear mid-corner. Road debris, slippery spills, and broken pavement all threaten to increase the risk of a crash. These types of hazards and unexpected changes in corner radius can be thwarted by an early look through the turn. Cornering lines are effective in increasing sight distance, but you will still encounter corners that are obscured by vegetation or some other roadside feature. This is why it is important to choose a conservative entry speed that keeps plenty of lean angle and traction in reserve. Savvy riders scan aggressively for information and choose cornering lines that help them get the best angle of view possible. (Cornering lines are discussed fully in a later chapter.)

Visual Direction Control

Seeing hazards is important for staying safe,

but your eyes also play a significant role in motorcycle control and confidence. You may have heard the phrase, "you go where you look." By pointing your eyes toward the corner exit, you help direct the motorcycle on the desired path. Riders who discover the power of "looking where they want to go" make great leaps in motorcycle control.

You may be thinking, "I already look ahead." Perhaps; but there is a difference between looking ahead in the mid-distance and *really* looking ahead all the way through the turn, toward the corner exit. On your next ride, try lengthening your vision to a point in the distance that is at least 4 seconds ahead. You'll find that looking deeper into corners will help you to enjoy the full benefits of visual direction control.

Part of the reason that visual direction control can increase confidence is because it puts your eyes and mind ahead of the situation and prepares you for what is about to happen. In contrast, near-distance scanning often leads to anxiety because you don't have the time to process what is about to happen. This leaves you less prepared for corner hazards and less able to select the proper lean angle and speed to complete the turn skillfully.

Even though you want to look well ahead, you will also need to get a closer look at possible road surface hazards as they approach. This means using quick downward glances but, once you've gotten a look at the possible problem, returning your eyes to the corner exit.

An effective way to look through a turn is to "ratchet" your eyes as you round the corner, looking for visual clues about road surface condition, camber, turn radius, and the like. Your eyes register the information early and signal that it is either okay to proceed at the given speed and path or alert you to the need to adjust speed or direction to manage a hazard or to stay in your lane.

Don't be surprised if looking far ahead is disorienting at first, but with practice it will become a natural part of your riding skill set. If you find yourself reverting back to looking in the near-distance, you may be experiencing anxiety—probably because you are riding a bit too fast for your comfort level. In this case, slow down to re-establish your wider vision and restore confidence.

Visual direction control helps you go where you want to go, but it is only one component of the turning process. Looking where you want to go simply makes the cornering process easier.

Visual Targets

To improve your visual precision, you must actively identify "visual targets" that can help you to direct your motorcycle. On the racetrack, visual targets are easy to spot. They often include bright cones at the entry, apex, and exit of the corner. Other visual targets might include pavement patches or cracks, curbing, and other trackside features. These targets help place the rider and bike in the preferred location, lap after lap.

On the street, visual targets help determine which way the road goes and how tight the radius is. Unfortunately, visual targets aren't as obvious here, which makes the characteristics of each approaching corner not as easily identified.

One helpful visual target is the road edge and painted road lines and how they visually converge into the distance. Essentially, when the lines converge in the near distance, the corner radius is tightening (decreasing) or the surface is sloping away, off-camber. If the lines converge in the far distance, then this indicates that the curve is straightening and/or is banked. There is a wide variation in how obviously the lines converge and what this means in terms of road characteristics. Even though this is an imperfect method, it can be a very powerful tool for "reading the road" so you can accurately adjust your cornering line

and entry speed. For the greatest margin of safety, enter unfamiliar turns more slowly.

Be Seen

The most common statement spoken by drivers involved in a motorcycle collision is "I didn't see him." This is because motorcycles are smaller in size and therefore command a much less visual impact compared to every other vehicle on the road. This small physical size means that drivers may subconsciously look past the motorcycle without even seeing it. Often, this is because they do not perceive the relatively tiny object as a threat and instead focus on more "important" vehicles.

Another reason why motorcyclists are not easily seen in traffic is because motorcycles can get lost behind other vehicles, inside blind spots, and hidden by roadside objects. This is the area where riders have the most

One helpful visual target is the road edge and painted road lines and how they visually converge into the distance.

RIDING TERM
CHANGE BLINDNESS

Situations when someone fails to notice rather obvious changes in the environment.

control. It is imperative that you have a sixth sense about how well you are seen by other drivers. You should be constantly evaluating your line of sight to determine whether you may be hidden from view.

It's easy to blame a driver who cuts you off for being inattentive, but maybe you need to share some of the blame. Perhaps you weren't using the best lane position to help the driver identify your presence. Or maybe you weren't paying attention to how the

driver was blinded by solar glare, or you were wearing inconspicuous riding gear without any reflective material. The point is that there is plenty you can do to be more visible.

In Plain Sight

I've heard many stories of drivers cutting riders off even though the driver was looking directly at them. What would cause someone to proceed even if the rider was in plain sight? Perhaps the driver was daydreaming, has poor eyesight, or was focusing on something else behind the rider. Whatever the reason, the driver *looked* but did not *see*.

One reason people don't see what they are looking at involves human perception. It's widely known that humans are influenced by what they believe to be true, even if all the evidence before them points to the contrary. One example is the driver who pulls out in front of a motorcycle rider in the early days or weeks of a new riding season because he did not expect to see a motorcycle on the road. It's understandable. The driver hasn't seen a single motorcycle on the road during the long winter months, so, when one appears, he mentally dismisses its importance and pulls out without ever *seeing* the rider.

Scientific studies abound that describe *perception blindness* and *inattentional blindness*, which is when a person does not see something that is in plain sight, usually because of environment distraction. A classic example of this is demonstrated in a video produced by the University of Illinois and Harvard University that shows several people in black or white clothes passing a basketball between themselves. The viewing audience is asked to count the number of passes. As the audience focuses on the action, a man in a gorilla suit does a moonwalk across the screen. The man in the gorilla suit goes unnoticed by about half the people watching. Asking the audience to count the passes provided adequate distraction to cause many to miss what was directly in their field of view. This is what happens when a driver pulls out in front of a motorcycle, even though the driver appears to be looking directly at the rider. It also is what happens when we miss important clues that can keep us out of harm's way.

Change blindness is similar to perception blindness. It is a term used to describe situations when someone fails to notice rather obvious changes in the environment. A Harvard University study filmed a scene with a man standing behind a counter. Prospective subjects speak with the man about participating in the study. What they don't know is that the interaction at the counter is the study. As they discuss the requirements and fill out some paperwork the man ducks below the counter, supposedly to retrieve another form. But a different man pops up with the form in hand. Most of the subjects do not notice the switch and carry on with the conversation, even though the second man is wearing a different colored shirt and has different hair. This demonstrates how we see what we expect to see, not necessarily what is actually going on.

Combat Motion Camouflage

Another phenomenon that affects our safety is *motion camouflage*. Motion camouflage is a term used to describe how an object can appear to be stationary to the observer, even though the object is approaching. If you ride directly toward a driver waiting at

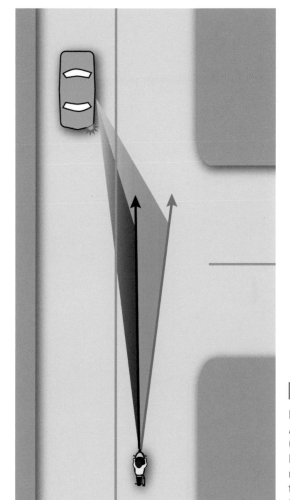

Figure 3.2

Figure 3.2
Avoid Motion
Camouflage
by gradually
moving across
the driver's
field of vision.

an intersection, then you risk appearing to be stationary against the distant landscape.

You can combat this by gradually moving from one side of your lane to the other to cross the driver's field of vision. Choose an approach angle that creates the greatest contrast of motion between you and the background. Even a lane width is often enough to separate you from the landscape and alert drivers that you are in motion and help them more accurately judge your approach speed.

Get Conspicuous

I mentioned earlier how the most reliable strategy for being seen is to be more visible. A driver who sees you and is able to

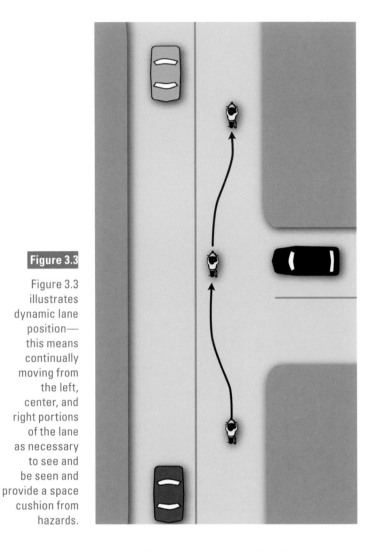

Figure 3.3 illustrates dynamic lane position—this means continually moving from the left, center, and right portions of the lane as necessary to see and be seen and provide a space cushion from hazards.

consider what you're communicating—or not communicating—can precipitate an accident. For instance, only using engine braking to slow and not activating your brake light until you are almost stopped can easily result in the driver behind you reacting too late and hitting you. (More about avoiding rear-end collisions is discussed in a later chapter.)

Turn signals are effective attention-getters as well as communicators of intent. Turn signals need to be activated early enough to give drivers plenty of time to respond. It's not much help to signal at the same instant you push on the grip. A good rule of thumb is to signal at least 3 seconds before slowing to turn or change lane position. Indicate that you are going to change speed or direction…and then pause. If you don't have time to pause, then you are waiting too long to indicate your intentions and putting yourself at unnecessary risk.

Lane Position to Be Seen

We talked a bit earlier about how lane position affects how well you can see past cars ahead. Well, lane position has an equally important role in helping drivers see you in traffic.

accurately judge your speed and distance is much less likely to pull out in front of you.

Sound is not a very reliable way to be noticed. This is why installing loud pipes is not a great strategy for increasing safety. Sure, loud pipes will increase the likelihood that drivers will know you are in the vicinity, but don't be fooled into thinking that sound will help a driver locate *where* you are in traffic. Thankfully, there are other strategies for being conspicuous.

It is important to be aware of other vehicles around you and to communicate your presence and intent and to act predictably to minimize miscommunication. Failure to

Lane position is dynamic and will change with varying conditions. This means continually moving from the left, center, and right portions of the lane as necessary to see and be seen. I mentioned earlier that, in many situations, riding in the left/center of your lane makes the most sense. This position gives other drivers in the oncoming lane ahead a good angle of view to see you. Remember that certain situations might require a change in lane position. If a car is waiting on your right, it makes sense to

move to the right portion of your lane, until you are confident that the driver sees you, and then move back toward the center of your lane to increase your buffer of space between you and the car.

When riding with other motorcyclists, riders ahead will move within their lane, so be sure to adjust your lane position as necessary to make yourself visible. A staggered formation makes this possible. (More about group riding in a later chapter.)

Hiding Away
One of the most common errors in lane positioning is when a rider hides behind a vehicle by tailgating in the center or right-hand portion of the lane. This is especially risky when following large trucks and vans.

Blind Spots
Motorcycles can easily get lost in driver's blind spots, which typically fall just behind a car's front doors all the way to the rear bumper, out of range of the mirrors. If you can't see the face of the driver in her mirror, she can't see you. Large trucks have very large blind spots, commonly referred to by

Figure 3.4

Figure 3.4 shows what can happen if you are "hiding away." The rider was tailgating behind a vehicle and therefore was hidden from view from the car making a turn across the lane.

Figure 3.5

Figure 3.5 shows the position of a car's blind spot.

Figure 3.6

Figure 3.6 illustrates the "No-Zone" for large trucks.

LESSON LEARNED

Hiding Away

Rusty is riding down a two-lane road. He usually rides in the middle of his lane thinking it's the best way to keep distance from oncoming cars and roadside hazards. A minivan is ahead of Rusty moving at what seems like a snail's pace, and his frustration causes him to ride closer than he should.

There are several side streets and intersections along the way, but Rusty pays them little attention, focusing on the minivan's rear bumper instead. As the minivan passes a side street on the right, a car suddenly appears to Rusty's left, accelerating hard across his lane to enter the street. The driver apparently did not notice Rusty hidden behind the van and thought it was safe to go. Once he sees the motorcycle, the driver slams on his brakes. Rusty swerves to the right, but it's too late as the car smashes into his motorcycle's rear wheel and fender.

Rusty was riding close behind the minivan and in a portion of the lane that did not allow oncoming cars to see him, nor could Rusty see that a car was waiting to turn across his lane to enter the side street. As soon as the minivan cleared the way, the driver made his move, not knowing that Rusty was there until the last moment.

WHAT'S THE LESSON?

Had Rusty been more aware that he was hidden from view, perhaps he would have selected the left-hand lane position. But the very first thing he should have done was to back away from the minivan for a greater angle of view to see approaching vehicles and to make it easier for drivers to see him.

Next time someone suddenly veers into your lane as if they never saw you, ask yourself why this happened. It could be that you were hiding away without even knowing it.

LESSON LEARNED

Blind Spot

You gather your things and pack your bike for the ride up North where you will meet family for an annual reunion. The route you select minimizes traffic, but unfortunately will require a stint on a section of road that is known for being crowded.

The ride is going well; the weather is nice, and the traffic is surprisingly light. However, traffic volume eventually picks up, and you find yourself among a mix of cars and trucks funneling to a crawl as the highway transforms to a surface artery. As you slow, you notice a truck in front of you and a silver sedan to your left. You don't think much about the surrounding vehicles because everyone is rolling at a steady 20 mph (32 kph) with no apparent intent on changing lanes.

Suddenly, the sedan moves to the right into your lane. You have little time to react. You try to swerve away from the car, but it's too late. Your front tire makes contact with the right rear bumper. You are thrown to the pavement in an instant. You wake up in an ambulance with a wicked headache and a searing pain in your left arm.

The driver who crossed into your lane did so because she thought the lane was clear. She claimed to have looked in her side mirror and even glanced over her shoulder before turning, but could not see you in her blind spot. The driver is responsible for making sure the lane was clear, but you are also responsible for making sure it was possible for her to see you. The problem would have been avoided if you had been riding slightly ahead of the driver's passenger door or dropping back so she could see you in her mirrors. Next time, be more aware of sight lines and use lane positions that ensure that other road users see you.

WHAT'S THE LESSON?

Develop a sixth sense about your surroundings, select lane positions that ensure the highest level of conspicuity, and avoid riding in drivers' blind spots or hiding behind other vehicles.

---

the cautionary moniker "The No-Zone." Continually monitor your position to avoid riding in this blind spot. Remind yourself to ride *through* blind spots by continuing to accelerate past the vehicle until you are in a position where you are seen.

Never make lane changes into the blind spot of a driver who is next to you because he might attempt to change lanes simultaneously as he tries to occupy the same lane. Change lanes gradually to allow drivers time to predict your intentions.

Motorcyclists have blind spots, too; unfortunately, typical motorcycle mirrors do a rather poor job of revealing what's behind and to the sides. Take a quick glance over your shoulder to be sure it's safe to merge or change lanes.

Chapter 4

Preventing Crashes: Awareness and Decision Making

Okay, so you choose to pilot a two-wheeler even though you know it is risky. What are you going to do about it? One really smart move is to develop strategies for minimizing the risk as much as you can.

Master the Traffic Game

Surviving on the road requires you to play nice with other drivers. But this can be difficult when drivers don't seem to care about their driving and are willing to let distractions get in the way of following the rules of the road or watching out for motorcyclists.

The best riders are able to evaluate the traffic or roadway scene and quickly identify when something is amiss. One way to develop these mental skills is to play an imaginary game in which your objective is to survive against careless drivers who are out to get you. As you ride, scan the roadway, identify possible hazards, and predict the actions of the other players who may be out to get you. You accumulate points for acting in a way that keeps you safe.

For instance, you approach an intersection with a car in the opposite lane that is waiting to turn left across your path. You get the following points for your actions:

- 30 points for being in the proper lane position and not tailgating the car ahead.
- 10 points for slowing by rolling off the throttle.
- 10 more points for covering your brakes.
- 20 points for realizing early that the driver does not see you and is about to turn.
- 50 points for applying your brakes without skidding and stopping in time.
- 20 points for checking your mirrors to prevent being rear-ended.

Adding up your total, you'll notice that the mental skills netted you a total of 90 points, whereas the physical skill of braking accounts for 50 points. Of course, if your physical skills had failed and you either collided with the car or skidded and fell, then you would have lost the game. However, excellent mental skills would have likely prevented you from needing to brake to the absolute edge of traction in the first place.

Time and Space

To play the game well, you need to understand that your survival strategies are what will keep you safe. Yes, superior physical skills are important, but they won't necessarily get you out of trouble. To illustrate the importance of good judgment, let's consider the timing and circumstances of a typical 30 mph (48 kph) crash. At that speed, you are traveling at 44 feet per second (1 mph = 1.47 ft/sec) [13 meters per second]. Getting a motorcycle stopped at 30 mph (48 kph) takes just over 2 seconds

When avoiding collisions, don't forget to factor in your reaction time.

and requires about 35 feet (11 m) of space. But braking distances include more than just the time and space to physically stop your motorcycle. It also includes *thinking time* and *reaction time*. At 30 mph (48 kph) you can count on using about .7 seconds or 31 feet (9 m) to realize that there is a problem. It then takes you another .3 seconds or 13 feet (4 m) to roll off the throttle and reach for the brakes. That means you traveled 44 feet (13 m) before even touching the brakes. Finally, it takes you about 2.2 seconds or 35 feet (9 m) with a typical deceleration rate achieved by the average rider to bring the motorcycle to a halt. Add this *braking time* to the *thinking time* and *reaction time* and you'll need a total of 3.2 seconds and 79 feet (24 m) with which to stop. (Note that this scenario applies to motorcycles with and without anti-lock braking systems.)

Let's say you are traveling at 30 mph (48 kph), and a car pulls out from a side street. It takes 1 second for you to perceive that action is required and for you to react. You execute a perfect quick stop, but did you have enough time and space to avoid a collision? The car would have to be at least 80 feet (24 m) (about 3.5 seconds) away when you noticed it as a threat. Unfortunately, you probably won't have that much time, which is why it's better to do all you can to avoid being faced with the need to use superhero skills in the first place.

Swerving is an alternative to emergency braking when there isn't enough time and space to stop. However, effective swerving requires excellent countersteering skill, which can be a real challenge for many motorcyclists. (We discuss swerving in depth a bit later.)

RIDING TERM
COUNTERSTEERING

Term used to describe the handlebar pressure to get the bike to go from upright to leaned. It is used whenever you need to change direction.

The message here is that it is unwise to rely solely on your braking or swerving skill to keep you safe.

Prevent Mental Impairment

One of the most significant factors that affect your ability to accurately judge and evaluate your surroundings is mental impairment. This can be from alcohol and drugs, but it also includes emotional upsets and stress or distraction caused by thoughts or mood. Any one of these conditions can affect judgment and your ability to manage hazards.

In addition to keeping your head clear, it is also very important to have a high level of attention and awareness. The best motorcyclists are able to evaluate their surroundings and adapt to changing situations, but this cannot happen if focus and attention is lacking. One indication that your awareness may not be as sharp as it should be is if you often find yourself being surprised by hazards. Small clues exist that tell you about possible hazards, and it's up to you to identify them.

Another mental block that can cause problems is overconfidence and complacency. Although confidence is usually a good thing, you must never assume

Physical skill can be developed by taking a safety course and then practicing in parking lots.

you are 100% safe and then let down your guard. Continually evaluate your mental and physical skills and be truthful about areas that may need improvement.

At the other end of the confidence spectrum is fear. Fear prevents us from taking unwise chances, but excessive fear can cause problems. It isn't uncommon to see a new rider put him- or herself at greater risk by traveling below the speed limit, timidly entering the roadway, or grasping the handlebars with a deathgrip. This type of fear must be overcome as soon as possible, and the best way to do this is to practice both physical and mental skills.

Visualization Training

Physical skill can be developed by taking a safety course and then practicing in parking lots and on lightly traveled roads, but practicing mental skills requires a different approach that involves imagining scenarios and solutions. This can be done when sitting in your easy chair or when driving in a car. The idea is to exercise your brain to keep your mental skills sharp and well rehearsed.

Soldiers, pilots, police officers, firefighters, and other people exposed to high-stress situations are trained using methods that emulate the real world so they can handle the inevitable first battle, conflict, or emergency situation. Without this part of the training process, the skills are likely to either become too delayed or go unused as the brain wastes valuable time processing what is happening.

The training includes sounds, smells, and sights that shock the ears, nose, and eyes. Explosions, live ammo, alarms, and life-threatening scenarios played by actors all prepare these trainees for the worst. That doesn't happen with motorcycle training courses.

Nobody dares to suggest that instructors drive a Chevy onto the practice range at random times, walk unpredictably in front of unsuspecting students, or secretly drop sand or diesel fuel on the parking lot. These scenarios would help condition students for real-world situations, but liability means this method just won't fly.

The next best thing to exposing riders to real-word scenarios is visualization. Racers use visualization to run laps in their mind before hitting the track. They can be seen closing their eyes or staring into space as they imagine every nuance of the racetrack and every braking, shifting, and cornering action with great precision. If you click a stopwatch as they begin and end a visualized lap, the best racers will be remarkably close to their real lap times. This exercise is known to be almost as effective as actually riding the machine on the track—without using up tires or fuel or risking a crash.

Street riders can also use visualization to train themselves to manage a car pulling out from a side street or a patch of sand appearing suddenly around a blind corner. The Motorcycle Saftey Foundation (MSF) attempts to have new riders visualize real-life hazards using videos and online simulators.

Close your eyes and visualize yourself riding to work. As you enter a familiar intersection, imagine a car suddenly running the stoplight or stop sign. Feel the panic as your muscles tense and your eyes widen. Now, imagine yourself squeezing the brakes fully, the G-forces pushing you forward in the saddle. How did you do? Did you avoid a collision? If not, then try again and again. You cannot do this too much.

Go back in time and plan better by slowing down and covering your brakes to reduce reaction time. Notice how more time allows you to respond with less drama. Now, imagine yourself swerving instead of stopping. Visualize other scenarios, like rounding a blind corner and needing to avoid an animal or realizing the corner is tightening and your speed is too fast.

This is a sort of mental rehearsal for a future performance. This idea is to desensitize and train your mind ahead of time. This training is not the same as having a car pull out in front of you, but it can be remarkably effective if done well—and it's safe.

Situational Awareness

How aware are you of your surroundings? To what degree can you take small clues and "connect the dots" to identify potential hazards? Are you conscious of your intuition? Answers to these questions can help you to identify your level of *situational awareness*.

Situational awareness is a concept used by the military, aviation industry, and emergency personnel to describe the level of awareness and perception of an immediate situation. Someone with well-developed situational awareness is able to "see the big picture" and to accurately evaluate likely outcomes.

One example of the importance of situational awareness is when a person walks through a bad neighborhood. Some walkers are at higher risk of being approached by assailants because they blindly stroll without tuning into whether there may be a threat in the vicinity. Those who are aware of their surroundings identify possible hazards to keep from becoming a victim.

Being aware of your surroundings is essential for reducing risk, but it's important not to be overly paranoid, either. It's smart to learn from past mishaps but not be overly

Threats are many, and managing these risks can easily become overwhelming. To minimize hazard overload and help simplify risk, it's beneficial to categorize hazards into the following:

- Vehicles
- Road and surface dangers
- Unpredictable hazards, such as pedestrians and animals

A typical commute in an urban area means that you will encounter each of the three hazard categories each and every day. Trucks, buses, taxicabs, and other commuters (many on cell phones), seem to conspire to mow you down. Potholes, construction plates, manhole covers, slick road markings, and spilled fuel are common road and surface dangers that you must also manage. You must also be aware of people exiting parked cars, as well as pedestrians crossing the street.

Being aware of your surroundings is essential for reducing risk.

influenced by old fears. Instead, keep your mind in the present and evaluate hazards based on the current situation. Fearful overreactions will reduce enjoyment and can hinder a rider's ability to accurately prioritize potential hazards.

It's important to be very skilled at recognizing when something doesn't look right. Well-honed senses allow you to gather important information, but don't forget the less tangible "sixth sense." Pay attention to a hunch that something isn't quite right and then respond by slowing down and scanning extra hard.

Threat Awareness

We've all heard the saying "ignorance is bliss," but when it comes to surviving on a motorcycle, ignorance can get you killed.

Before going into battle, it's important to have as much knowledge about your "enemy" as possible. For instance, transit buses are aggressive about re-entering traffic after picking up and dropping off passengers. This may mean you must slow down and position yourself away from the bus in case the driver suddenly pulls out.

Another significant threat when commuting is the potential of being rear-ended at a stoplight. Deal with this by keeping your eyes on the rearview mirrors and keep the motorcycle in gear in case an inattentive driver doesn't stop in time.

A ride in the country requires you to shift awareness to different dangers. Instead of buses and taxis, you'll encounter fast-moving cars and trucks. Instead of manhole covers, you'll see sand, gravel, and blind corners. Unpredictable hazards in the country are less likely to be pedestrians, but may include wild animals and unleashed pets.

Accurate Perception

Sometimes, we unconsciously convince ourselves that situations are less risky than they really are. This *confirmation bias* leads to decisions that are based on preconceived perceptions that may not be true. People tend to look for and accept information that supports what they want to believe and reject evidence that disproves these beliefs. Motorcyclists may believe that only those who ride fast are at risk and find comfort in the fact that they will be fine as long as they ride slowly. Others may believe that wearing full protective gear will make them safer, so they accept greater amounts of risk, thinking that if something does happen they will be protected. A rider who has an accurate perception of his or her abilities and of the risks of riding will make good decisions and behave accordingly.

Awareness Impairment

There are many factors that can impair your ability to gather necessary information and to make accurate decisions. Some of these factors are external, such as fog, rain, darkness, or solar glare that can hinder your visual sense, while other factors are internal, such as distraction or degradation of the senses due to age.

Fixation is another factor that can impair situational awareness if we become

Be aware of all the potential hazards on your commute.

preoccupied with relatively unimportant hazards. New riders are particularly susceptible to this type of impairment because they are easily overloaded with relatively simple tasks, such as starting on a hill, maneuvering in tight spaces, or cornering through a tricky set of curves.

Boredom can cause us to lose focus, which can happen when we travel many long highway miles (km). Other factors that impair situational awareness are things that affect our judgment, such as fatigue and stress. Sometimes, our minds fixate on matters not even related to riding a motorcycle, such as job or home worries.

The most likely cause of awareness problems comes from using alcohol and drugs. Alcohol consumption contributes greatly to missed clues about hazards and contributes to inaccurate judgment that can make a rider believe she can do things that she really can't handle. Drinking and riding is not only illegal; it can kill.

If you're smart enough not to drink and ride, you will likely live long enough to experience how the years dull our senses. As we age, the ability of our eyes, ears, and mind to quickly gather and perceive information slowly deteriorates. The result is a rider who cannot process information accurately and fails to judge distance for stopping at intersections, selecting cornering lines, or maintaining following distances. (Aging is discussed later.)

Multitasking

Riding a motorcycle requires a certain amount of multitasking to safely thread through traffic, carve a series of corners, or simply cruise down the highway. An efficient, well-developed ability to multitask maintains a reserve of brain capacity for dealing with compounding events.

Overtasking

Multitasking is necessary to ride a motorcycle safely, but inappropriate multitasking can increase danger if you try to do too much at once. Recent studies have concluded that a constant state of managing simultaneous actions leads to an overstimulated mind that is unable to focus deeply. One task is sacrificed as another is introduced, which itself is cut short as a third task is taken on.

Your brain can become overtasked by a simple thing like listening to music or using communicators to chat with fellow riders. Daydreaming can also lead to exceeding the limit of your brain to manage a difficult situation. The message is that trying to do too much or allowing mental distractions to be present can easily lead to task overload.

It's also smart to recognize that car drivers have multitasking limitations as well. Driving while texting or talking on a cell phone is a serious hazard. A lot of car drivers attempt other tasks as well, such as eating, reading, arguing, or adjusting the radio. Keep an extra keen eye out for four-wheeled overtaskers.

Proficient motorcyclists can perform important tasks without becoming overwhelmed. They keep situations in perspective, know how to prioritize, keep a wide view of situations, and act as efficiently as possible. They also understand the importance of not multitasking to the point of distraction. Keeping multitasking in balance is a skill

LESSON LEARNED

Compounding Problems

Carl is on his way to work. As he approaches a busy intersection, he spies a driver wanting to take a left turn across his lane. Carl knows that this hazard is a serious one, so he gives the driver extra attention as he slows down and covers his brakes, just in case. But, in the corner of his eye, Carl sees a car rolling into his lane from the right. His attention is now divided between the two hazards as his brain calculates the most immediate problem and what to do about it.

Carl decides a quick swerve away from the nearby car on the right is the first action to take, but as soon as he starts pushing on the handlebar, he sees that he's headed for a recessed manhole cover ringed with broken pavement. Yikes! Another change in plan is called for—and quick. He alters his swerve to avoid the road hazard and, using his peripheral vision, keeps just enough attention on the car on the right.

The car stops before pulling into Carl's path, and he narrowly avoids the massive hole around the manhole cover. But before he can relax, the left-hand turner decides to go. Carl needs to get on the brakes hard to avoid colliding with the car. But, traction is limited because of the crumbled pavement strewn down the road from around the manhole cover. Fortunately, Carl regularly practices maximum braking technique, so his fingers know exactly how much brake pressure his tires can handle without skidding. He stops in time to avoid hitting the car as it crosses in front of him.

Carl's quick responses averted a collision, but he knows it's not yet time to relax and celebrate his good skills. Carl takes a quick glance in his mirrors because he remembers a car was close behind him before approaching the intersection. Good thing he does, because the car is hard on the brakes trying to avoid rear-ending him. Part of Carl's braking practice involves downshifting to first gear, so he is already prepared to accelerate hard to avoid being hit from behind. Carl finds an escape route ahead and aims for it with a quick twist of the throttle. He hears tires squeal behind him as he rockets ahead.

This may sound like an extreme example of compounding hazards, but this type of scenario is more common than you might think. Intersections often have multiple hazards coming from several directions. A single successful hazard avoidance maneuver may not be enough if you have two vehicles and a road hazard each vying for your limited attention. Remember that collisions usually are the result of a series of factors, rather than a single cause.

WHAT'S THE LESSON?

Motorcyclists who can't effectively manage multiple hazards find themselves riding from one close call to another. In contrast, the best riders are able to scan the environment and predict likely problems well ahead of time and are rarely involved in close calls.

like any other that takes conscious effort to improve. First, recognize the level of proficiency you have for managing several tasks at once, then eliminate unnecessary undertakings.

Prioritizing

We must learn to prioritize hazards because we only have a finite amount of brain bandwidth to handle all that we need to do and also try to deal with unnecessary stimulus.

Accurately perceiving risk allows you to prioritize whether a hazard is significant or not, which avoids the trap of devoting too much attention to a hazard with relatively little risk and missing a more critical hazard. It's important to give a potential hazard only the amount of attention it deserves, no more, no less.

Juggling Controls

Even the most multitasking-challenged people are able to perform the mundane, mechanical tasks necessary to ride a motorcycle in typical nonthreatening situations. However, there are times when factors converge, and we must juggle many tasks at once: for example, when you must simultaneously brake and downshift while trying to stay in your lane after entering a corner too fast. This can be too much if you haven't mastered each of these tasks individually beforehand and also have difficulty multitasking.

Decisions, Decisions

Decisions are made during almost every moment of every ride you take. These decisions range from mundane to potentially life-changing. Each person makes decisions in his or her own unique way. Some people

Accurately perceiving risk allows you to prioritize whether a hazard is significant or not.

evaluate factors rationally, while others base decisions on their instinct or feelings. There are three methods for making decisions:

1. *Rational decision making* usually involves a process of listing several options and identifying the pros and cons of each choice. This way of making decisions considers the cause and effect of multiple options. People who want to "get it right" often rely on this style of decision making.

   The rational method is useful when a decision is not time sensitive. You may take all the time you want to decide what motorcycle to buy or where to go on a motorcycle trip by listing all the possibilities and analyzing each one. But you don't have this luxury when a car is about to pull out in front of you.

2. *Intuitive decision making* relies on a person's "sixth sense" or gut feelings. Intuition can be a very effective tool for identifying problems, but it requires the ability to tune into the subtle voices that warn of impending danger and tell you to pay attention because something isn't quite right.

3. *Experiential decision making* combines both the rational and intuitive methods by utilizing past experiences and environmental recognition to form an educated guess about what might be the best way to proceed. This method usually produces the best outcomes. One example might be how we choose the best lane position and travel speed. Basing decisions on surroundings and the expected behavior of other drivers allows you to arrive at conclusions that are both logical and feel right.

DECIDE TO RIDE SOBER

Alcohol is a powerful elixir capable of bringing the worst decisions to life. Almost half of all motorcycle fatalities are alcohol-related. The effects of alcohol are well known, so there is no need for me to preach about how alcohol impairs judgment, vision, and coordination. Unfortunately, even very sensible people sometimes allow themselves to be exposed to this potentially deadly combination.

Too many times, alcohol or drug impairment has turned an otherwise manageable situation into a disastrous mishap. Experienced riders can fall into the trap of thinking they can ride just fine with a couple of drinks in their system because they are so highly accomplished. But this confidence is often the thing that gets experienced riders into trouble. They think they can handle the motorcycle just as competently as when they are sober. They may perform very familiar maneuvers pretty well, but as soon as they are faced with a split-second decision that requires a high level of precision and coordination, things often turn out badly. It's a rookie move to think that you can ride with even a small amount of alcohol in your system...so don't!

LESSON LEARNED

So Many Decisions

You are meeting some friends at the beach today and really want to take your motorcycle. But the weatherman reports that today will be oppressively hot. You would be more comfortable in your air-conditioned car, but you decide to take the bike anyway.

The beach is about an hour away. Unfortunately, the most direct route is a highway that is notorious for heavy traffic. You could choose another route, but you chose to sleep late, which caused you to run behind schedule. The idea of wearing your leather jacket and riding pants in heavy traffic and blistering heat seems foolish, so you decide to wear a t-shirt and lightweight pants instead. In hindsight, you should have bought the mesh jacket you saw in the local dealership last month, but the weather was cool at the time, which made it hard to justify spending the money.

As expected, the traffic is heavy and slow. The sun bakes your arms and the hot wind blows unmercifully across your skin, causing your sweat to evaporate as quickly as it can exit your pores. Soon, you become very thirsty, and your concentration begins to whither, but there is no easy place to stop so you soldier on.

You are traveling in the middle lane when suddenly a driver to your left cuts across your front wheel to try and make an exit. He is obviously unaware of your presence because you are in his blind spot. You freeze for a moment and then overreact with too much brake force, which causes your tires to skid and you fall. Your t-shirt shreds within 30 feet (9 m) and exposes your skin to the brutal abrasion of the hot pavement.

WHAT'S THE LESSON?

Several unfortunate decisions contributed to your pain and misery. The first occurred weeks earlier when you decided not to buy a protective jacket designed for hot weather. The second was your decision to go ahead and ride on such a hot day. Third, you decided to forego protective gear. Fourth, you chose a route congested with slow-moving traffic that exposed you to the risk of dehydration and the resultant distraction. And fifth, your poor choice of riding in the driver's blind spot made you virtually invisible.

The true cause of most mishaps can be traced to several small, seemingly insignificant missteps. Unfortunately, a lot of riders fail to see their role in preventing close calls and crashes and are destined to repeat their misfortune.

Make good decisions, like not riding in a driver's blind spot, to avoid accidents.

Sometimes decisions must be made without the benefit of forethought, like when you're faced with a hazard that requires split-second reactions. Without time, you will likely react with a knee-jerk response. Unfortunately, our reflexes often cause us to panic, usually leading to unhappy outcomes.

Short-Term, Long-Term

There are three types of decisions: *immediate*, *short-term*, and *long-term*. Avoiding a collision requires an immediate response about whether to brake or swerve. These urgent decisions affect your immediate survival and command your full attention. Short-term decisions are less dramatic but still affect your safety, such as deciding your lane position and speed. Long-term decisions hold little drama and include such things as bike, gear, and insurance purchases and where to go on a summer trip. However, long-term decisions do affect

our safety. Deciding to forego rider training is one example of a long-term decision that can lead to regret.

Impulsive Decisions

Impulsive decisions can ensnare even the most safety-conscious rider, like when you get caught up in the moment trying to keep up with friends or accelerate into an intersection in an attempt to make the light.

Most of us have made questionable decisions at one time or another and then immediately felt the sting of regret. I once made an unwise pass on a car because I was determined to take full advantage of a particularly sumptuous stretch of serpentine road. Maturity is the remedy for such impulsive decision making, but inside all of us is an impetuous youngster poised to overrule reason. Understand that this alter ego exists and try to resist its influence.

LESSON LEARNED

Unfamiliar Ride

You're on your way to meet a few friends for a long weekend ride. The weather is terrific for the overnight excursion, and your motorcycle is running great. You arrive at the designated meeting spot to find the other riders having their breakfast and engaged in a lively conversation about their respective bikes.

During the conversation, one friend insists that his new motorcycle is worlds better than the older-generation bike you own. The owner of the new model wants to prove his position, so you both agree to switch bikes sometime during the ride. Everyone finishes their breakfast and suits up to go.

During a rest stop, you and your friend decide that it's a good time to switch bikes. At first you ride cautiously, not wanting to risk crashing your friend's motorcycle. But the new motorcycle seems to ask to be ridden harder through the twisty sections of road. You oblige by turning the throttle.

You dart into a blind right-hand corner when you are surprised to see that the turn's radius decreases significantly toward the exit. You press hard to lean the bike more, but this motorcycle turns quicker and sharper than yours, and you end up in the dirt on the inside of the turn. The next few moments are a blur. Eventually, you notice the new bike laying on its side. You are mostly okay, thanks to your full complement of riding gear, but you're horrified at what you've done. You jump up to assess the damage while the rest of the riders park their bikes and run over to assist. The damaged motorcycle's owner looks in disbelief at his now scraped and broken machine.

WHAT'S THE LESSON?

Statistics suggest that crashes occur more often when an unfamiliar motorcycle is involved, whether borrowed or newly purchased. Handling, power, and braking characteristics are different between different types of motorcycles and even between two different examples of the same model. One motorcycle may respond differently than another simply because of different tire profile or suspension setup.

When you do chose to test a demo bike or take the offer to ride a different motorcycle owned by a generous fellow rider, take time to get a feel for the differences the unfamiliar bike possesses. And consider declining the offer if you are uncomfortable with the risks.

One segment of the Motorcycle Safety Foundation's *Advanced RiderCourse-Sportbike Techniques* is called "Voices and Choices," which identifies three types of "voices" behind the decisions we make: the *rule-oriented parent*; the *selfish, impulsive child*; and the *wise, responsible adult*. The parent says "I should," the child says "I want to," and the adult says "I'll do what's right." Students discuss this concept as a way to understand why they make certain decisions and how to avoid negative behavior. What voice do you listen to?

Beware of Strange Bikes

If you decide to ride other people's bikes, beware! Swinging a leg over a new or unfamiliar motorcycle can be dangerous. I've seen what happens when a rider doesn't respect the variations in power delivery, handling, and braking power between different bikes. Whenever you choose to ride someone else's motorcycle or when you are familiarizing yourself with a new bike, keep in mind that it takes time to reset your mind and muscles so you will apply the proper amount of throttle, steering, or braking force.

Also, consider that even your trusty motorcycle becomes an unfamiliar mount after sitting in the garage over a long winter. Be sure to take some time during your first ride to refamiliarize yourself with your bike. A bit of practice in a parking lot is a good start.

Sensory Intelligence

Your sense of smell, hearing, touch, sight, and taste make safe and enjoyable riding possible by dutifully providing information about your surroundings.

The information you get from these five senses is tangible. However, there is other sensory intelligence that is less tangible, often referred to as a "sixth sense." Let's hear Alan's story to see how each sense is used.

Staying alert to all types of potential hazards will help prevent accidents.

LESSON LEARNED

Alan's Ride

Alan is gearing up in preparation for a daylong tour through the mountains. He slips on his boots, zips his jacket, and straps his helmet, anxious to get out of town and onto the open road. The morning air smells fresh, and the sound and throbbing pulses of his rumbling V-twin make the beginning of the ride quite satisfying.

Traffic is light at this time of morning with most people still in bed. Even so, Alan is aware that he needs to keep a keen eye out for errant drivers, many who are still under the effects of sleepiness. Alan encounters one such driver on his left waiting to turn onto the main road from a shopping center. Alan sees from the driver's body language that he is distracted by something inside his large SUV. As Alan nears, the driver quickly looks left then right for an opportunity to proceed onto the main road. Alan is sure the driver didn't see his approaching motorcycle during the hasty traffic check, so he slows and covers his brakes. Sure enough, the driver darts in front of Alan on what would have been a collision course had Alan not seen and anticipated the violation.

Further down the road, Alan pulls into a gas station entrance and is ready to park next to a pump when he hears a car rev abruptly. It's hard to identify exactly where the noise is coming from, but Alan quickly scans to see a car on the other side of the pumps beginning to move toward him. He notices that the driver can't see him because the pumps are blocking his view, so Alan decides to stop. It's a good thing, because the driver accelerates quickly right where Alan would have been if he had ignored the audible clue.

After filling his tank, Alan gets back on the road. A few miles up the road, he sees the entrance ramp onto the highway that leads him to the mountains so he decelerates, gears down, and leans into the curve. Suddenly, Alan gets a whiff of a pungent scent that he immediately recognizes as diesel fuel. He knows the dangers of this slippery substance, so he smoothly reduces speed while searching for the source of the odor. Sure enough, just ahead is a glossy area spread along about 30 feet (9 m) of the ramp. Fortunately, Alan is able to maneuver around the mess and continue on his way.

Let's learn about how your senses relate to riding a motorcycle and talk about how you can further develop your ability to take full advantage of what your senses have to tell you.

Sight

Vision is the most reliable source for gathering information. Your eyes scan a "visual map" of a situation, telling you whether what you see hints of a threat or not. Visual clues help you judge appropriate speed, determine whether a car is about to cross your path, or evaluate if the road conditions will provide enough traction. Also, monitoring your mirrors while sitting at a red traffic light will help determine if

After an hour or so, Alan exits the highway onto the twisty mountain roads. One of Alan's destinations is a local restaurant known for the best charbroiled burgers around. He savors the flavor and aroma of the culinary treat as it mixes with the fresh air. After lunch is finished, Alan is back on his bike ready to return home.

Less than a mile (km) up the road, Alan feels an unusual vibration through the handlebars and seat, and it seems as if the tires are wandering from side to side. He pulls off the road to investigate the cause. A quick inspection reveals an almost flat rear tire. Alan finds that the source of the puncture is a nail in the center of the tread. Fortunately, Alan has a tire repair kit in his tank bag. It takes Alan about 20 minutes to make the fix and reinflate the tire with the CO_2 cartridge included in the kit. He is a few pounds short of the recommended pressure, so he rides carefully to the next gas station to top off the tire with air. Once he is confident that the plug will hold, Alan is back under way. It's a good thing Alan was sensitive to the abnormal handlebar vibrations and pulled over when he did.

On his ride back home through the busy part of town near his house, Alan notices a feeling of uneasiness. The source of this discord comes from the somewhat frantic behavior of the car drivers around him. Moments later, Alan's senses are piqued by several drivers jockeying aggressively for position in traffic. He makes sure to cover his brakes and horn, just in case, which is a good thing because a blue sedan begins to move into Alan's lane. Alan beeps his horn, but the driver doesn't seem to notice. Alan recognizes that he'll have to brake hard to avoid the sedan. Fortunately, his response was quick enough so that the sedan's rear bumper misses Alan's front wheel by only a few feet (m).

WHAT'S THE LESSON?

Even though there were several situations where Alan could have gotten into trouble, his senses alerted him to the hazards. Alan knows that these sorts of scenarios play out on almost every ride, which is why he has become attuned to his senses and developed strategies for handling such hazards. You can too!

approaching traffic is stopping safely behind you.

To be able to see traffic hazards, it's critical to position yourself so you can maximize your angle of sight. This means increasing following distance and choosing lane positions that allow you to see past vehicles ahead and so others

can see you. Remember that if you can't see them, they can't see you.

Since there is so much to look out for, you must learn to aggressively scan the environment, putting extra attention toward the most serious hazards. And don't forget to use your mirrors and peripheral vision to detect hazards from all around. Quick, efficient head checks (what Europeans call "Life Savers") are also important for identifying vehicles that might be in your blind spots. (Visual skills are discussed in detail a bit later.)

Hearing

Sounds, such as revving motors, squealing brakes, honking horns, and sirens from emergency vehicles can alert you to possible hazards. But you should recognize that hearing is not as reliable as sight for gathering information and making accurate decisions. Alan was able to use his hearing to determine that a car was about to drive away from the fuel pumps, but it was difficult for him to pinpoint the exact source of the sound.

A large reason why he was able to hear the car at all was because he was riding at a slow speed with no wind noise to obstruct the sound. At higher speeds, sound becomes less helpful for spotting hazards. This is why relying on horns or loud pipes to alert a driver of your presence isn't a great idea. As mentioned previously, loud pipes will alert drivers (and the general public) of your presence, but the sound doesn't make clear the exact location of the motorcycle. Part of the reason it's difficult to pinpoint a nearby motorcycle is because low-frequency sounds, such as the slow bangs emanating from a V-twin's exhaust, tend to spread in all directions compared to high-frequency sounds that travel mostly in one direction.

Another characteristic of sound that makes loud pipes less effective is that it travels in directional waves away from its source. Because motorcycle exhausts point rearward, the sound doesn't easily get to the ears of drivers that pose the most risk—the vast majority of motorcycle collisions occur from *ahead*. In other words, an exhaust pipe pointed rearward is opposite

Relying on horns or loud pipes to alert a driver of your presence isn't a great idea.

the direction from where the vast majority of collisions occur.

The location of a sound's source can be hard to determine for other reasons, too. Sound can bounce off buildings and pavement, which can also help to disguise the location of the sound's source. In city traffic, a driver may be able to hear a bike with loud pipes but have a difficult time recognizing where the noise is coming from. Rural areas aren't any better, because vegetation absorbs and dissipates low-frequency sounds.

There are many riders who swear that their loud pipes saved them from being involved in an accident. Arguably, the louder exhaust may have provided added conspicuity, but evidence suggests that it is better to make yourself more visible by wearing brightly colored clothing and using lane positions that keep you in sight.

Touch

We don't often think of touch as a significant factor in information gathering, but your sense of touch is related to your ability to sense vibration and pressure. This sensory information can help you notice mechanical problems and can even indicate imminent traction loss.

Alan noticed a change in how his motorcycle felt, so he pulled off the road to investigate. The nail he discovered that was stuck in the rear tire caused an unusual vibration and a vague feeling coming from his tires that Alan was able to detect.

Another example of sensory information contributing to safety is the ability to detect visceral sensations from the tires

PROTECT YOUR SENSES

As we age, our senses become dulled, especially our eyesight and hearing. Save your eyesight by wearing durable eye protection and protect your hearing by wearing earplugs that guard against the harmful effects of wind noise. (I discuss more about the effects of aging later in the book.)

Recognize when your senses are dulled, which can happen when you are sick or when weather conditions obscure sight distance and clarity. It can also happen if you're impaired by drugs, alcohol, discomfort, or emotions.

and chassis and feedback from the road. This communication is transmitted through the tires and suspension to your hands, seat, and feet. Keen awareness of this information can tell you whether traction has changed or whether you're on the edge of losing grip. Slight changes in handlebar feel may indicate that front tire grip may be at its limit. Determining traction levels is useful when cornering and to prevent a skid in emergency braking situations where maximum brake force is needed.

Smell

Smell is often relegated to the pleasant aroma of passing vegetation and is not usually associated with motorcycle safety, but smell plays a role in environmental awareness. Alan was alerted to a diesel fuel spill when the pungent aroma passed his nose.

Other odors that might trigger an alert are the smell of marijuana from a nearby car or the smell of alcohol on a fellow rider's breath. Burning oil or antifreeze has a distinct smell and should prompt a thorough inspection of your bike.

Taste

Taste plays no significant role in motorcycling; however, let's not ignore the simple pleasure of a delicious meal enjoyed during a ride with friends as a noteworthy element of motorcycling.

Smart riders separate drinking from riding.

Sixth Sense: Predicting the Future

Beyond our five senses is the less tangible "sixth sense," which includes subtle feelings processed by our intellect at a subliminal level. This "sense" is much less understood, and the interpretation of the data is much less objective. Alan's sixth sense of survival prompted him to pay attention to the hard acceleration of other drivers, their failure to use turn signals, and their erratic lane changes.

This sixth sense is also useful for managing less obvious hazards. For instance, you might sense tension when negotiating a series of curves. This stress is trying to tell you that you're going a bit too fast for the conditions or your comfort level. Another example might be a voice whispering inside your helmet saying that you should get ready to stop— just before an animal darts from the roadside brush. Listening to these insightful messages is a good idea.

Common Sense

The last sense that I want to talk about is common sense, which is really a concept more than a sense. As common as this sense may be, it is too often ignored. A few examples of poor common sense include trying to keep up with faster riding friends, choosing to drink alcohol before or during a ride, and not wearing your helmet because it's not "cool." Listen to your inner voice when it tells you "This isn't such a good idea."

Stay Fully Alert

To benefit from what your senses have to offer, you must pay

LESSON LEARNED

Don't Look Now

You're on a long trip far from home. The other people you are riding with are on motorcycles with a fairly short fuel range, so it is important to take advantage of the few fuel stops that are available in this remote part of the country. You see an exit coming up that looks like it may have a gas station, so you signal for the group to follow you off the highway.

You notice a line of cars stopped at the end of the exit ramp. You slow to about 25 mph as you scan the adjoining roadway to the left and right to see if there actually is a gas station at this exit. It becomes apparent that no fuel is available, so you look over your shoulder to signal the group of your mistake and your intention to reenter the highway.

When you return your vision ahead, you are shocked to see that the car in front of you has come to a complete stop. You immediately hit the brakes hard. The rear tire skids as you swerve the bike to the left. You are able to miss the car's rear bumper by inches and stop next to the driver's side door. The driver gives you a dirty look. You give him a "sorry" gesture as he proceeds to roll forward toward the stop sign at the end of the ramp. Your heart is pounding as you and your riding partners get back onto the highway to find an exit with fuel.

WHAT'S THE LESSON?

Your attention was occupied as you tried to determine whether you made a good decision about exiting. This fixation caused you to pay more attention to looking for gas than to the traffic that was stopping ahead of you. It would have been better to wait until you were stopped in line to scan the surroundings for a gas station. Instead, you were rolling at a speed that could have caused some serious damage to you and your machine.

attention, otherwise the messages go unheard. It takes only a small lapse of attention to find yourself in the midst of a dangerous situation. We've all experienced times when we spaced out. Distracting thoughts triggered by anxiety, fatigue, or boredom are often to blame. This drifting concentration can cause you to miss the often-subtle hints about potential hazards.

Another factor that contributes greatly to inattention is alcohol or drug impairment. For some, alcohol is a part of the motorcycling culture, where a few drinks before or during a ride is common. Smart riders separate drinking from riding, but it can be tough to maintain this policy when peer pressure encourages participation. The best way to avoid being involved in an alcohol-related crash is to remain

LESSON LEARNED

Device Distraction

You and your friend are far from home on secondary roads that are not known to either of you. You are leading the way with your buddy riding behind. The road you're on was selected by your friend's GPS, but is looking more and more like a road best suited for tractors than motorcycles. You stop at an intersecting road to confer with your navigator. His GPS suggests that taking a right-hand turn might provide a better route with an improved road surface.

With a nod, you both point your front wheels to the right and accelerate briskly. The road ahead quickly rises uphill. As you crest the hill, you are shocked to see the road turn to loose dirt and gravel. You brake quickly to slow before reaching the loose surface. That's when you feel a violent impact from behind. The next thing you remember is lying face up on the edge of the road with your friend lying about 20 feet (6 m) away near the fallen bikes. You assess your condition as mostly shaken, so you crawl over to your friend to offer assistance. Your friend will need medical help, and both motorcycles are in a heap of wreckage and will need towing.

After quizzing your friend about what happened, you find out that he was still messing with his GPS while you both were accelerating up the hill. With his eyes glued to the GPS screen and his left hand punching the buttons, he never noticed your brake light and proceeded to plow into the back of your bike.

WHAT'S THE LESSON?

GPS devices can really help you find the way during riding adventures. But it's important not to let them draw your attention away from the immediate need to watch what's going on ahead. It's best to refer to any navigational aid when stopped and resist the temptation to read a map or GPS while rolling.

steadfast against any form of drinking and riding.

Visual Distractions

There are many visual distractions that can grab your attention. The problem with visual distractions is that they can cause you to look away from where you're going. This has obvious consequences if the road bends unexpectedly or a car crosses your path at that moment. Not only that, but where you look influences where you go. It's common for riders to veer off course when looking over their shoulder, especially when traveling at slower speeds.

Other visual distractions include consulting a map or a GPS, fiddling with your phone, adjusting your riding gear, or looking behind when doing a blind-spot "head check." Minimize the amount of time that your eyes are off the road.

Fatigue

Fatigue affects your ability to process information and react to hazards. When riding to work in the morning, be aware of residual slumber, and make sure to keep speeds low at the end of a long, tiring day.

Another situation that can lead to poor judgment is when a rider pushes his endurance limits a bit too far. This typically occurs during long trips when a schedule or destination is followed too rigidly. Instead of pulling over for a refreshing break, the rider pushes on hoping to make it just one more exit. Not only is this risky, it also diminishes enjoyment.

Be flexible with time, and take breaks as often as needed. And remember that more breaks are needed when you are uncomfortable because of hot or cold temperatures or inclement weather. Also, recognize when you aren't at your physical or emotional best and adjust break schedules accordingly.

Chapter 5

Maintain Your Ride: Maintenance and Packing to Help Manage Risk

I t's easy to ignore your motorcycle's maintenance, but neglecting certain maintenance chores can lead to serious trouble. In addition, packing is an often overlooked risk when riding.

Maintenance

Let's take a closer look at the maintenance items that must be taken care of if you are to manage risk.

Tires

Your motorcycle's tires are an important facet of handling and safety. Yet, a surprising number of riders neglect their tires. I'm constantly surprised at how many riders I survey admit to checking their tire pressures only once a year, usually at the beginning of the riding season. The problem is that air escapes slowly over time, and you may not recognize deteriorating handling. Low tire pressures can also lead to more rapid and uneven wear as excessive flex creates too much heat. Enough deflection and heat can even lead to a blowout.

So, how often should you check tire pressures? I recommend checking pressures at least twice a month, but once a week is better. Also, adjust pressures whenever you carry a passenger or a heavy load for any significant distance. Another advantage of making regular tire monitoring a habit is early detection of slow leaking punctures.

The manufacturer's suggested tire pressures can be modified somewhat to enhance handling and traction levels. For instance, performance riders who want a bit more grip at the expense of wear may choose to lower pressure a few pounds. But, take care not to decrease pressures below what a knowledgeable tire vendor suggests, or you may experience worse performance and excessive wear. Conversely, too high pressures can result in reduced grip and poor bump absorption.

The first thing people check when determining whether a tire needs replacing or not is the tire tread depth. Many tires have several small raised tread wear indicator bars molded into the bottom of the tread. As the tire surface wears, the tread wear indicator appears closer and closer to the tire's surface. Not all tires have these built-in indicators. If you can't find indicators, measure thread depth using a U.S. penny. Place Lincoln headfirst in a groove, and if you can just see the top of his hair, it's time to order new rubber.

It's best not to wait until your tires are worn to the indicators. Shallow tread depth directly affects traction, especially when riding in the rain. The grooves in the tread are there to allow water to squeeze sideways out from under the tire. A worn tire with shallower grooves cannot shed water as efficiently, thus increasing the risk of hydroplaning.

While you're looking at your tires, check to see if the tire is wearing evenly. Often, tires will suffer from various maladies, such as *cupping* or *scalloping*, where the tread blocks make uneven contact with the road. Incorrect inflation, suspension problems, hard braking, and many other factors can cause this. Many times, there is nothing you can do except replace oddly worn tires. It's possible that you will get better wear characteristics with a different brand or model of tire. You may want to check model-specific Internet forums for advice on what tires work best on your bike.

Tread depth and uneven wear are not the only considerations when it comes to determining whether it's time to order new tires. Over time, the rubber can become harder and less pliable. There may also be cracking. Most professionals recommend you buy fresh tires if your current tires are more than 5 years old, even if the tread isn't worn down to the wear bars. You can identify when the tires were manufactured by looking for a series of three or four numbers stamped inside an oval on the tire sidewall indicating the week and year of manufacture. For example, 2209 indicates that the tire was made in the twenty-second week of 2009. Note that tires made before 2000 have only 1 digit for the year.

Brakes

The condition of your brake system can easily go unnoticed because brake pads and brake fluid are mostly out of sight. It takes a conscious effort to examine brake pad wear, requiring you to get onto your knees and peer into the brake calipers. Look for wear indicator grooves located in the middle or edges of the brake pads. If the pads have worn down so the depth of the grooves are very shallow, it's time to replace your pads. If your brake pads lack these grooves, refer to your owner's manual for minimum

Your motorcycle's tires are an important facet of handling and safety.

thickness specifications. Replacing brake pads is rather simple, but requires care. A good shop manual will walk you through the procedure. After replacing the pads, tighten the caliper bolts to the proper torque specification and make absolutely sure the pins that hold the brake pads in the calipers are secure.

Check brake fluid by identifying its color and opacity. Clean brake fluid looks like apple juice, whereas old fluid looks like molasses. Monitoring brake fluid is easy if your brake master cylinder reservoir has a translucent body or a small window. Even if your fluid looks okay, you should change it at least every 2 years, because water from the atmosphere contaminates brake fluid, which causes corrosion and a spongy-feeling lever and reduced performance. Changing brake fluid can be a do-it-yourself task, although it can be tricky to expel all the air from the system.

Final Drive

Touring bikes and many cruiser-style motorcycles have shaft-driven final drive, which requires little attention, but even these systems need occasional care. Check your owner's manual for the maintenance schedules for fluid replacement or lubrication. Belt-driven motorcycles require little care as well, but belts will need to be inspected at regular intervals and will eventually need replacing.

Unlike shaft drive, chain drive systems need regular attention to prevent premature wear. Modern O-ring chains are quite durable, but require regular cleaning and lubrication to ensure a long life. There are many theories about the best way to maintain a drive chain, but many riders

have luck spraying the chain with WD40 to dissolve the grime, wiping it off with a shop towel, then spraying a light coating of chain lube or chain wax every few hundred miles. Do this after a ride when the chain is warm for maximum coverage. You may consider installing an automatic chain oiler, such as Scottoiler system, to ensure a healthy chain.

Adjusting the drive chain slack is another important task. The tools for adjusting the chain are included with most motorcycles' basic tool kit. Chains wear unevenly, which means you must find the tightest spot of the chain run and adjust slack to this section of chain. Refer to your owner's manual for adjustment specifications.

Chain wear can be evaluated by pulling the chain away from the rear sprocket; a new chain will not pull away. Chain replacement is a messy and relatively difficult job requiring some special tools for cutting, removing, and assembling links. Note that it's a good idea to replace sprockets as well for longer chain life.

Engine Fluids

Most riders follow the almost universal 3,000-mile (4828 km) interval for changing the oil and filter. However, hard-ridden motorcycles may need more frequent oil changes. Changing the oil and filter is a project you should learn to do yourself. Not only will you save money, you will also become familiar with the hidden regions of your motorcycle where fluid leaks and loose fasteners can easily go unnoticed.

Liquid-cooled engines require occasional coolant checks. Refer to your owner's manual for information about when coolant must be changed. Old coolant can cause scale to build

Adjusting the drive chain slack is an important maintenance task.

up inside the radiator and the engine. Be sure to replace the coolant with a brand that is designed for motorcycle engines.

This and That

Throttle, clutch, and choke cables need to be lubricated periodically. For less mess and a more effective treatment, consider purchasing a cable lubing tool that clamps onto the cable end and directs the cable lube into and down the casing. It is possible to get lubrication down the cable casing without a special tool by removing the cable ends from their connections and patiently spraying or pouring lube inside the casing, then sliding the cable back and forth to coat the cable. Don't forget other parts that need lubrication, including lever pivot points and gearshift linkage.

Loose or corroded electrical components cause all sorts of problems, including intermittent power loss or a complete shutdown that can leave you stranded. Periodically cleaning and tightening all

accessible connectors can prevent this from happening. Also, an application of electrical grease or a water dispersant spray will help keep water away.

Vibration causes nuts, bolts, and screws to come loose. Take a bit of extra time after a cleaning session to go around the bike to make sure all fasteners are snug. Apply a drop of thread lock to secure critical fasteners or drill a small hole in the bolt and lock-wire it to a nearby bracket or neighboring bolt.

You'll find a maintenance schedule inside your owner's manual that will tell you when it's time to give attention to specific areas. Find a place in the manual where you can make notes about when procedures were done by date and mileage. Include chain, sprocket, and tire changes, as well as any modifications. This documentation can help you track component wear intervals and becomes evidence that the motorcycle was well cared for when it comes time to sell.

Preemptive Care

Taking care of your motorcycle also involves detecting unexpected problems before they become a hazard. Many issues can be thwarted through regular cleaning and attention and with a simple pre-ride check. Perform a quick walk-around, checking tire condition and pressures as well as chain slack and oil level. Also, look for escaping fluids. Turn on the key and check that lights are working, then clean your windscreen and mirrors.

Mount the bike and turn the handlebars full lock left and right. Listen and feel for indications of poorly routed cables or dry steering head bearings. Creaking sounds or resistance while turning the handlebars warrant further investigation. While you're mounted, apply both brakes to be sure there is firm resistance. After you've adjusted your mirrors and checked fuel level, you're almost ready to go.

If you are about to carry a passenger or a significant amount of extra weight, be sure to increase tire pressures and adjust suspension settings. See your owner's manual for appropriate settings.

After you've taken care of the motorcycle, clean the shield on your helmet and get your riding gear together. Performing this pre-ride routine allows the opportunity to head off any mechanically related issues and gets your mind prepared for a safe ride.

Roadside Repairs

Even with meticulous care, you may experience a mechanical problem while on the road. Fortunately, many roadside breakdowns require simple fixes. A basic understanding of how engines run and how brake and electrical systems work can mean the difference between being stranded and getting back on the road in short order.

To make roadside repairs possible, you may want to read up on basic motorcycle mechanics. Even if you can't perform a roadside repair, this knowledge can help you decide whether you should attempt to fix the problem yourself, call for a ride, or summon expert help.

Tools

Almost every motorcycle comes with a basic toolkit, but these kits may not include all the items you need to make some roadside repairs. It's a good idea to take inventory of the most common sized bolt heads on your motorcycle and buy a set of small sockets and a socket wrench. Carrying a multitool is also a good idea. It's also smart to carry a few common fasteners, extra bulbs, fuses, a small amount of safety wire, electrical wire, electrical tape, and some wire ties. A small pair of locking pliers is quite useful, and a flashlight or headlamp is useful for peering into dark recesses and for illuminating the darkness when stranded on the side of the road at night. And don't forget your cell phone.

Before you begin your roadside repairs, make sure you are safely situated to prevent being hit by a passing car. Also, park the motorcycle so it will be stable enough to stay upright while being worked on.

Tire Punctures

Other roadside mechanical issues may come up that aren't related to the engine, such as a flat tire. Tire punctures occur often enough that you may want to consider

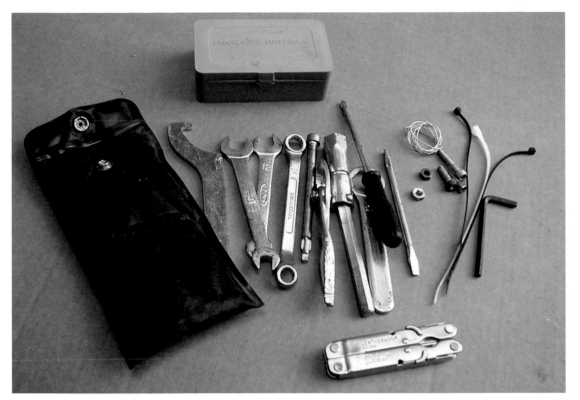

Almost every motorcycle comes with a basic toolkit.

packing a tire repair kit. It's not a bad idea to practice using the repair kit by drilling a hole in an old tire and plugging the hole. This practice will be very helpful if you're ever stuck on the side of the road.

There are several types of repair kits, some with tar-like strings, others with rubber plugs. Each kit will have a tool to insert the plug and cement to secure it. Some kits include CO_2 cartridges to inflate your tire. If yours does not, then consider purchasing a supply to add to your kit or packing a small bicycle pump. There is wide debate about whether it's safe to ride on repaired tires. Many riders risk riding on plugged tires and have had no problems, while others value the peace of mind a new tire brings. Many dealers will not plug tires due to liability.

Taking care of your bike will reward you with many trouble-free miles. Good preparation is key to preventing mechanical problems and for making a potentially depressing roadside breakdown a minor event. You can learn about motorcycle mechanics by reading or taking a course, but the best way to gain knowledge and confidence is to get your hands dirty. You may be surprised just how easy some procedures are, and the value of the experience will last a long time.

Pack Smart

You may not think that your luggage can increase the risk of a crash, but there have been many incidents of riders falling as the result of a jacket sleeve or some other item coming loose and getting caught in the chain or rear wheel. Do not take your packing for granted!

Containment is one of the most important aspects of a safe, secure load. The simple act of putting various items inside a container or bag greatly reduces the

SMART BIKE CHOICES FOR NEWER RIDERS

Many people ask which motorcycle is best for new riders. I almost always recommend small displacement machines: a sport bike in the 250cc to 500cc range, a 650cc adventure bike, or a 800cc cruiser. One reason behind this recommendation is that new riders shouldn't be pressured to ride faster than their skills will allow. Also, a big, powerful machine can be intimidating and cause unnecessary and distracting anxiety. It's tempting to want the hottest sport bike or the biggest, baddest road burner on the planet, but there are better choices.

From my perspective, the best bikes include the following criteria:

Reliable: A machine that you can always count on to start and run reliably all day long.

Not very powerful: A moderately powerful bike is one of the most important criteria for novice and intermediate riders.

Inexpensive: The newest machines are amazing, but you don't need a $10,000 or $20,000 machine to have a great time. As a matter of fact, if you spend all your money on your bike, then you will not have as much money available for other things like quality riding gear, rider education, or trip expenses. Also, forgo unnecessary bling and resist making any engine performance modifications. Sometimes spending a bit more is worthwhile. The newest motorcycles are coming equipped with advanced electronics that improve safety, such as anti-lock brakes, traction control, and power modes. These safety features will cost more but are usually worth the extra money.

likelihood of something coming loose in transit. But not any bag will do. Plastic grocery bags can slip easily from beneath the most tenacious bungee cord, whereas a canvas or nylon bag with a coarse texture will give a better hold. Common sense is your best source of information when it comes to containment choices. Of course, the best containment solution is motorcycle-specific luggage.

Soft Luggage

The advantages of soft luggage are its light weight and temporary installment. The disadvantages are that soft luggage does not provide security or much weather protection. Soft luggage can also scuff paint.

There are many choices when it comes to soft motorcycle luggage, including tank bags, tail packs, and saddlebags. The features to look for are sturdy zippers that will endure a lot of yanking and stuffing, a semi-ridged body for easy loading and good looks when not packed, and a well-designed system for securing the luggage to the bike. Additional features include protection for your bike's paint, rain covers, reflective material, additional pockets, and styling to match your bike.

Hard Luggage

Hard luggage is the way to go for the motorcyclist who tours regularly in all kinds of weather. Most touring bikes come from the manufacturer with hard saddlebags and possibly a tail trunk, whereas many sport tourers have optional factory-available hard bags. For those with bikes that don't come with hard luggage, there are manufacturers of aftermarket hard luggage.

Containment is one of the most important aspects of a safe, secure load.

Hard bags carry a pretty generous amount of gear with the added benefit of weather and theft protection. The disadvantages are that hard luggage is expensive, relatively heavy, and can add a lot of girth to the profile of an otherwise slim motorcycle. Although many hard bags are removable, some are not, requiring bag liners that can be brought into a hotel room. Bags that are removable allow the bike to be less encumbered when not on touring duty. Some bags can be difficult to remove, depending on the system's design, and reveal ugly brackets when the bags are left home.

Overloaded

No matter what type of luggage you use, it's important that you don't overload the motorcycle. Every motorcycle manufacturer and maker of luggage will have a weight limit for their product. Motorcycle manufacturers assign a *gross vehicle weight restriction* (GVWR), which is the maximum allowable weight, including the combined weight of the motorcycle, rider, passenger, fuel, and any gear.

The manufacturers assign the GVWR to prevent the frame, drivetrain, and transmission from becoming overly stressed and to help avoid overheating the bearings and brakes, which can cause premature wear. Suspension components will suffer trying to control the extra weight, which can result in an ill-handling beast that wallows and scrapes hard parts in corners. And suspension that is compressed toward its maximum will be hard-pressed to keep the tires in contact with the road as it struggles to follow the dips and rises of the road surface. If the suspension bottoms, the wheels can actually lift off the surface on rebound.

Most owners' manuals list the GVWR as well as the maximum weight allowed for you, your gear, and a passenger. A motorcycle with a GVWR of 902 pounds (409 kg) and a load capacity of 386 pounds (175 kg) can handle a 150-pound (68-kg) rider and a similarly sized passenger along with 86 pounds (39 kg) of riding gear and cargo. Considering that one set of riding gear can weigh as much as 20 pounds (9 kg), not much is left for cargo. Larger bikes will accommodate larger people and more gear.

Now you can see why it's important to follow the manufacturer's suggested GVWR and consider the GVWR of any motorcycle you consider purchasing for its ability to handle what you're likely to ask of it.

The Right Stuff

Even without knowing our motorcycle's GVWR, most of us know that it's best to take the four-wheeler when it comes to carrying heavy or awkward loads. But some may attempt to carry things that tax the carrying capacity of a motorcycle. Tent campers may endeavor to carry a full-sized camp stove, lantern, jumbo tent, tarp, and folding chair, as well as a few extra changes of clothes. Full-sized gear and other large items can shift around, distracting the rider and possibly destabilizing the bike.

A better strategy is to prioritize and eliminate all but the most essential pieces of equipment. It's good to make a list of needed items and put the gear on the floor in front of you. Divide the gear into three piles: one pile will contain your "most important" items, one will contain "somewhat important" items, and the last pile is for items that are "nice to have." Now determine what can be eliminated and what can be downsized with a smaller version. For instance, full-sized toiletries can be replaced with drugstore samples of toothpaste, soap, and shampoo.

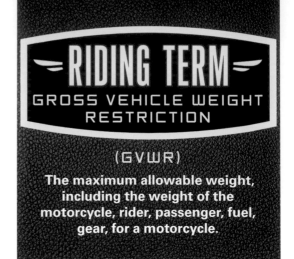

RIDING TERM
GROSS VEHICLE WEIGHT RESTRICTION
(GVWR)
The maximum allowable weight, including the weight of the motorcycle, rider, passenger, fuel, gear, for a motorcycle.

A typical 2-foot (60-cm) wide camp stove that weighs 5 pounds (2 kg) can be replaced with a hikers stove, which collapses down to 6 inches (15 cm) and weighs less than 1 pound (.5 kg). Sure, the cooking capacity is reduced, but it may allow you to take along some other "somewhat important" and "nice to have" items. Small-sized mess kits and lanterns are also available, as are lightweight tents and sleeping bags that can help manage the overall size of the load and keep weight down.

Some riders mount stuff on top of the front fender or strapped onto the front fender, but this can cause adverse handling effects and block cooling air from reaching the radiator or engine, so don't do it.

Straps

Now that you've pared down your luggage to the bare necessities, it's time to get it onto the motorcycle and make sure it stays there. Bungee cords have been around for many years and were a huge advancement in convenience and security. Several years ago, the bungee cord concept was expanded (pun intended) to include the bungee net. I remember the first time I saw a bungee net—I thought the world of motorcycling as I knew it had changed. I bought one for myself and for my two riding buddies, and, from that day on, our packing leaped from a precarious pile to a secure bundle. But I soon realized that bungee nets weren't perfect. Holding a large sleeping bag, a duffel, and raingear soon stretched these nets to a point where the space between cords was large enough to allow items to slip from its matrix. It seemed that the venerable bungee cord still had a purpose. A stout bungee cord will cinch down the load while the net helps contain the various items.

Recently, more high-tech straps have hit the market with hassle-free hooks and easy cinching methods. I really like Rok™ straps that combine cinchable plastic clips with stretch-cord material for very secure packing.

Balancing Act

Once you've figured out what to bring and how to carry it, it is important to distribute the weight to keep it from negatively affecting stability. The rule of thumb is to keep weight as low and toward the motorcycle's center of gravity (CG) as possible. Saddlebags are located low and a bit rearward, which makes them a good choice for heavier items. The tank bag is a great place for items you need to get to quickly. It's not the best place for heavy items because, even though it is close to the CG, it is also rather high. It's a good idea to keep middle-to-lightweight items in tank bags, because they can shift from side to side. Also, you wouldn't want anything hard and sharp in a tank

RIDING TERM
CENTER OF GRAVITY

(CG)
The average location of the weight of any object.

bag in case of a crash. Luggage racks and tail boxes have the disadvantage of being far from the CG and up high. This location would be fine for lightweight items, especially since some racks are designed to handle as little as 3 pounds (1 kg)! Some riders use backpacks, which are convenient, but can cause shoulder and back fatigue on longer rides and can encumber movement. Be wise about what you choose to put in a backpack because whatever is inside your backpack will go tumbling with you in a crash.

Many riders often overlook proper, safe loading, but a secure load is just as important as possessing proficient riding skills.

The cargo on this fully loaded bike is about to fall off; don't underestimate the importance of good packing.

Chapter 6

Managing Traction

C ar drivers have few concerns about tar snakes, wet road markings, sand, railroad tracks, pavement drop-offs, or raised construction plates. But for a motorcycle rider, these seemingly benign surface characteristics become serious hazards that can land you in the hospital. Anyone who is new to motorcycling needs to go through the transition from car driver to motorcycle rider, and an important part of this transition includes knowing whether there is enough traction to prevent a crash.

On the one hand, traction management is rather straightforward— recognizing when traction is limited and then doing nothing that could cause a skid. However, that's easier said than done. This section will help you recognize factors that affect traction so you can better judge if it is possible to brake, swerve, or corner without crashing. Let's start by describing exactly what traction is.

Traction 101

Simply put, traction is friction between the tire contact patch and the road surface. The technical measurement of traction potential is called the *coefficient of friction*. Several factors determine how much traction is available, including road condition, the tires' ability to grip the road, and the amount of load or pressure pressing the tires onto the road surface.

The quality and quantity of traction depends on several factors, and it changes continually. This means that we must always be alert to factors that affect how much grip we have, including surface debris, water, contaminants, broken pavement, large cracks, and other hazards, such as raised structures. Traction changes quickly from one section of pavement to the next, and it's up to you to recognize these changes and maintain a healthy amount of traction in your account. It also means monitoring tire condition and inflation pressures.

Tires and Traction

Tire compound, temperature, and condition directly affect traction potential. Tires grip the road through friction and by mechanically bonding with the surface as the rubber conforms to the surface texture. A softer compound allows for the best coefficient of friction partly because it more easily interlocks with the voids in the pavement surface. That said, a touring tire with a harder rubber compound does a commendable job of providing acceptable traction along with the benefit of exceptionally long wear. Soft-compound sport tires generally provide more grip, but at the expense of a shorter tire life. Positioned between long-distance touring tires and sport rubber are sport-touring tires that offer a good compromise, providing wet and dry road grip and decent wear life.

Tire technology has improved to a point where it is possible to buy a tire with the grip that sport tires provided a decade ago combined with a fairly long life. Much of this is due to new rubber compounds and the introduction of multiple compounds used in the same tire, which feature more durable rubber in the center to manage

RIDING TERM

TRACTION

Friction between the tire contact patch and the road surface.

long highway miles and a softer rubber compound on the outer regions of the tread for cornering grip.

I talked earlier about how proper inflation pressures are necessary for your tires to operate within their intended temperature range by controlling tire flex. Maintaining optimal heat range extends tire life, decreases risk of tire failure, and provides the best grip in the widest range of conditions. Investigations have revealed that close to 50% of the bikes on the road have underinflated tires. A good rule of thumb is to check pressures weekly, whenever air temperature changes appreciably, and before any significant road trip. Remember that tire inflation pressures must be raised to support additional load from a passenger or luggage. Check your owner's manual for details.

Traction and Surface Quality

Traction quality and quantity is constantly changing with variations in the road surface. As mentioned earlier, tire rubber mechanically bonds to the road as the rubber squeezes into the little nooks and crannies that are present in the textured pavement surface. Roads with a coarse texture offer more dimples and voids for the rubber to squeeze into, whereas very smooth surfaces, such as a steel construction plate, have very little roughness for tires to grip.

Proper inflation pressures are necessary for your tires to operate within their intended temperature range.

Moisture and surface debris will reduce the amount of available traction, no matter what surface you're on. Rain-slick roads have reduced traction because the water lubricates the surface. However, there is usually more than enough traction for normal riding situations, providing you use smooth braking, turning, and acceleration inputs.

Be aware that moisture can accumulate due to sudden changes in ambient temperature causing condensation to collect on the roadway, even if the sky is clear. This can happen when the road temperature is colder than the air temperature and is most common in shady areas, on humid days.

The first step in managing traction is to identify areas that may not provide sufficient grip for braking, accelerating, or cornering. Unfortunately, it can be difficult to spot some surface hazards, especially at night or when the sun reflects sharply

off the surface. One thing to look for to determine a potential change in traction potential is any variation in surface color or texture. A surface that is glossy reflects light differently than a textured surface, causing either a lighter or darker color depending on the exact makeup of the surface and angle of light.

Sometimes, spotting surface contamination can be almost impossible. A light scattering of sand that covers the entire lane may not have enough change in color or texture to be identified. Fluid spills are another contaminant that can be tough to see. Keep in mind that the presence of fluid spills may be recognized by smell, so keep all of your senses on high alert. If you must ride over traction-robbing hazards, do so as upright as possible and avoid braking, turning, or accelerating.

Broken pavement, construction plates, manhole covers, and surface debris are

LESSON LEARNED

Cold Tire Lowside

You have become an avid track day enthusiast ever since your first experience riding on a racetrack a few years ago. Not only has your riding skill improved, but you've made several new friends who enjoy riding with.

Today, you and your friends anxiously wait in the garage for your next riding session to begin. Your bike has been sitting in the cool garage for almost 40 minutes since your last session. You hear the announcement that your group is on deck, so you pull on your leathers and thumb the starter. Your friends have tire warmers on their bikes, so it takes a few more moments before they are ready to go.

You have a video camera mounted to your gas tank with the intention of filming your friends. You line up behind them and are soon signaled to enter the track. The three of you accelerate briskly to the pit exit. Your friends charge through the first corner faster than you expect them to, so you twist the throttle a bit more so that they don't get away. The first couple of corners are stressful as you try to keep up.

You charge ahead toward the first left-hand turn. You quickly realize that your speed is a bit too high. You know that trail braking is risky, but you remain on the brakes a bit longer to scrub off more speed as you lean into the turn. Suddenly, you feel the front wheel slip, and, before you know it, you are sliding on the ground. You are well protected with full a leather suit and race-grade boots and gloves, so you are unhurt. And because there was plenty of runoff, your bike simply comes to rest in the grass with minimal damage.

WHAT'S THE LESSON?

Your tires had cooled after the last riding session and were not warmed up enough to handle the braking and cornering forces you introduced. You know it usually takes a couple of laps before your tires are up to full operating temperature, but you trail-braked hard in an effort to keep up with your friends whose tires were already warm from their tire warmers.

The desire to video your friends also contributed to the crash. You could have asked your friends to wait a bit longer before achieving full speed. Next time, take a couple of laps to warm up your tires and resist keeping up with other riders.

often easier to spot, but may be hard to avoid. Look for an escape route around the hazard that does not lead you toward a second, perhaps more threatening hazard. Keep your vision well ahead and constantly scan aggressively for surface issues.

The trick to preventing traction loss caused by hidden hazards is to predict that a hazard is likely to exist. For instance, you should expect oil and coolant to accumulate where vehicles typically idle in place, such as tollbooths, stoplights, and drive thru lanes.

Some hazards like gravel on the road are hard to spot.

And, you should not be surprised to find sand, gravel, and other debris on rural roads and near construction sites.

Load Management

Another important aspect that affects the amount of available traction is the load on your tires. Even the stickiest tire cannot grip the road if it isn't making good contact with the road. More force pressing the tire contact patch onto the road means more traction. This can be illustrated simply by sliding the palm of your hand on a table surface with only minimal pressure. Now do it again, but this time press vertically down into the table surface. The vertical force creates more friction, pressing your skin into the minute voids in the table surface and preventing your hand from sliding easily.

Although the amount of grip from your tires remains more or less constant during a ride, the load placed on your tires changes constantly with variations in surface slope, camber, and irregularities, such as bumps and pavement drop-offs. Ascending hills places load on the rear tire, and descending hills places load on the front tire.

The load placed on your tires also changes with every action you take. Accelerating causes the load to shift rearward, and braking causes the load to pitch forward. Handlebar inputs load the sides of the tires, and cornering also plays a role in causing shifts in tire load. Let's look at actions that use traction so we can understand how to maintain grip.

Traction Expenditures

Available traction can be thought of as a bank balance. The amount of funds in your account is the traction you have available. Certain "expenses" require you to withdraw these funds, which are the forces that make your motorcycle accelerate, turn, and stop. Acceleration introduces driving forces, which can spin the rear wheel, while braking force can cause a skid. Cornering forces will slide your tires out from under you if available traction is exceeded.

Any one of these forces can eat up the entire traction balance (available grip), leaving your account empty. Spend all your traction, and you'll crash. You can also drain the traction account by spending for two needs at once. For example, if you spent 70% of your savings on cornering, and you try to spend another 40% on braking, you will overdraw from your account and lose traction. But, it's important to have traction in reserve, which means that you should allow at least 20% to remain in your account at all times, just in case.

Traction and control are directly affected by how skillfully you perform braking, accelerating, and cornering actions. Ham-fisted handlebar inputs can cause abrupt spikes in load that squander available

traction. Let's take a closer look at how braking and cornering affect traction.

Braking Traction

Let's talk about how traction is used for braking. When you apply the brakes, weight pitches forward, increasing load and traction on the front tire. This means the front brakes provide the most braking power and is why most bikes have larger front brakes. Unfortunately, this forward load transfer also means there is less grip available for rear wheel braking.

Sport bikes have a taller center of gravity and a shorter wheelbase, which causes the bike to pitch forward more easily when braking. Compare this to a cruiser, with its long wheelbase, and you'll see that the cruiser exhibits less forward load transfer, meaning that the rear brake becomes more important. Note that the total traction between the front and rear does not change, but the amount of rear traction is reduced as the front is increased.

To stop in the shortest distance, you must progressively apply more front brake force to take advantage of the increasing traction, especially on dry pavement. Since the forward load transfer lightens the rear, we must reduce rear brake pressure to avoid a rear wheel skid. Anti-lock braking systems (ABS) are helpful in preventing skids in an emergency situation, but most systems work only when the bike is upright and not leaned.

No matter what kind of bike you ride, you can't brake as hard when the road surface is compromised; therefore, load transfer is reduced and traction distribution is more balanced front to rear. This means that

when braking on slippery surfaces, you can rely a bit more on rear brake power.

Braking over bumps can make traction management difficult because the load on the tires changes momentarily. When you hit a bump, the suspension is compressed so it cannot as effectively absorb the impact. Depending on the size of the bump or the depth of the pothole, you can easily find yourself with a locked front brake. For this reason, if you must brake, do it before the bump(s) or wait until your front tire is clear of the bumpy surface. (Braking techniques are discussed in a later chapter.)

Braking in Corners
One of the most common rider errors that result in traction loss in corners is braking to avoid a mid-corner hazard. The scenario usually goes like this: you round a corner at a comfortable pace at a moderate lean angle when you suddenly see a branch that

One of the most common rider errors that result in traction loss in corners is braking to avoid a mid-corner hazard.

has fallen completely across your lane. You instinctively go for the brakes. But if you jam on the brakes, you will exceed the amount of traction available in your traction account and cause your tires to slide out from under you.

It's certainly possible to apply the brakes while leaned, but you won't have much traction to brake very hard. In an emergency situation, it's often best to straighten the bike as much as you can (without going out of your lane) and then apply the brakes. This will transfer some of your traction "funds" from the "cornering account" to the "braking account" so you don't become overdrawn and crash. Once the side forces are reduced, you can apply more brake power. If this isn't possible, then you're stuck trying to simply apply the brakes as much as you can without skidding. Brake lightly at first and increase brake force as the bike stands up. Unfortunately, most ABS cannot detect sideways slips and are therefore not useful in preventing sideways traction loss due to braking while cornering.

Cornering Traction

Cornering is discussed fully in a later chapter, but for now, let's talk about how cornering affects traction. You use handlebar pressure to initiate lean to corner, which creates side forces that use traction. Once the bike is banked into the corner, traction is used to keep the bike carving the arc. The greater the speed and the greater the lean angle, the more traction is consumed. If traction is lost, as happens when you hit a patch of mid-corner sand, then the bike stops turning and slides straight to the outside of the curve. This can result in a collision with a guardrail or an oncoming car.

Abrupt handlebar inputs can also cause traction loss. Depending on your speed and lean angle, cornering can use almost all of the available tire traction. This means that there is precious little traction in reserve for mid-corner correction, braking, or, in extreme situations, even a flinch at the handlebars.

Here's a common scenario: let's say you are very confident at cornering and really enjoy the thrill of deep lean angles at an invigorating pace. All is well until you feel your boot begin to grind on the pavement. You instinctively flinch at the handlebars, and the next thing you know, you are sliding on the ground in a shower of sparks. The tire would have had a decent chance of maintaining grip if you had remained relaxed.

Tire Trust

One of the reasons inexperienced and untrained riders are afraid of cornering is because of a lack of trust in their tires' ability to grip the road. It's certainly possible to lose traction in a corner if you ask too much from your tires, but there is usually plenty of grip for cornering at normal speeds. The most likely condition that can overtax tires while cornering is excessive speed. Depending on the tire type, condition, and age, it is possible that speed alone is enough to cause traction loss. But when it comes to the average street rider, more times than not, traction loss happens because of fast speeds combined with a surface hazard or a seemingly small mistake from the rider.

One technique for managing traction in corners is to follow the straightest path through a curve, which requires less lean angle compared to simply following the contour dictated by the road engineer. (I'll discuss cornering and cornering lines in more detail in a later chapter.)

Throttle Traction

Remaining relaxed when in a corner is one way to help the tires maintain grip. Another is to gradually accelerate once you are leaned in the curve. This *maintenance throttle* also helps balance available traction between both tires and keeps the suspension in its "sweet spot" to maintain tire contact with the road.

Acceleration is good, but too much throttle will increase cornering forces, compress the rear shock, and extend the front suspension enough to cause the bike to drift away from the intended path of travel. Too much acceleration can also overtax the rear tire, especially if the bike is leaning. Careful throttle modulation is the key to avoiding rear tire spins.

Throttle Ratchet

One method that can help manage throttle application and rear tire traction is the "ratchet" technique. Most people use the throttle like a rheostat light switch, simply rolling on the gas in a continuous motion. But, you will be less likely to go too far if you imagine the throttle barrel as having tiny detents along its path from off throttle to full throttle. "Click" through the series of detents to monitor tire grip. Each click is a measure of throttle application that incrementally feeds power. If you sense the rear tire beginning to slide, stop clicking on the throttle. The tire will likely regain its grip without much drama. This technique is particularly useful when riding aggressively out of corners or when the road surface is wet or otherwise compromised. Click, click, click for more precise throttle control.

Remaining relaxed when in a corner is one way to help the tires maintain grip.

Chapter 7

Shifting and Braking the Right Way

Learning to ride a motorcycle includes learning to shift gears and brake properly.

Shifting

Shifting can be a challenge to new riders, especially for those who have never driven a manual transmission. Some people struggle with the coordination of clutching and shifting, but most get past the difficulties and go on to do fine.

New riders learn early that the reason for shifting from one gear to another is to match the *road speed* (mph/kmh) with the *engine speed* (rpm). Higher gears are used as speeds increase, and lower gears are selected as the bike slows. Being in too high a gear can cause the motor to "lug" if you attempt to accelerate, and being in too low a gear can cause over-revving.

Shifting up or down requires disengaging and reengaging power to the rear wheel through the use of a manual clutch. This is where new riders have trouble. People who have no previous experience using a manual

Some people struggle with the coordination of clutching and shifting.

transmission struggle with the concept of engaging and disengaging power to the rear wheel. Add the need to roll off the throttle and click the gearshift lever, and the whole process can be overwhelming.

To manage the relative complexity of learning to shift, beginner courses introduce the shifting skill one step at a time. First, the student shifts into gear and then rolls the bike forward using the clutch to learn about the mechanism and how to control it. They also learn how to shift into neutral, which is not an easy task for a lot of newbies. Before they are allowed to ride, each student simply rocks the motorcycle back and forth by putting the bike into first gear and easing the clutch into the "friction zone" to feel how the clutch transfers power to the rear wheel.

With this drill under their belt, they are ready to go to the next step and ride across the parking lot. If the student puts what he

learned into practice, he will be able get under way without stalling. This may take a few attempts because anxiety causes muscles to lose coordination, but, with a little practice, shifting becomes more and more of an unconscious task as the day goes on. As a new rider gains more experience and seat time, he or she can soon devote less thinking capacity on gear shifting and instead focus on more immediate issues, such as balance, traction management, and surviving in traffic.

Poor shifting skill can be a problem, of course. Lousy coordination and timing leads to abrupt gear transitions and lurching that can compromise control and traction. Poor shifting will also cause a passenger to have a poor experience as he or she braces for each gear change. To become proficient, a rider must pay attention to how he or she can refine shifting skill. Let's take a look at some advanced shifting techniques that can increase both control and riding satisfaction.

Advanced Upshifting

Upshifting is often done in a relaxed manner, with throttle and clutch actions done rather leisurely. The problem with slow upshifting is that it allows the engine rpm to drop so that, when the clutch is released, the spinning rear wheel forces the engine to rev to match the higher road speed. This can lead to abrupt lurching and unwanted engine braking.

To control this abruptness, keep the revs elevated while shifting. The best way to do this is to upshift quickly. Your goal should be to prevent the revs from dropping more than about 500–1,000 rpm between the time you squeeze the clutch to when you release it.

To perform this technique, roll off the throttle only slightly instead of closing it fully. This keeps the revs from falling to idle. When you disengage the clutch, squeeze the lever only enough to interrupt power to the rear wheel and then shift the transmission into the higher gear with a quick flick. Preload the shifter with bit of pressure on the lever for speedy lever action. As soon as the transmission is in the higher gear, immediately release the clutch and roll on the throttle to maintain speed. Done correctly, the quick-shift technique should take about 1 second, and forward drive should remain steady.

Clutchless Upshifts

Another advanced upshifting technique used by racers and sport riders is the *clutchless upshift* procedure. This technique eliminates the clutch from the upshifting process and offers the potential for very

RIDING TERM
CLUTCHLESS UPSHIFTING

The act of shifting into a higher gear without using the clutch.

quick upshifts. A well-timed, rapid throttle closing, in combination with a ready left foot, can upshift most modern transmissions with buttery smooth precision to maintain forward drive with virtually no chassis pitch.

Clutchless upshifts involve the same steps as the quick upshift, but *without squeezing the clutch*. To perform this technique, close the throttle as you instantaneously shift to the next higher gear and then immediately open the throttle. Each step is done simultaneously, with the entire technique taking less than a second.

Done correctly, the machine will experience no added wear and tear. That said, I would limit clutchless upshifts to times when rapid acceleration is required. It may take a bit of practice before you can perform this technique skillfully, but it's a worthwhile tool to master.

More and more manufacturers are shipping their latest performance motorcycles with optional electric shifters that allow full-throttle upshifts. This device momentarily cuts the ignition when the shift lever is moved, thus eliminating the need to close the throttle at all. You would expect this option to be available only on sport bikes, but BMW's latest

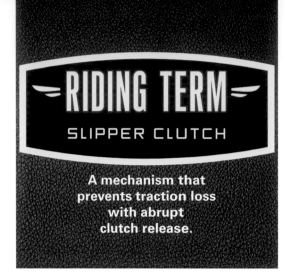
usually causes abrupt engine braking that can lead to a brief but potentially dangerous rear tire skid. Quickly letting go of the clutch after downshifting forces the engine rpm to instantly match the road speed, causing you to lurch forward and skid. It may even cause the rear tire to "hop" as the rear wheel is forced to slow as the engine rpm catches up to the rear wheel speed. By easing the clutch out slowly, the engine is allowed to match the rear tire speed without any of this drama.

Manufacturers understand that miscued downshifts are a hazard, and they mount slipper clutches on many high-performance motorcycles to reduce the danger of locking the rear wheel during a high rpm downshift.

R1200RT is available with an electric quick shifter that they call the Gearshift Assistant Pro. Times are changing.

Advanced Downshifting

Good downshifting technique is essential for maintaining control.

Good downshifting technique is arguably more important than upshifting for maintaining control. Poor downshifting

Throttle Blipping

To execute smooth downshifts, it is important to match the engine speed with the road speed. You can do this by slowly easing out the clutch, but sometimes a rapid downshift is necessary or desirable. Unfortunately, releasing the clutch quickly can lead to abrupt re-engagement. To downshift quickly, you must keep the rpm elevated as you downshift. This can be done by either keeping the throttle open slightly or by "blipping" the throttle during the downshift.

The throttle blipping technique is done by quickly cracking the throttle open, then closed (blip), while you simultaneously squeeze the clutch and click the gearshift lever. The point is to get engine rpm matched to the lower gear ratio before you release the clutch. The rapid blipping technique occurs within the span of less than 1 second. The clutch is quickly squeezed and released as the transmission is shifted down, and the right hand blips the throttle. This is repeated with every downshift, one gear at a time.

You can blip the throttle rapidly to reduce the time between gears, or you can be leisurely. High-performance riders blip the throttle very quickly when downshifting between gears as they set up for a corner. Street riders may choose to blip the throttle more slowly when coming to a stop.

Brake and Blip

Often, you need to brake while downshifting, but trying to simultaneously brake and blip is a difficult skill to master. The problem is that moving the right hand to blip also causes the fingers to move, which invariably changes brake pressure.

RIDING TERM

THROTTLE BLIPPING

A method for executing smooth downshifts by quickly twisting the throttle to match the engine speed with the road speed before releasing the clutch.

Combining braking and throttle blipping can be done with less difficulty if you apply the front brake with your index and middle fingers while you close and open the throttle with your thumb and two outside fingers.

The point is to blip the throttle while keeping consistent brake lever pressure. This is most easily done when using very firm braking pressure, where brake lever movements translate into relatively minor brake force changes.

Which Gear?

Higher gears provide a more relaxed ride but do not offer immediate acceleration. Lower gears ensure decent driving force when you roll on the throttle, but will harm fuel mileage. Every bike is different, and what may be the right gear for one machine may not be right for another. You must identify your bike's engine power characteristics to be able to take advantage of the power it has to offer.

Small-displacement bikes typically need more frequent shifting and are more demanding on the rider to pay attention to gear selection. Large-displacement bikes have a wider power range and allow less shifting. One isn't better than the other, but they need to be ridden differently.

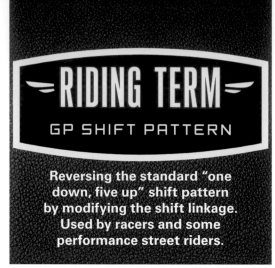

No matter what bike you ride, it's a good idea to be in a low enough gear for ready acceleration. This is especially important if you need to get out of trouble when riding in traffic or trying to outrun a dog. It's also important when cornering. The right gear will provide enough drive through the corner to stabilize the suspension and carve a predictable path. It also increases rearward weight transfer, which causes your motorcycle to drift slightly to the outside and "finish" the turn when using the "outside-inside-outside" cornering line. Master your bike's power characteristics by experimenting with different gears in various situations. As you experiment, notice how various rpm help you refine your bike's handling.

Braking

Most riders understand that braking is an important skill to learn. But, as you're about to find out, there is much more to braking than just squeezing a lever on the right handlebar and pressing a foot pedal on the right.

Braking Basics

To ride well, you must feel confident that you can slow and stop your motorcycle. To do this, you must understand a bit of motorcycle physics and then practice to make braking mastery an integral part of your skillset.

First, let's consider the various ways to slow a motorcycle. You can use the front brake, the rear brake, and engine braking as a supplement—or any combination of the three. You can use one finger, four fingers, or any number in between on the front brake lever. You can brake quickly or smoothly. You can brake hard or soft. Each method has its place, depending on the situation.

Braking Intensity

When slowing for a corner or just for a stop sign, you must determine how hard to brake. Often, how hard you must brake is based on timing. Wait too long to apply the brakes, and you'll need to brake hard to stop in time, possibly causing the tires to slide. Brake earlier, and you introduce less brake force for more control.

Brake Adjustments

Did you know you can adjust your front brake lever and rear brake pedal? You can adjust your front brake by rotating the lever mount on the handlebar. Choose a position that allows your forearm and wrist to be flat when applying the brake. A lot of brake levers allow you to adjust the reach by turning a numbered dial.

Rear brake pedals may be adjustable as well by removing the pedal and repositioning it onto the splined shaft at a different location. Be sure to adjust your rear brake light switch if necessary.

Engine Braking

We all use engine braking from time to time to slow our motorcycle. This is appropriate when minor speed adjustment is required. However, for significant speed reduction, it's best not to use engine braking alone. Relying on engine braking to slow rapidly can lead to uncontrolled rear wheel braking force and loss of rear tire traction. Instead, use the brakes and let engine braking merely assist the process. As a rule of thumb, brake first to slow the bike and then downshift once road speed is reduced to minimize this risk and to ensure a smooth downshift.

The Power of the Front Brake

An important concept that all motorcycle riders must know is that the majority of braking power occurs at the front tire.

This is because the load supported by the front tire contact patch increases as the motorcycle pitches forward under braking. More forward load transfer means increased traction at the front tire, thus allowing the rider to use more front brake.

Unfortunately, there is a myth about the danger of using the front brake that won't seem to die. Perhaps this myth started with tales of hapless kids flipping over a bicycle's handlebars or from horror stories told by riders who fell because they skidded the front tire, usually because they locked the front brake in a fit of panic. Whatever the source, too many riders still believe that the front brake should be avoided.

AUTOMATIC MOTORCYCLES?

There are some signs that suggest that choosing the right gear may become less relevant in the future. Until very recently, motorcyclists have not been faced with the choice of whether to purchase a manual or automatic transmission because all motorcycles came with a manual clutch and gearshift lever. However, manufacturers are now offering models with automatic transmissions, such as the Honda VFR 1200.

Past examples of automatic motorcycles never sold well, so why would they bring them back? Perhaps it has to do with the changing demands of new riders. Very few manual shift cars are being sold in the United States, which means that there are fewer potential new riders who know how to shift a manual transmission. The fact is that manual transmissions intimidate potential new riders who see the clutch and shifter as a barrier to learning to ride.

With fewer new riders entering motorcycling, it is important to entice them in any way possible. If motorcycling is to grow (or even maintain its numbers), then manufacturers need to provide machines with automatic transmissions. By offering full-sized automatic models (not scooters), new riders inexperienced in manual shifting just might be enticed to enter the world of motorcycling.

Older, experienced motorcyclists may also be attracted to automatics as a way to simplify motorcycling as age challenges their ability to multitask. Of course, most veteran riders have no interest in eliminating shifting from the riding experience. They understand that shifting is an integral part of riding a motorcycle and that the act of shifting a motorcycle skillfully can enhance riding enjoyment.

In most situations, this couldn't be further from the truth. While it is possible to flip over the handlebars on certain motorcycles, the chances are very remote on most machines. Riders of long wheelbase cruiser and touring motorcycles really have nothing to worry about because the center of gravity is low and far back from the front wheel. However, sport bike riders are more likely to lift the rear wheel because of the short wheelbase and high center of gravity. But traction must be optimal to lift the rear tire completely off the ground into a "stoppie." It's more likely that you will skid the front tire than flip over the handlebars. Skidding the front tire is something you must prevent because you lose directional control and often "tuck" the front tire underneath the bike and crash almost instantly. If you do lock the front wheel, release the brake immediately and reapply more gently.

To avoid skidding the front tire, it's important to remember that an increase in tire load increases traction. By squeezing the brake lever progressively, you allow time for the weight of the bike and rider to shift onto the front tire so it is less likely to skid. "Set" the front brake and load the front tire before squeezing fully so the forks start compressing. It's a two-step process: squeeze, and then squeeze more. In an emergency situation, you may not feel as though you have time to set the brakes, but if you simply grab the lever without settling the bike onto the front tire, you risk skidding the front tire and falling. (Emergency braking technique is discussed later.)

In most situations, the front brake is the primary brake to use. However, there are times when you want to avoid using the front brake, like when riding at very slow speeds and riding over very loose sand or gravel. In these situations, the powerful front brake can cause a slow-moving motorcycle to lurch to an abrupt stop or skid. In these situations, use mostly rear brake.

In most situations, the front brake is the primary brake to use.

How Many Fingers?

Most new riders are taught to use four fingers on the front brake when braking. This is a good idea if you ride a vintage bike, an older large tourer, or a cruiser with relatively weak front brakes or a lot of weight to a stop. However, most modern brake systems deliver impressive stopping power, which means maximum brake force can be had with two-finger front brake operation.

There are a lot of advantages to using two fingers, including being able to leave two digits on the throttle grip (usually the ring and pinkie). This is useful when implementing advanced throttle/brake techniques, such as throttle blipping (discussed earlier) or brake and throttle overlapping (discussed later). Whether you use two, three, or four fingers to brake (I don't recommend using only one finger), your goal is to find the best combination of power, feedback, and braking control.

The Rear Brake Is Good

Emphasizing the importance of the front brake might make you think that the rear brake is unimportant. That would be wrong. As a matter of fact, the rear brake plays a large role in reducing stopping distances if both front and rear brakes are used together.

The rear brake also plays a role in stabilizing the motorcycle. Applying the rear brake helps keep the rear of the motorcycle from lifting and "pulls" the rear of the motorcycle in line with the front wheel and the direction of travel. Pressing the rear brake pedal just before applying the front brake minimizes load transfer and increases stability.

The rear brake can be a powerful tool, but it must be used carefully to avoid skidding. Rear tire skids are common because weight pitches forward under braking, which means less traction is available at the rear tire. Many riders think that a skidding tire

There are a lot of advantages to using two fingers to brake, including being able to leave two digits on the throttle grip.

This makes sense since the rear tire has little load during maximum braking to accept rear brake force without skidding. But for a street rider, it makes no sense to forego the rear brake and forfeit the benefit of shorter stopping distances.

It is important to know that there are times when you will favor the rear brake over the front, or use the rear brake only. I mentioned earlier that you should avoid the front brake over very loose sand or gravel and when making slow maneuvers because the front brake can be overly powerful for fine control. Instead, drag the rear brake to control your speed (and help with balance in slow-speed maneuvers).

provides comparable stopping distances to a nonskidding tire. But, a skidding tire creates excessive heat, tread deformation, and tearing of rubber at the contact patch, thus reducing grip and contributing to longer stopping distances. Also, a skidding tire leads to loss of lateral grip, allowing the rear tire to fishtail and making it difficult to control the motorcycle.

Because the rear wheel can lock under extreme braking, most road racers and track day riders avoid the rear brake altogether.

If you happen to skid your rear tire on gravel, dirt, or a wet surface, you may be able to successfully release the rear brake without incident.

You may be tempted to avoid the front brake on surfaces with less traction, like a rain-soaked roadway, but, in most situations, there is ample traction to use both brakes. This is important because the majority of brake force still comes from the front tire, although you won't be able to brake as hard as in the dry. And braking with less force means less weight transfer occurs so that the rear tire has good contact with the road for braking traction. A heavy load or a passenger makes the rear brake even more effective by keeping weight over the rear wheel.

If you happen to skid your rear tire on gravel, dirt, or a wet surface, you may be able to successfully release the rear brake without incident. However, it is risky to immediately release the rear brake if you skid on surfaces where traction is abundant because you could get flung up and over the high side of the bike if the rear tire suddenly regains traction while the bike is pointed sideways and instantly tries to align itself

with the direction of travel. This turns the bike into a catapult and can spit you into the weeds.

If your tires happen to be aligned at the moment you release the rear brake, you may not highside. But another way to manage a rear tire skid is to keep the rear tire locked while you steer through the inevitable fishtailing. Unfortunately, keeping the tire skidding can also result in a crash. However, you are more likely to lowside, which is preferable to a highside any day. If you decide to ride it out, keep your eyes on the horizon to help maintain direction control and balance. Next time, don't skid!

To prevent rear wheel skids, you've got to know how much pressure it takes to lock your bike's rear brake. The technique for stopping quickly without skidding the rear tire is to apply the rear brake firmly at first, but then gradually reduce rear brake power as the weight transfers forward. Essentially, begin with a firm rear brake and, as you increase front brake power, decrease rear brake power. This allows you to achieve full braking potential while remaining in control. This technique will take practice to master, so spend some time in a parking lot and be patient.

With all this talk about skidding tires, what about anti-lock braking systems (ABS)? Just because your bike has ABS doesn't mean you're excused from practice! Yes, ABS can help maintain control and virtually eliminate the risk of skidding, but the system doesn't apply the brakes for you. That's why you need to practice… because a surprising number of riders whose machines have ABS fail to use their brakes hard enough to avoid a collision.

RIDING TERM
LOWSIDE

A crash that occurs when traction is lost while leaned in a corner, and the motorcycle slides out from under the rider.

Laying it Down

"Laying it down" is a phrase that describes deliberately sliding a motorcycle on its side to avoid hitting a vehicle or some solid object. Why would someone think this was a good idea? Good question!

There was a time when motorcycle brakes and tires didn't perform very well, which made "laying it down" a potentially viable option for getting a bike stopped in an emergency. Even though motorcycle brakes and tires have evolved remarkably over the years, there are riders out there who still think that laying it down is a reasonable option. While it is possible that there may be some freak occurrences that might justify laying it down, I cannot think of any.

More times than not, laying a motorcycle down is the result of braking errors or because the rider panicked and overreacted. Often, the rider skids and falls without impacting the obstacle. What may follow next is the rider claiming that he "meant to do that" and that all he could do was "lay it down." In reality, he would have been better off remaining on two wheels and using proper braking technique.

Emergency Braking Practice

Instead of using ineffective techniques for avoiding collisions, why not learn the proper way to stop in the shortest possible distance? The natural, knee-jerk response of the untrained rider to an emergency situation is to jam on the rear brake while either grabbing the front lever abruptly or using it too lightly.

Since the need to use emergency braking technique is relatively rare, most riders aren't very good at it. Regular parking lot practice will help you master emergency braking technique and provide you the opportunity to discover your bike's full braking potential.

Unfortunately, many motorcycle riders never experience the full power of their brakes. This is apparent when they fail to stop in time to avoid a vehicle or other

Regular parking lot practice will help you master emergency braking technique and provide you the opportunity to discover your bike's full braking potential.

hazard. People may avoid learning how to use maximum braking power because they are afraid they will skid or flip over the bars. Learning proper braking technique will minimize these concerns.

Practicing correct emergency braking technique allows you to:
- Experience what extreme braking feels like
- Learn to apply the brakes to their maximum potential without skidding
- Engrain emergency braking technique in your mind and muscles so you will perform correctly even in the heat of battle

Here's what you do: Find a clean parking lot where you can safely accelerate up to

about 25 mph (40 kph) with lots of runoff space at both ends. Mark a stopping zone with a "begin braking" marker (a bottle cap will do) and then measure and mark braking distances of 13 feet (4 m), 23 feet (7 m), and 34 feet (10 m), representing stopping distances for 15 mph (24 kph), 20 mph (32 kph), and 25 mph (40 kph), respectively. A skilled rider can easily stop short of these standards.

To stop in the shortest distance, apply both brakes firmly without grabbing or stomping. Apply more front brake lever pressure as you slow; squeeze, then squeeze more. You'll feel your eyeballs press forward in your skull when you get it right. If you skid the front tire, release it immediately. If you skid the rear tire, release it if you're more-or-less upright and try again, this time reducing pressure on the rear brake pedal as weight transfers forward. Repeat often until emergency braking is well-engrained and second nature.

Brake or Swerve?

Coming face-to-face with a car turning left in front of you means you have a decision to make: should you brake or swerve? Braking gives you the chance to stop before reaching the hazard, or at least to reduce speed and minimize impact if you cannot stop in time. On the other hand, swerving may allow you to ride around the problem.

When faced with a seemingly imminent collision, you will likely react with the method with which you are most familiar or comfortable. Many people choose emergency braking by default, but stopping quickly requires an intimate familiarity with maximum braking—a skill that few riders practice.

Some riders attempt to swerve, but this maneuver requires precise timing and assertive handlebar inputs. And, even if they manage to avoid the hazard, many fail to recover and run off the road. To effectively execute a swerve, you must know how to countersteer (press right, go right, press left, go left). You must also have a good sense of timing in order to avoid hitting the obstacle. Press too late or fail to hold the countersteer input long enough, and you'll hit the hazard. Hold the countersteer too long, and you'll need to act quickly and forcefully to stay on the road, which can compromise traction, especially on a dirty or wet surface.

You may think that applying the brakes and swerving at the same time is a possible option. But braking while performing a swerve can also result in the front tire sliding because the tires do not have enough traction to manage simultaneous braking and swerving forces. Precise timing is important for managing traction when swerving. Either brake first and release the brakes before swerving, or swerve first and then brake.

Corner Braking

Most times, you enter a corner at a safe speed and glide safely to the corner exit. However, you may encounter a mid-corner hazard like sand, a rockslide, or fallen branches that require advanced cornering and braking techniques.

We talked earlier about what you can do if you enter a turn too fast and that most times you can simply lean the bike more to complete the corner. (How to salvage a too-fast corner is covered at the end of this chapter.) First, let's discuss what you can do if you encounter a hazard in the middle of a corner.

Predict and Prepare

To help manage mid-corner hazards, you must predict and prepare. First, accept that there could very well be something around every corner you encounter. Yes, more often than not the coast will be clear, but resist complacency. It's usually the one time that you assume nothing is around the corner that bad things happen. Being mentally prepared for the possibility of a mid-corner obstacle is half the battle.

Once you accept that an obstacle or surface hazard may be present, then you are more likely to ride according to the laws of probability. This means approaching corners with a bit of skepticism. Look carefully for clues that indicate possible problems, such as questionable pavement with varying changes in color and texture that can indicate surface contamination, broken asphalt, or some other traction-robbing hazard. Also, consider the environment. If the area has a lot of construction traffic, expect dirt in the corners, diesel fuel spills, or even chunks of wood or metal on the road. In urban areas, expect to encounter pedestrians, bicyclists, dogs, and other vehicles.

For most riders, cornering is challenging enough without an unexpected problem appearing, which can overtax their mental and physical ability. If you have the time and space, you can simply slow down and steer around the problem. If your speed is too high, you may have to pull out your

It's a good idea to practice swerving because it requires precise timing and assertive handlebar inputs.

superhero skills and perform a quick stop or swerve abruptly to avoid colliding with the obstacle. Can you handle such an extreme maneuver? Most cannot.

Try to see as far into the corner as possible by putting your tires near the outside of your lane at the corner entrance. We talked earlier about how the "outside-inside-outside" cornering line can provide precious sight distance to allow you to see a problem moments earlier than if you hugged the inside of the curve. If you can't see far enough into the corner to evaluate whether there is a problem, then slow more.

How to Avoid Mid-Corner Hazards

Many times, the better choice is to maneuver around the problem. Let's look at your options. Say you lean into a turn and about halfway around the curve you spot a 4-foot (1-m) wide tree branch lying in your lane. You have to make a quick choice about whether to maneuver left or right. If you have the room, you may be able to go around the outside of the problem. This requires less traction and does not call on your maximum leaning skills. However, this may be a poor choice if it means that you risk going off the road or into the oncoming lane. Also, once past the obstacle, you will have to lean quickly to stay in your lane.

The other option is to tighten your line and go to the inside of the obstacle. This requires you to lean more by pressing firmly on the inside handlebar. Done correctly, this option keeps you in your lane, but asks a lot from your tires and your confidence to achieve more extreme lean angles. Also, in a left-hand turn, this may bring you dangerously close to the oncoming lane as your upper body hangs well over the

centerline. Another reason why this option may not turn out well is if you fail to turn tightly enough to actually avoid the hazard. Not leaning quite enough means that your tire will hit the object at a greater lean angle, which will likely result in a crash.

It may be tempting to swerve abruptly while leaned to avoid a hazard. But remember that your tires are already working hard just trying to handle the cornering forces that are required to keep your motorcycle tracking around the curve. Adding handlebar input risks overwhelming available traction, and the front tire can slide out from under you. Another factor that can overwhelm traction is abruptly chopping off the throttle. Depending on how much engine braking your motorcycle produces, even just decelerating while at full lean can cause a loss of traction. Also, consider the surface quality and slope of the road—will it allow significant handlebar input? If it's raining, you have much less traction available for mid-corner maneuvers.

Braking in a Curve

Sometimes, steering around the hazard isn't an option, and you'll need to slow down or come to a complete stop in the middle of a corner. Unfortunately, slowing or stopping while leaned can cause a skid. This is because traction is already being used to keep the bike tracking around the curve, and adding significant brake force will likely overwhelm the tires. To safely introduce stopping power, you must first make traction available by reducing cornering forces.

There are two basic techniques for stopping quickly in a curve:

- **Straighten, then Brake:** If the situation is urgent, you'll need to use the "straighten first" option, in which you first reduce lean angle (by pushing on the *upper* handlebar) to make traction available and then apply the brakes hard without skidding (see the section on emergency braking in this chapter). The problem with this option is that straightening the bike will cause you to shoot to the outside of your lane and no longer be on a curved path. This makes the "straighten, then brake" technique a poor choice if the road is narrow or if your tires are already near the centerline or edge of the road.

- **Brake while Straightening:** When the "straighten, then brake" technique is not possible, or when you have a bit more time to stop, you have the option of using the "brake while straightening" technique. This technique involves applying the brakes as much as possible to slow down, but not so much that traction is

exceeded. Lean angle will decrease as the motorcycle slows, making more traction available for braking. Brake progressively harder as the motorcycle straightens fully. A hybrid version of these two techniques involves partially straightening the motorcycle before braking. This allows stronger initial brake force compared to the gradual straightening method, and it allows the motorcycle to stay on a curved path.

Some riders are under the impression that the ABS found on many touring and sport touring motorcycles can prevent a cornering slide due to overbraking. But most ABS cannot detect sideward slides, only wheel rotation. Some motorcycles are just now coming to market with ABS that can detect lean angle and reduce the chance of a skid in a corner, but it's still best to rely on your skills and not on electronics to save you.

Corner braking can be a challenge.

As you can see, handling mid-corner obstacles can be tricky. The best way to manage these hazards is to predict them and ride so that you always have options of either maneuvering or stopping with minimal drama. This usually means entering turns a bit slower than you think you need to and practicing your leaning skills so both become second nature.

Advanced Corner Braking Techniques

I'd like to share some other braking techniques used by performance riders on the racetrack.

Trail Braking

Usually, you do the majority of your braking while the bike is still upright and release the brakes just as you countersteer into the turn. But sometimes delayed braking can be a useful tool. *Trail braking* is a technique for adjusting corner entry speed that involves continuing to brake beyond the turn-in point and then "trailing" off the brakes gradually until the brakes are fully released at or before mid-corner. Trail braking is most useful for tighter turns with a relatively high approach speed. Trail braking is typically done using the front brake only, with the rear brake released before turn-in, although trail braking can be done with either or both brakes.

One advantage to trail braking is that it allows you to extend the distance used to establish entry speed, giving you the option to slow over a greater amount of time and distance for smoother, less hurried braking. This extra time also allows you to adjust corner entry speed with more accuracy. By entering a turn with light brake pressure, you are less likely to upset the chassis if you

need to slow a bit more. For minor speed adjustments, simply remain on the brakes a bit longer. On the other hand, if you release the brakes completely before leaning, you have committed to that entry speed. If you need to slow more, you'll have to begin braking again, which can easily upset the bike and tires. To maintain traction, avoid increasing brake force and lean angle at the same time.

Another benefit of trail braking is that it enhances stability and control by minimizing the forward and rearward chassis pitch that occurs when applying and then releasing the brakes. When the front brake is applied, the forks compress, and when the brakes are released, they rebound and extend. The forks compress once again when the bike is leaned into the curve. When trail braking, the forks remain compressed as the bike is leaned, and the "off-brake" rebound action is eliminated. The suspension stays compressed as the bike leans and then rebounds gradually as the brakes are released and the throttle is rolled on.

Because trail braking is a technique that combines both cornering and braking forces, you must use light brake pressure. This is why it is best to get most, if not all, of your braking done before the turn. Trail braking can be risky; therefore, it should be used judiciously and avoided when traction is limited.

Practice trail braking only where traction is excellent. Learning how to trail brake starts with overcoming the anxiety that the tires will slide. Use light front brake pressure, and decrease brake pressure as you increase lean angle.

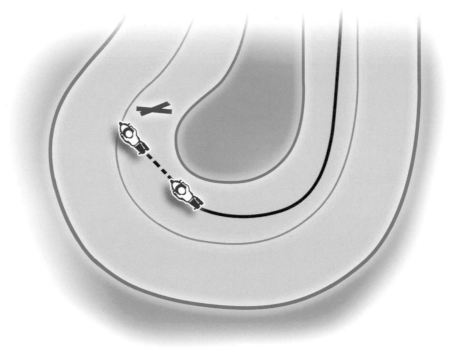

Figure 7.1

Figure 7.1 illustrates the "straighten first" option, in which you first reduce lean angle to make traction available and then apply the brakes hard without skidding. This will cause you to shoot to the outside of your lane and no longer be on a curved path.

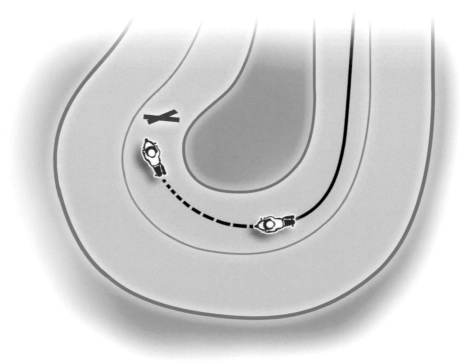

Figure 7.2

Figure 7.2 illustrates the "brake while straightening" technique, which involves applying the brakes as much as possible to slow down, but not so much that traction is exceeded.

One way to help refine the trail braking technique is to use two fingers on the front brake. This allows the use of both the brake and the throttle, which is useful for transitioning smoothly between braking and acceleration.

Overlapping Brake and Throttle

Overlapping braking and acceleration is a way to smooth the transition between the two. This is done by progressively rolling on the throttle as you release the brakes. The overlap is momentary and is designed to eliminate the often abrupt switch from brakes to throttle that can cause abrupt fork extension and compression. This may seem like an unnecessary level of control for typical street riding, but once you feel the benefits of such smooth transitions, you will find more and more situations where it provides superior control.

Use the brake/throttle/brake overlap technique when cornering. Proper cornering technique involves slowing before the turn, leaning into the turn, and accelerating through the turn. Most riders perform these tasks individually, but overlapping the brakes and throttle keeps the bike stable and helps preserve traction.

Handling a Too-Fast Entry Speed

You may one day face a situation where you enter a turn way too fast and leaning further is not an option. This can occur if your motorcycle has insufficient ground clearance, or you lose traction because the tires are unable to adhere to the pavement. This condition may cause your motorcycle to slide even if you are doing all the right things to manage traction, including looking through the turn, remaining light on

RIDING TERM

TRAIL BRAKING

A technique for adjusting corner entry speed.

the handlebars, and maintaining smooth throttle application. In these situations, you need to consider other options. For slightly overspeed corners, you can probably decelerate by gently rolling off the throttle. However, doing so can reduce ground clearance further and overtax the tires so that a slide out will occur.

Another option is to straighten the motorcycle and brake, then quickly lean the bike again before running off the road or into the oncoming lane. The idea is to scrub off speed so the motorcycle can carve a tighter path. Because there isn't enough traction to simply brake while leaned, you must first straighten the motorcycle, brake, release the brakes, and then return to maximum lean. This requires precise timing and control.

The last and most risky option is to straighten the bike and ride off the road or racetrack. Let's be clear: deliberately riding off the road is not a recommended technique and should only be considered when all hope of staying on the pavement is exhausted. Of course, this is not a viable option if a solid object is in the way, such as a guardrail. But, if the runoff is clear, it may be a feasible way to salvage a crash. Just be sure to straighten the motorcycle before you ride off the pavement to avoid losing traction.

Chapter 8

Cornering
the Right Way

Cornering is one of the most challenging and enjoyable parts of motorcycling. But consider that single-vehicle cornering crashes account for about half of all incidents, meaning that cornering is a challenge that is greater than some people can handle.

These mishaps are often the result of motorcycle riders flirting with the edge of their abilities, often charging into corners only to find themselves in "too hot." They usually respond by chopping off the throttle and braking mid-corner. The result is erratic control, with the bike possibly drifting too close to the edge of the road or crossing the centerline.

To execute the ideal corner means selecting the perfect entry speed, initiating the proper lean angle with a single handlebar input, relaxing your handlebar grip, and gradually accelerating throughout the turn to the exit. If you find yourself entering turns too fast, adjusting your path mid-corner, or delaying acceleration until well past the middle of the turn, then you've got some work to do.

One way to advance your cornering prowess and confidence is to think about you and your bike as dance partners and the road as your dance floor. Just like dancing, a graceful, well-trained partner makes the activity more enjoyable and, in the case of motorcycle riding, safer. This partnership begins by understanding the pitfalls and common solutions. Let's begin with basic cornering comprehension.

Cornering Comprehension

Truly skillful riders are able to "read" the road and adjust speed as each corner dictates—not too slow, not too fast. They know when and how much to lean and can place their tires' contact patch precisely on an intentional path. They also know when and how to modulate the throttle to maintain traction and execute a smooth exit. These riders feel less stressed and never rushed when cornering.

Cornering Process

An important lesson to learn is that optimum cornering, safety, control, and confidence is achieved when all facets of the cornering process are executed with precision. Let's discuss the basic steps to proper cornering:

- Entry speed
- Leaning
- Throttle application

By identifying each of these actions individually, you can refine your ability to manage the forces that use traction, which results in greater safety and confidence.

Entry Speed

Quite often, the reason for crashes in corners is simply because the rider did not accurately judge the proper entry speed. What exactly is a "proper" speed? It is a speed that allows you to negotiate the turn comfortably while applying

Remember the importance of keeping your eyes pointed where you want to go.

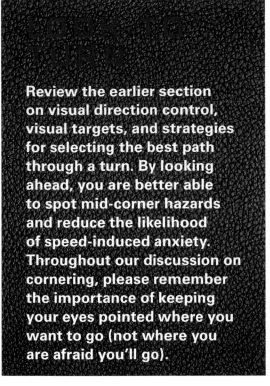

Look to Turn

Review the earlier section on visual direction control, visual targets, and strategies for selecting the best path through a turn. By looking ahead, you are better able to spot mid-corner hazards and reduce the likelihood of speed-induced anxiety. Throughout our discussion on cornering, please remember the importance of keeping your eyes pointed where you want to go (not where you are afraid you'll go).

gradual acceleration without the need for deceleration or braking.

Steady acceleration keeps the bike stable and makes the bike corner predictably, so entry speed should allow for this steady drive through the curve. Most cornering issues can be avoided by entering turns a bit slower than necessary. Always select cornering speeds that allow enough traction reserve for you to make a small mistake or to slow if necessary without losing traction. Remember, you can always accelerate once you can see that the coast is clear.

When cornering, you lean the motorcycle to the degree that is necessary to match the speed and cornering forces with the radius of the curve. The faster you go and/or the tighter you turn, the more you must lean. If you are afraid to lean, then you must reduce speed or only ride in big, sweeping arcs. Of course, in the real world, it's impossible to

avoid the occasional tight turn. The fact is that you will eventually have to deal with corners that challenge your ability. Let's talk about how to lean the bike.

Countersteering

To cause a motorcycle to turn, you must lean it into the corner. Handlebar pressure is used to get the bike to go from upright to leaned. *Countersteering* is the term used to describe this handlebar pressure and is used whenever you need to change direction. This applies to basic cornering maneuvers, as well as evasive maneuvers like swerving. It's important to be able to countersteer with authority when a corner suddenly tightens more than you expected or when you approach a tight corner at a too-fast speed.

Countersteering is done by pressing forward (and to a lesser degree, down) on the handlebar in the direction you want to go. Press on the right handlebar to initiate a lean to the right, and press on the left handlebar to turn left. This steers the front tire in the opposite direction, which unbalances the bike and causes it to "fall" into the turn. Got it? For quicker changes in direction you can simultaneously pull on the other handlebar. This "push-pull" technique is how racers achieve quick changes in direction in chicanes on the racetrack.

Some riders think that they turn their motorcycle by shifting body weight to the inside of the turn. Body position can help the bike change direction, but the effect is not significant.

Prove it to yourself by getting your bike up to about 20 mph (32 kph) in a clean and clear parking lot and then hold onto the bars with

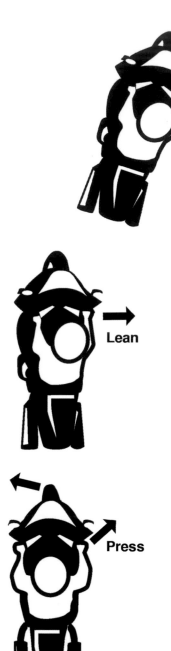

Turn

Lean

Press

Figure 8.1

Figure 8.1 identifies how to countersteer by using handlebar pressure.

off course but offers nowhere near the level of accuracy and quickness necessary for safe and effective cornering. It's difficult to avoid putting some pressure on the inside handlebar, but if you can truly isolate your body from the handlebars you should be convinced.

Body weight has even less influence as speeds rise. Try using body position to turn at 50 mph (80 kph), and you'll find that it has very little effect. The message is that body positioning alone is not effective at initiating precise lean angle and that countersteering is the primary method for turning.

Roll On the Throttle

Once the bike is leaned in a turn, the geometry of the chassis, the rounded profile of the tires, and several hard-to-describe forces cause the machine to arc around the curve. But this self-steering effect needs steady forward drive to work well and be predictable.

As I said earlier, the definition of correct corner entry speed is a speed that allows you to feel comfortable rolling on the throttle as soon as you lean the bike into the turn. This doesn't mean grabbing a handful of gas. It means gradually and progressively introducing drive to the rear wheel as you round the corner.

Rolling on the throttle stabilizes the bike and distributes load to help manage traction. Gradually introducing driving force as soon as you tip into a turn results in a predictable path of travel. It also extends the suspension into the middle of its travel, which helps it manage bumps. Without this steady drive, the bike will feel reluctant to turn. Just the right amount of throttle keeps

just your fingertips, keeping enough finger force on the throttle to maintain speed. Now, try to lean the motorcycle using your body weight only. Move your shoulders toward the direction of the turn as far as necessary to get the bike to lean and turn. You will notice that your bike slowly drifts

the traction load shared between both tires and the suspension in the right position for optimal stability.

The amount of drive force being applied affects path of travel. Acceleration causes the motorcycle's load to transfer rearward, reducing the front tire's load and its ability to maintain a tight arc around a curve. The result is a bike that drifts wide. This can actually be helpful in steering the motorcycle to the outside of the curve to a wide exit (as is used in the outside-inside-outside cornering line discussed later). By using the throttle, you can direct the bike to the outside without any significant handlebar steering input that uses front tire traction. You can think of this as "finishing the turn with the throttle."

Cornering Mistakes

One of the most common cornering mistakes is assuming the curve is easier than it actually is, when in fact the corner radius tightens mid-corner. This can happen if vegetation or some other vision blocker is hiding important information about the curve's character. Without seeing into the curve, the radius of the corner won't become apparent until after you are already committed to an entry speed.

The ideal solution to a tightening turn is to lean more by pressing on the inside handgrip enough to increase lean angle (countersteering). The throttle should be kept steady to stabilize the chassis, and you should look well into the turn to help direct the motorcycle.

This scenario will trigger varying levels of anxiety depending on entry speed, how tight the curve is, and how much cornering

Direction control and balance is maintained primarily with the handlebars.

skill the rider has in reserve. If you enter a corner a bit too fast, but are comfortable leaning the bike, you will experience little anxiety. However, you will experience significant anxiety if the curve tightens a lot and requires a lean angle that is beyond your comfort level. This usually results in an off-road excursion or collision with an oncoming car. Yikes!

To avoid putting yourself in such a precarious situation, you must always have speed and skill in reserve. Here is my advice:

1. Slow down enough to ensure that you can safely negotiate the curve (but not so slow as to cause problems behind

you). If you end up slowing too much, you can always get on the gas. But, remember that the speed at which you enter the turn is your "committed speed." Slowing down once you are already in the curve risks upsetting the chassis and compromising traction.

2. **Understand proper cornering technique.** Getting a motorcycle from upright to leaned requires an understanding of countersteering. Initiate lean by pressing forward on the inside handlebar (press right to go right and vice versa). A motorcycle handles and tracks best if you are relaxed and apply steady throttle once lean angle is established. Getting on the throttle too late can cause the bike to handle poorly and make it feel as though you must wrestle the motorcycle through the turn. This results in a sensation that the bike is uncooperative, which quickly erodes confidence.

3. **Practice to increase cornering confidence**. Imagine yourself in a situation where you are asked to perform a maneuver with mastery that you've never performed before. That usually does not turn out well. The same holds true with cornering. If you've never leaned your motorcycle beyond your comfort level, what makes you think you will do it when a corner tightens unexpectedly? A tightening corner may require you to lean farther than you have before—perhaps far enough for your footpegs or floorboards to drag. Practice leaning your motorcycle in a clean and clear parking lot until you have established a new comfort level. Practice regularly to keep this ability fresh.

Following these steps is no guarantee that the next decreasing radius will turn out fine. But you will have increased the odds that it will. Understanding how cornering stability is achieved is the first step. With this information, it is possible for you to develop your cornering and traction sense to a very high level for maximum safety, control, and confidence.

Learning to Lean More

Street riders never, or rarely ever, experience their motorcycle's cornering potential, which means that they are susceptible to failing to lean enough when necessary. Unless you are prepared both mentally and physically, you may very likely fail to perform well. That's why it's important that this skill remain sharp through practice.

If you perceive your corner speed to be too great, you will likely panic. This may cause you to freeze at the handlebars and run off the road instead of tightening the turn radius by adding a bit more lean angle. Although it may sound simple to just "lean further," it is not realistic to expect a rider to lean more than she has experienced previously, which is why many simply give up. A person who has only leaned her motorcycle to 30 degrees from vertical will not likely lean the extra 5 degrees that is necessary to stay in the lane.

Every rider has his or her own "lean limit," which is defined largely by previous experience. According to Berndt Spiegel, author of *The Upper Half of the Motorcycle*, humans are hardwired to lean no further than about 20 degrees, which is the maximum angle of lean achieved when running around a tight curve on natural surfaces. Anything beyond that angle of lean results in anxiety. This personal lean limit can prevent you from salvaging an overspeed turn, and it can also prevent you from reaching the next level of cornering proficiency.

Learning to lean a motorcycle to its full potential takes knowledge, skill, and practice to make it part of your muscle memory. You don't have to go fast to experience greater lean angles. A large parking lot that is clean and clear of obstacles can be an excellent venue for learning to lean. Simply ride in a circle, keeping the throttle steady at about 25 mph (40 kph). Look through the circle and relax as you lean the bike further and further as you gradually increase lean angles. You will gain a ton of cornering confidence once your brain and body develop a "trust" in this new sensation.

It's a significant accomplishment if you can lean enough to touch the footpegs or floorboards, but remember to respect the limits of the motorcycle you are riding. How far a motorcycle can safely lean depends on the motorcycle's ground clearance and handling capabilities, as well as on the traction the tires provide. Street motorcycles have built-in lean-angle warning devices in the form of footpeg "feelers" or folding floorboards. Depending on the motorcycle, you can usually touch these indicators without exceeding the limits of the bike (as long as the tires are in excellent condition and properly inflated and warmed). However, you must heed the warning these lean-angle indicators are giving you and not push much further because touching a stand or frame member can lever the tires off the ground.

Practice leaning to increase cornering confidence.

This practice leaning is critical for salvaging a too-fast corner. However, the very best way to avoid cornering problems is to use strategies that prevent you from needing these high-level skills in the first place. Always slow more than you feel is necessary when entering corners; that way, you are much more likely to handle unseen mid-corner hazards or changes in radius. You can always get on the throttle if the corner is clear, but it's difficult to recover when you are already in the curve too fast.

Quick Turning

One way to increase cornering confidence is to be able to quickly initiate a turn. You will use this technique anytime you must get the bike turned immediately, either because of a miscalculation or as a way to achieve a higher level of cornering precision. Quick turns are necessary at higher speeds because you don't have as much time and space to get the bike from upright to leaned.

One advantage of getting the motorcycle turned quickly is that it allows you to

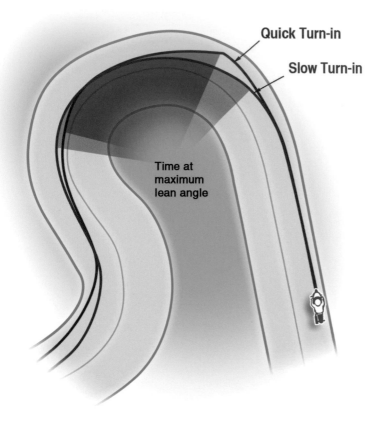

Quick Turn-in

Slow Turn-in

Time at
maximum
lean angle

Executing a precise cornering line requires coordination between the timing of your turn-in and the amount of countersteering intensity. Turning in too late and with not enough handlebar force can result in a "missed" apex, causing your motorcycle to stay in the middle or even outside portion of the lane, not near the inside as desired.

A quick turn uses more traction at the beginning of the turn, but uses less at the apex and exit. Even though more traction is used when turning quickly, good tires in dry conditions have more than enough grip to handle the extra force. However, a quick-turn technique should be avoided in the rain or at any time traction is limited.

Figure 8.2

Figure 8.2 illustrates the difference between a quick turn-in and a slow turn-in.

complete the majority of the directional change early in the curve and within a shorter distance and period of time. In comparison, a slower turn-in requires the lean angle to be held longer.

A quick turn is also useful as a way to achieve a delayed apex cornering line. Delaying turn-in by a half-second or so gives the rider a wider angle of view at the turn entry and points the motorcycle toward the turn exit, rather than toward the edge of the lane. Learning to turn quickly isn't difficult, but it does require firm countersteering inputs. The harder you press on the inside handgrip, the quicker you will turn. To aid the quick-turn process, pull on the outside handgrip while pushing on the inside grip (push-pull) and pre-position your body to the inside to help the motorcycle fall into the corner with less effort.

Cornering Lines

A *cornering line* is the path you take through a corner. A lot of riders simply ride down the middle of the road, echoing the shape of the curve. But remember, you have the option to ride in the left, center, or right portion of your lane, which offers several benefits not available to car drivers.

The basic cornering line is accomplished by entering the turn at the outside edge of the lane, turning toward the apex (the innermost part of the curve near the middle of the corner), and then exiting toward the outside of the lane. This "outside-inside-outside" path straightens the corner radius, which uses less lean angle and keeps more traction in reserve in case you must increase lean angle or execute mid-corner braking or swerving maneuvers.

LESSON LEARNED

Cornering Lines

Ralph doesn't think much about cornering lines, believing that simply keeping his bike in between the painted lines is good enough. He usually enters and exits turns in the center portion of his lane, only changing this routine when he needs to avoid something in the road.

Today, Ralph is riding on an unfamiliar road that twists and turns around blind curves. Ralph becomes tense trying to manage some of these corners. As he approaches one corner, he slows to what he thinks is an appropriate speed and begins to lean into the turn. But as Ralph begins to round the blind turn, he notices that the radius is much tighter than he expected, and his motorcycle is heading toward the oncoming lane. Panic burns as he tries to lean his bike further, but his floorboards begin to drag hard. Ralph is not turning sharply enough to stay in his lane so he decides to decelerate, but then the sound of hard parts on pavement becomes much louder. The next thing Ralph knows, he is on the ground.

WHAT'S THE LESSON?

This is a classic example of what can happen when cornering lines are not utilized. Ralph couldn't see much of the curve because it was obscured by roadside vegetation, and he was positioned too far to the inside of his lane. He would have seen further into the turn and made a better decision about his entry speed had he been positioned at the outside of his lane. By entering the curve from the inside, Ralph's motorcycle was pointed too much toward the outside of the turn so that much more lean angle was required to remain in his lane. Unfortunately, his motorcycle was already near its cornering limit so that when Ralph tried to lean further, it used what cornering clearance remained. This prompted him to decelerate, which compressed his suspension and ground the frame hard enough to cause a slide.

Entering a turn from the outside also allows a better angle of view into the curve to identify a corner's characteristics and any mid-corner hazards. Approaching from this location increases the likelihood that you will see problems early so you can adjust your entry speed if necessary.

Take a look at the "Lesson Learned" box on this page to see how an imaginary rider struggles when he does not use cornering lines.

Corner Types

The ideal line varies depending on the type of corner you encounter. There are three basic types of corners: *constant radius turns*, *increasing radius turns*, and *decreasing radius turns*. It's important to be familiar with the different corner types so you can determine the best line to take for maximum traction and control.

- **Constant radius turns** resemble a section of a circle and are usually easy to negotiate because the turn maintains a constant arc from beginning to end. A constant radius turn calls for the most basic cornering line, one in which you enter from the outside of the turn, apex mid-corner, and exit wide (outside-inside-outside).

- **Increasing radius turns** begin with a smaller radius and end with a larger radius. You enter these turns slowly, where the turn is sharpest, and accelerate early as the corner straightens out. Follow the outside-inside-outside path as you would with a constant radius turn, but plan on turning in earlier and apexing sooner.

- **Decreasing radius turns** are the most dangerous type of corner because they tighten from the corner entry to the exit. On and off ramps

are often decreasing radius turns, but these types of corners can be found anywhere. Many riders make the mistake of entering decreasing radius turns assuming the radius will remain constant. But this optimism can be deadly if they enter the corner too fast. A too-fast entry speed often results in a panicked rider responding poorly by locking the brakes or freezing at a lean angle that is insufficient to keep him or her from careening off the road. Decreasing radius turns are negotiated with the outside-inside-outside path, but it is important to turn in later so that the apex can be located further around the curve. This is referred to as a *delayed apex* cornering line.

Delayed Apex

A delayed apex is when you locate the innermost part of the turn (the apex) *around* the middle of the corner. Delaying your turn-in and using a delayed apex line will gain the best angle of view for determining turn characteristics and spotting potential hazards. The delayed apex also points the bike toward the outside portion of the lane at the exit. In contrast, an earlier apex location points the motorcycle dangerously close to the edge of the road and requires more lean angle as you near the exit to stay in the lane.

Figure 8.3

Figure 8.3 shows two cornering line options. The dashed line is the preferred path.

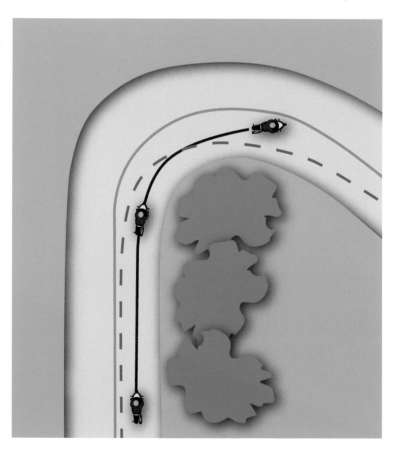

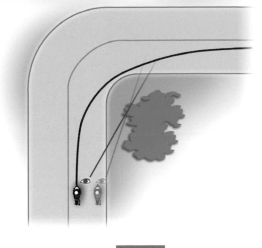

Figure 8.4. A constant radius turn.

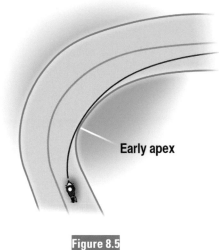

Early apex

Figure 8.5. An increasing radius turn.

The basic outside-inside-outside cornering line creates the largest possible radius and is a good choice if the corner is isolated from other corners with a straight before and after the curve. But multiple corners strung together can make the outside exit location used with the basic line unusable and dangerous. An outside exit that is appropriate for a single turn may prove too wide if the next corner bends in the opposite direction. You must determine what the exit location of the first turn should be so that the next corner can be handled safely.

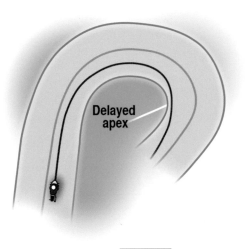

Delayed apex

Figure 8.6. A decreasing radius turn.

Turns in Sequence

Both increasing and constant radius turns are relatively easy to negotiate. However, even these relatively simple types of corners can become a problem if they are strung together into a series of turns. A rider who gets the first few turns wrong will have an increasingly difficult time negotiating each successive corner. The more corners in the series, the more likely that problems will compound. Add in a decreasing radius turn or two into the series, and the rider may encounter more than he or she can handle.

The preferred line through one particular series of corners that starts with a right-hand turn and then exits immediately into a left-hand turn and then into another right-hand turn is to stay right at the first turn's exit so you are set up for the immediate left-hand turn. This will keep your front wheel pointed away from the edge of the road and reduce the risk of crossing the centerline or running out of pavement on the road edge.

The trick is to string a series of corners together seamlessly by identifying each corner's characteristics and determining what the proper entry is for the following corner. Do this by looking well ahead.

Line Caveats

Whether dealing with a single corner or a series of corners, the ideal cornering line cannot always be utilized. A narrow lane can prevent the use of the ideal line, as can a road surface hazard or an oncoming vehicle. In these situations, a different plan must be considered.

Using the outside-inside-outside line means that you will be near the outside of your lane as you enter and exit the curve. Be careful not to hug the edge of the lane too closely to avoid a close call with a roadside obstacle or an oncoming car.

This cornering line also means you will near the inside of the curve at the apex. It is very important that this inside location not be too close to the oncoming lane or the edge of the roadway. When you lean into a turn,

you hang further to the left or right from where the tires are on the road. The more lean angle used, the more you overhang the oncoming lane or road edge. For left-hand turns, place your tires no closer than the left third of your lane to minimize the risk of a close call with an oncoming vehicle. If the road is narrow or your lean angle is significant, your tires must remain in the middle of the lane.

Corner Camber

Camber and slope are corner characteristics that must also be considered when selecting your path through a curve because of the way rises and dips can affect traction and limit ground clearance. Properly cambered corners are sloped to help vehicles stay on the road. *Positive cambered* or *banked* surfaces decrease the likelihood of sliding out because the cornering forces press the tires into the road surface at an angle that is closer to perpendicular.

Unfortunately, not all roads feature properly banked turns. Many corners are flat or have a *negative camber* or *off-camber* surface, which offers reduced traction compared to a properly banked corner. The slope of an off-camber curve requires an increase in tire side force and allows gravity to pull or slide the motorcycle down the slope more easily.

Even if the road is mostly flat, you are likely to encounter off-camber surfaces. Most roads have some amount of *crown*, which refers to the downhill slope from the center of the road to the edge to allow for drainage. This slope can cause traction (and ground clearance) problems when a motorcycle leans to the left when traveling in the right-

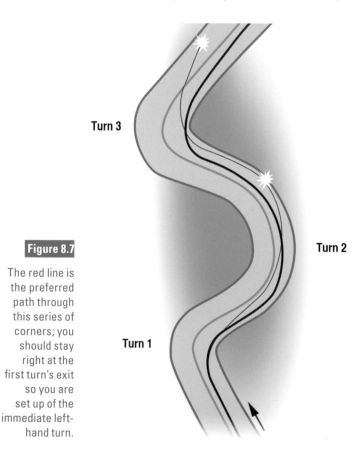

Turn 3

Turn 2

Turn 1

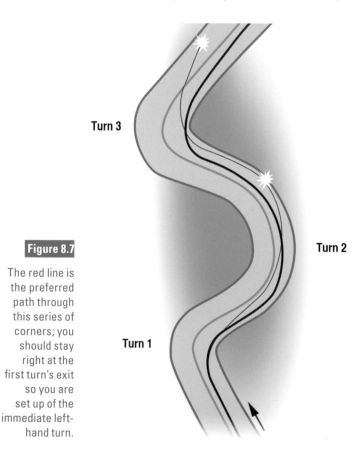

Figure 8.7

The red line is the preferred path through this series of corners; you should stay right at the first turn's exit so you are set up of the immediate left-hand turn.

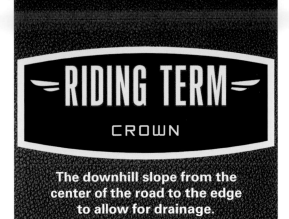

hand lane (off-camber), but can aid traction in right-hand turns (on-camber). Keep an eye out for these corner characteristics to determine the best line and entry speed. If possible, place your tires on positive-cambered banking.

It's not always clear whether a corner is flat or cambered or whether the radius is constant, increasing, or decreasing. But there are clues that you can look for to help determine the nature of the corner you're about to encounter. One technique mentioned earlier is to recognize how the sides of the road visually converge in the distance. If the road edges converge quickly, you can be sure that the radius is tightening and/or the slope is going off camber. If the road edges converge farther away, then the road is straightening and/or the camber is positive. Tree lines and telephone poles may give some indication of where the road is going, but they aren't as reliable as the road edge. If the corner characteristics are not easily identified, slow down.

A Deeper Connection

There is another excellent reason for utilizing the cornering lines and that is the enjoyment that results from interacting with the road. If you choose to simply follow the obvious radius of each corner, you miss a special interaction with the road that comes from consciously slicing through a series of turns. Using cornering lines feels more involved and focused.

It goes back to the idea that you and your motorcycle are dance partners, and the road is the dance floor. A series of turns become a ballet that brings a great deal of satisfaction, a deeper relationship with riding, and a feeling of cornering mastery.

Body Position for Cornering

Body position is also useful for initiating lean, stabilizing the bike, and increasing ground clearance when cornering.

Relax

Relaxed posture allows you to have a more enjoyable ride, but it also helps your motorcycle handle better and delivers feedback that increases cornering confidence. Relaxed arms are particularly important because they allow fluid handlebar movement so the suspension and tires can manage variations in surface quality that can affect available grip. For maximum control, it is best to isolate the upper body from the bars as much as possible by supporting body weight with the torso and legs.

Camber and slope are corner characteristics that must be considered when selecting your path through a curve.

Unfortunately, many people support much of their body weight with their arms. When I work with track day students, one of the first things I observe is their level of arm tension. Tense riders struggle to get their motorcycle turned and maintain a smooth path. I often give track day students the "loosen up" signal illustrated by me flapping my arms like a chicken. They report a huge increase in control and confidence and a decrease in fatigue after relaxing their arms.

Body Position to Initiate Lean

We learned earlier that countersteering is the primary way to initiate lean, but if you combine countersteering with body positioning, you can initiate turns quickly, efficiently, and accurately. Positioning your upper body toward the inside of the turn shifts the center of gravity toward the corner, puts weight on your inside handlebar, and causes you to pull on the outside handlebar, which enhances the countersteering effect. The result is a sense of "power steering."

Body position is really helpful when initiating a quick turn. Lee Parks describes a useful body "pre-load" technique in his book *Total Control* that involves pre-positioning your body before a turn while the bike is still upright. This will cause the bike to drift toward the curve, but you won't be ready to turn just yet. To keep the bike heading straight, put pressure on the outside handlebar until you reach the exact turn-in location, then release pressure on the outside bar and press on the inside bar. The bike will fall quickly into the turn. This technique may be scary at first because the effect is often dramatic, but a bit of practice will increase confidence.

Once you get the motorcycle leaned to the proper angle for the corner, your best tactic is to relax and be a good passenger.

There is one more good reason to use the inside body position technique. By leading with your shoulders and head, you are essentially telling your mind, muscles, and motorcycle where you want to go. Combining body position with visual direction control greatly increases cornering confidence and efficiency.

When you brake for a corner, try to have your inner thigh in contact with the rear of the fuel tank. This will happen naturally if you are leaning your body toward the inside of the turn. By supporting your thigh against the tank, you prevent your lower body from sliding forward on the seat when you brake, thus allowing your arms to remain light on the handlebars. On sport bikes with a lower fairing, you can position your inside knee so that it contacts the back of the mid-fairing for extra support. This technique not only minimizes handlebar pressure, but it also preserves energy by concentrating the substantial braking force low and at the center of the rider/bike center of mass.

Better Handling

Another, lesser known advantage of leaning your body off the inside of the motorcycle is the positive effect on handling. As a motorcycle leans, the tire's point of contact (*contact ring*) moves from the tire's center toward the smaller diameter sidewall. Rolling on this smaller diameter part of the tire causes the wheel and the motor to rotate faster to match the road speed. On your next ride, maintain steady speed and throttle setting, then weave side-to-side. You will be able to hear the motor rev as your lean onto the tire's smaller diameter contact ring. You are essentially forcing the motor to rev to match the road speed. You are also forcing the wheels to rotate

faster. This increased friction between the tires and the road uses more traction, conspires to countersteer the bike upright, and increases steering effort. Keeping the motorcycle more upright reduces these forces while allowing the motorcycle to carve its cornering path.

Mid-Corner Posture

Once you get the motorcycle leaned to the proper angle for the corner, your best tactic is to relax and be a good passenger. Motorcycle geometry varies from bike to bike, but, in most cases, the motorcycle will corner pretty much on its own once you are at the right lean angle. Relax and add only minimal input as needed to adjust the path of travel.

We discussed the advantages of leaning your body to initiate lean, but there are also many advantages to maintaining this position throughout the turn. Most riders stay perpendicular to the motorcycle, which is fine in most street-riding situations. But leaning your upper body inside of the bike's centerline has several advantages.

First, it relocates the center of mass so that the motorcycle does not have to lean as far for a given speed and turn radius, thus providing more ground clearance. In contrast, if you lean in the *opposite* direction of the motorcycle (counterleaning) with your body "on top" of the motorcycle, you will need more lean angle for a given curve at a given speed. This may be a useful technique for slow-speed maneuvers, but it is detrimental at higher speeds.

Using active body positioning when cornering also enhances the interactions among you, your motorcycle, and the road.

Lead fluidly with your eyes, arms, and upper body, and your motorcycle will willingly follow your lead.

Body Position Techniques

Let's discuss three body position levels: The *basic*, *intermediate*, and *full* hang-off techniques. Each provides varying degrees of influence on corner turn-in and lean angle.

- **Basic:** The basic body position technique is what I've been talking about so far. This technique is beneficial to all street riders. It simply involves leaning your upper body off-center, toward the inside of the turn. Position your inside shoulder low and forward toward the turn while your eyes look through the curve.

- **Intermediate:** The intermediate body position technique is appropriate when riding more aggressively. To do this, unweight your outside sit-bone by rocking your hips so that your inside sit-bone supports much of your body weight. Use this technique in combination with the upper body position described above.

- **Full:** The full hang-off technique is used by track day riders and racers to allow a quicker turn-in and maximum ground clearance. It involves positioning half of your butt off the inside of the seat while positioning your shoulders inside and low. To do this, get your weight on the balls of your feet, and then use your legs to lift your body into position with the edge of the seat resting in the middle of your buttocks. Avoid rotating the hips around the tank, which can result in an undesirable "crossed" body position where the upper torso is positioned on top of the bike. Keep your hips

perpendicular to the motorcycle with the inner thigh of your outside leg resting against the back of the gas tank. For maximum support, have the ball of your outside foot on the footpeg and lift your heel to raise and press your outside knee into the fuel tank. This gives firm contact between the footpeg and the tank to help support your body with your legs, not your arms. The indents found on the sides of many sport bike fuel tanks provide a place to press the inner knee against the tank. For added grip, apply stick-on rubber panels available from Stomp Grip® or Tec-Spec®.

Knee Dragging

When using the full hang-off technique, the inside leg can be kept close to the bike or extended into the turn to drag a knee. Knee dragging is used on the racetrack primarily as a lean-angle gauge. How early and how long the knee touches down can indicate whether a lap is slow or fast. If the knee touches early in a corner and remains in contact with the pavement longer, then it's a fast lap. Touching the knee down in the same place lap after lap also helps the rider develop consistency.

Many first-time track day riders are eager to drag a knee. Although knee dragging is a notable accomplishment, it is important to recognize that knee dragging is a result of advanced cornering skill that takes time and effort to achieve. Dragging a knee also requires more corner speed than most new track riders can safely reach. If you are one of these riders who aspire to drag a knee, I encourage you to first take the time to develop excellent body dynamics and cornering technique rather than push too hard in an attempt to shortcut the process. Let the pavement *come* to your knee rather than attempt to *reach* the pavement. Remember that extreme lean angles are necessary to drag a knee—lean angles you should not attempt on public roads.

Foot Position while Cornering

When riding aggressively, it is smart to move your feet back so the ball of the foot rests on the peg to prevent dragging a toe. Riding on the balls of your feet also makes it easier to maneuver fluidly when changing body positions. Think of how basketball or tennis players stand when ready for action, and you'll get the idea.

When initiating lean, it is beneficial to weight the inside footpeg to help lever the bike into the turn. This is easy if you pre-position your body to the inside before turning in (as discussed earlier). When using the full hang-off technique with the knee out, position your inside foot with the end of the footpeg located between the toes and the ball of the foot. The heel can then rest against the heel guard. This position facilitates lower body support and allows the hips to remain perpendicular to the bike.

Once leaned, street riders should not worry about which peg to weight when cornering because it offers little benefit in most situations. However, for those seeking the highest level of control when approaching the limits, there is benefit in experimenting with various peg-weighting options. Put more weight on the inside peg at the beginning of the turn and then shift weight to the outside peg about mid-corner. Weighting the outside peg as you reach the corner exit can help the bike stand up to reduce lean angle.

Riding a motorcycle is much more than simply sitting in the saddle. Learning to use these body position techniques can lead to significant increases in control. Parking lot practice sessions are a great way to learn this skill and to keep it sharp, but track days are the best venue for developing cornering confidence.

Photo 1 shows the basic body position.

Photo 2 is intermediate.

And Photo 3 is the full hang-off technique.

Chapter 9

Mastering Essential Skills

There are certain skills that are necessary if you are to ride a motorcycle well. They may seem simple at first, but you just may find yourself on your side or in an ambulance if you aren't prepared.

Slow-Speed Riding

Slow-speed maneuvers can stir fear into the hearts of even the best riders. It's understandable because motorcycles are unstable at slow speeds. The solution many riders employ is to drag their feet or paddle-walk, but there is a better way. The reason parking lot speeds are so intimidating is because of the instability inherent with a slow-moving motorcycle. It's worth learning to handle slow-speed maneuvers not only to minimize the risk of broken turn signals and bruised egos, but also to increase overall confidence.

Slow-speed maneuvers, such as negotiating stop-and-go traffic, maneuvering into a tight parking space, or making tight U-turns require specific slow-speed control skills. The right way to think about slow-speed maneuvers is to accept them as part of riding a motorcycle and then learn and practice these skills. Let's distill the key points of successfully executing slow-speed maneuvers.

Why Slow Is Difficult

It's easy to keep a motorcycle balanced at highway speeds because inertia from the bike/rider mass and gyroscopic force generated by the fast spinning wheels, as well as the righting effect of front-end geometry all combine to generate stability. Inertia describes the tendency for objects to stay at rest or in motion. A motorcycle rolling down the highway at 60 mph (96 kph) continues at 60 mph (kph) unless forces intervene. Inertia also contributes to stability by resisting changes in direction by pulling the motorcycle's mass straight ahead. The effect of this force diminishes with a decrease in speed.

Gyroscopic forces from the spinning wheels also contribute to keeping the bike upright and moving straight ahead—the faster the wheels spin, the more stabilizing effect they provide, which is why it's easy to fall over at slow speeds. If you were to hold a spinning wheel by its axle and try to turn it left or right, you'd feel gyroscopic resistance as the wheel tries to remain spinning on its current plane. Try turning the spinning wheel to the right and the wheel will react by leaning to the left. This reaction has a role in leaning a motorcycle into a turn. But, gyroscopic precession has almost no effect when the wheels are turning at slow speeds.

Slow-Speed Balance

To keep the bike on two wheels without the benefit of inertia and gyroscopic forces, you need to balance the center of gravity (CG) directly above the tire contact patches so gravity doesn't get an overwhelming hold on one side of the motorcycle. Imagine trying to balance a broomstick on your palm. It takes continual adjustment to keep the broom's contact point vertically below the CG so the broomstick remains upright—react too slowly, and the broomstick falls to the floor.

You need to do the same thing when trying to stay upright on a slow-moving motorcycle. The difference is that the motorcycle is the broomstick, and you must move the tire's contact patch to keep in balance by turning the handlebars left and right, which causes the steering head—and the motorcycle's CG—to from shift side-to-side. Shifting your body weight left or right is another way to move the combined CG to help keep the bike upright.

Feet Up

When riding slowly, many riders drag their feet for fear of falling over. However, to maintain stability and balance, you're better

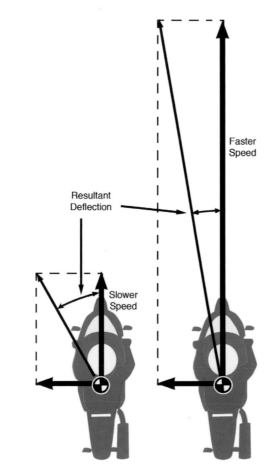

Figure 9.1

Figure 9.1 illustrates the effect of force on diminishing speed.

When riding slowly, many riders drag their feet for fear of falling over, but to maintain stability and balance, you're better off keeping your feet on the pegs and your knees against the tank.

off keeping your feet on the pegs and your knees against the tank. This posture helps stabilize the combined motorcycle/rider mass.

We mentioned earlier how you can use body positioning to help keep the CG over the contact patches (remember, you are part of the CG when mounted on the bike). By keeping the feet on the footpegs, you can lean the bike more-or-less independently of your body for rapid adjustments. One way to help the bike respond quickly is to support more weight on the footpegs and to relax your upper body. This allows you to quickly shift body weight, turn the handlebars, or lean the bike to regain balance.

When making tight turns, position your weight on the outside footpeg (the right peg for left turns) to let the motorcycle lean. For the tightest turns, shift your butt off the outside portion of the seat and lean the bike beneath you.

Rear Brake Control

One other reason for keeping your feet on the footpegs is so your right foot can apply rear brake pressure to control speed (without chopping the throttle off). Dragging the rear brake also gives the drivetrain a tension force to pull against, which stabilizes the chassis and helps pivot the bike around when making tight U-turns.

If you feel the need to slow down, apply rear brake pressure while avoiding the front brake. Most motorcycle front brakes are rather touchy when riding at a snail's pace and can easily cause a slow-moving motorcycle to lurch to an abrupt stop. And if the bike is leaning even slightly, it will likely drop faster than you can react. The solution is to avoid front brake use and use the rear brake only.

Be aware that some motorcycles have integrated brake systems that don't allow rear-brake-only application and some have power-assisted brakes that make slow-speed braking a particularly touchy affair.

Eyes Up

We learned earlier about how visual direction control can help direct your motorcycle where you want it to go. Under nonthreatening conditions, your eyes naturally scan ahead. But when anxiety takes hold, most people narrow their vision and focus on the near distance directly in front of them.

Get up out of your chair and walk around your house, maneuvering around furniture and through doorways. Now, walk the same route, but this time look down at the floor directly in front of you as you walk. Looking down will likely make you anxious about crashing into a piece of furniture or a wall and will cause disorientation. Now, picture yourself doing this exercise in a house you've never been in before, and you can see the importance of good visual habits. The same anxiety applies if your eyes were glued to the ground in front of your front wheel while attempting a tight U-turn on your motorcycle. If you cringe at the thought, you're not alone.

Not only do your eyes direct you through turns, they also gather information about where you'll be in the next few seconds.

This is critical for planning exactly where you want your bike to go to avoid a patch of sand or a vehicle intent on occupying the parking spot you were about to claim. Without looking ahead, you can easily be taken by surprise by unseen hazards, which can lead to abrupt use of the brakes and a sudden loss of forward momentum and balance.

Target fixation is a big problem when trying to perform a tight U-turn. A common scenario is when a rider attempts a slow-speed U-turn across the width of a road. As the rider gets close to the opposite edge of the pavement, he panics and instinctively looks down at what he so desperately wants to avoid—the edge of the road. Consciously tell yourself to look at your desired path, not at the edge of the pavement.

Drive Control

When making tight maneuvers, forward drive must be steady and smooth. Imagine how difficult it would be to make a tight U-turn with the motorcycle lurching abruptly from on-and-off application of the throttle.

Make sure your eyes are looking at the desired path and not looking at the ground, especially when executing a U-turn at slow speeds.

Unfortunately, a lot of throttles are sensitive at slow speeds, and riding in low gear only adds to that sensitivity. So, what's the best way to control speed? Your first instinct may be to roll on and off the throttle, but that usually results in abrupt acceleration and deceleration. Instead, "slip" the clutch in the zone between disengaged and fully engaged while maintaining a steady throttle. Ease out the clutch to increase speed and squeeze it as needed to decrease speed. A trick to help minimize throttle movement is to "lock" your right wrist in a low position. You can also "anchor" your thumb or forefinger on the control pod or lightly apply the rear brake to adjust speed.

Tight Turn Demo

Let's put all the parts together to perform a tight, slow-speed turn:

1. Slow to a suitable speed.

2. Position your weight on the seat toward the outside of the turn.

3. Ease out the clutch about halfway.

4. Drag the rear brake lightly and keep the clutch slipped for speed control.

5. Turn your head like a barn owl.

6. Lean the bike and turn the handlebars.

7. Keep looking over your shoulder toward the exit of your turn.

8. Ease out the clutch a bit more to pull the bike around the turn.

Depending on your speed and how tight the turn is, you may have to lean quite a bit. That's okay, as long as you maintain steady drive. Minimize throttle movement by keeping your wrist down and anchoring your thumb or index finger to your handlebar control pod. Slow-speed handling doesn't have to cause anxiety. A bit of knowledge and practice can increase confidence and

decrease the likelihood of a slow-speed tipover and possible injury.

Turning from a Stop

Turning from a stop is a slow-speed maneuver that causes a lot of riders trouble because it requires making a rather tight turn to avoid crossing into the oncoming lane. This maneuver is used when moving from a stop at an intersection or leaving a parking lot and turning to enter the roadway.

Planning ahead can ease the difficulty of this maneuver. If you stop so your motorcycle is pointed in the direction of the turn, then much of your turn is already completed. Unfortunately, this is not always practical or possible. To make a 90-degree turn, rotate your handlebars and lean the bike in the direction of the turn before easing out the clutch. Get up to speed smoothly but quickly to minimize instability.

This pre-turn/lean technique allows you to make the turn in the shortest area. However, you can make a tight turn from a stop without first leaning the bike. But it requires you to lean the motorcycle and turn the handlebars quickly once the bike is in motion. To execute either technique successfully, you must ease out the clutch smoothly and look toward your desired path of travel.

Hills and Slopes

Your motorcycle must overcome the force of gravity as it climbs or descends hills. Hills usually aren't a big deal, but there are times when a slope can affect the way your bike handles. For instance, descending a hill with a passenger on board will require more brake force, and ascending a hill will require more power (but not so much as to cause your passenger to fall off the back).

LESSON LEARNED

Exit Error

You just finished fueling your bike and are stopped at the gas station's exit waiting to turn right onto the main road. Traffic is heavy and moving briskly, with few opportunities to enter, which means you'll have to act quickly. To make things more difficult, your motorcycle is pointed perpendicular to the roadway, meaning you have to make a right-angle turn within a fairly tight area to avoid crossing into the far lane.

You finally see an opening between two cars. You quickly release your clutch and attempt to merge into the traffic flow. But, instead of turning right, your motorcycle goes straight across the lane. You try desperately to turn the motorcycle, but it doesn't seem to go where you want. You grab the front brake hard in a desperate attempt to stop. This causes the front tire to skid, and you fall to the ground with your helmet and shoulder smashing to the pavement.

You are knocked unconscious, and when you awake, there are people standing over you. Later, in the hospital, you find out that your motorcycle is in ruins. A car collided with it as it slid into the oncoming lane. Thankfully, you weren't hit, but it will take a fair amount of time to recover from your injuries.

WHAT'S THE LESSON?

One thing that would have helped prevent the mishap was early planning. Had you planned ahead, you could have stopped with your motorcycle at an angle that pointed you in the direction that you needed to go. That way, your turn would not have needed to be so sharp.

You also lacked the ability to physically turn your motorcycle sharply from a stop. You needed to turn your handlebars and lean your bike before easing out the clutch.

Practice the "turn from a stop" technique in a parking lot. Learn to maintain steady throttle while dipping your bike into a steep lean and look ahead to carve a tight 90-degree arc. Next time, you'll have little trouble entering the roadway.

Starting on Hills

Unless you own one of the few motorcycles with a hill holder feature, getting under way when pointed uphill can be a challenge. This situation can be quite unnerving because you must balance the bike while preventing it from rolling backward. When it's time to go, you must do so without creeping backward or stalling the engine and losing balance.

One method for starting on hills involves having both feet on the ground and using the front brake to keep the bike from rolling backward. The problem is that the right hand now has two jobs to do: releasing the front brake at the same time you must roll on the throttle. It's easier to perform this technique if you use your index and middle fingers to hold the brake and ring and pinkie fingers to control the throttle.

The alternative method is to have one foot on the ground and one foot on the rear brake. Release the rear brake as the clutch is engaged. This method frees your right hand to turn the throttle without having to control the front brake as you release the clutch. But you must feel comfortable balancing the motorcycle with one foot. Those with a short inseam might find this one-foot method difficult. Even long-legged riders could have problems touching their left foot on the ground if the surface slopes away to the left. Practice both techniques to see which one suits you best.

Descending Hills

Load distribution and the resulting effect on traction put extra stress onto the front tire when descending hills. The steeper the hill, the more downhill force your front tire has to manage. Be sure to place your tires where you have enough traction so you don't skid. Carrying a heavy load or a passenger can make it difficult to keep the motorcycle from accelerating more than you want, which means you'll need to use even more brake power.

It's natural to grip the handlebars and stiffen your arms to brace against the downward force. Unfortunately, stiff arms resist the motorcycle's ability to manage surface irregularities and also transfer the rider's upper body weight onto the front tire's contact patch, which may be enough stress to cause traction loss.

Downhill Curves

To manage traction when descending hills, slow *before* the hill. Choose a speed that takes into account the likelihood of downhill acceleration. If the hill features a corner, then slow more. Ideally, you will slow enough to roll on the throttle slightly throughout the turn to transfer some load off the front tire to preserve traction.

There are times when a slope can affect the way your bike handles.

One method for starting on hills involves having both feet on the ground and using the front brake to keep the bike from rolling backward.

Let's apply the basic cornering technique to downhill curves.

1. **Look Ahead:** Look for telltale signs of a downhill curve: pavement sloping away from you, indicated by how the centerline and edge of the pavement visually converge in the distance. If these visual clues come together in the near distance, then the hill is steeper than if they converge farther away. Also, look for roadside objects to help you determine how tight the curve is and how steep the hill is.

2. **Slow:** The main difference between a flat curve and a descending curve is how gravity pulls you and your bike's mass down the hill. This means that you need to scrub more speed before the curve, otherwise you will find yourself going too fast mid-corner.

3. **Lean:** Initiate lean using countersteering. A quicker turn-in is often needed to avoid running wide. I often coach riders to "let the bike drop" into the curve when entering a downhill curve. Will your ability and experience with lean angles allow you to do this? Or will you ride off the road?

4. **Accelerate:** Even though gravity is going to cause your bike to speed up, you still need to stabilize the bike and manage traction. The trick is to slow down enough before the curve so you can crack the throttle ever so slightly and hold that throttle setting or accelerate as you round the bend. This will get some of the weight off the front tire so the bike will track easily around the corner. If you decelerate all the way around the curve, then the bike will fight you, and the front tire may wash out. Note that the steeper the curve, the later you will pick up the throttle and the less you will accelerate, but you still need to accelerate.

When cornering at normal speeds, you want to drop your inside shoulder to engage with the bike. This helps you lean with confidence, but also allows the bike to remain a bit more upright.

Surmounting Obstacles

It's always best to avoid riding over an object or road hazard. But, if the obstacle cannot be avoided, you must understand how to manage the hazard while maintaining traction and stability.

Determining

The first thing you need to do is quickly determine if the obstacle is surmountable. Any object that is taller than your front axle is not a candidate for attempting this maneuver. Also, you should consider another plan if the object is very slippery or might move out from under you as you roll over it.

Surmounting

Once you determine that the obstacle is surmountable, then you can proceed to follow the steps for surmounting:

1. **Approach Upright and Perpendicular:** Approach the object as close to 90 degrees as possible and with the bike completely upright. This minimizes the chance that your front tire will slide along the edge and out from under you.

   Many obstacles have an obvious straight edge, such as 2 × 4 lumber or a railroad track, but some obstacles have less defined edges. A pothole, for instance, may not have an obvious long edge for you to approach at 90 degrees. In this case, do the best you can to identify the best place for your front tire to make contact so that it hits the obstacle edge as close to perpendicular as possible.

   Sometimes you encounter embedded railroad tracks that cross the road at an acute angle. In this case, slow down and swing a bit wide so that you can cross the tracks at closer to a right angle. Not

only does this minimize the chance that the front tire will slide out, it also avoids getting your wheel caught in an "edge trap" where the wheel is forced to roll along the length of the obstacle. Edge traps are discussed a bit later.

2. **Rise off the Seat:** Help your motorcycle handle the impact by letting your legs become additional shock absorbers. Do this by weighting the footpegs and rising slightly off the seat to isolate your body weight.

   Look at how dirt riders manage bumps, fallen trees, rocks, and other obstacles. Even with the long suspension travel found on off-road bikes, dirt riders still need to stand so their legs absorb the hits caused by riding over large obstacles. Dirt bikes are designed to allow the rider to sit atop the machine in an upright position that enables an easy standing posture.

   With the exception of adventure bikes that offer better suspension travel, most street bikes are not ergonomically designed for the rider to easily rise off the seat. Cruisers with forward foot controls make it particularly difficult to

It's best to avoid riding over a road hazard, but if you can't avoid it, you need to determine if it is surmountable.

It is a good idea to practice surmounting obstacles.

rise off the seat, so do the best you can by simply weighting the footpegs.

3. **Transfer Weight Rearward:** When the front wheel makes contact with the object, the suspension will compress in reaction to the impact. To help the front suspension manage this impact, shift your body position rearward just before making contact with the object.

4. **Accelerate Slightly:** Accelerate slightly prior to impact to help take weight off the front suspension. Keep the throttle on until the front tire clears the object and then decelerate before the rear tire makes contact. That way, you reduce the risk of the rear tire spinning on the object and possibly spitting the rear end sideways.

5. **Keep Arms Loose and Avoid the Brakes:** Loose arms allow the front end to absorb the impact. Position yourself with your elbows bent, but with a firm grasp on the handgrips. It will be tempting to grab the brakes, either before or after you make contact with the object. But it's important to avoid introducing braking force while bouncing over an obstacle, which can result in loss of traction and control. The only time you should consider braking is if you can do so while upright and well before or well after you make contact with the hazard.

As with any skill, you must practice if you have any hope of executing the maneuver correctly when you need it. I suggest you practice surmounting obstacles by bringing a section of 2 × 4 to a clear parking lot and riding over it using the correct technique.

Highway Riding

Highway, freeway, interstate, turnpike— whatever you call it, these mostly straight, level stretches of asphalt or concrete have transformed the way America gets from one place to another. Highways aren't the most exiting venue for motorcyclists, but they serve to help us span large distances in a relatively short amount of time.

Some riders find highways intimidating because of the high speeds and congestion, but highways are statistically safer than most other riding environments, with almost 75% of motorcyclist fatalities occurring on undivided roadways. Even though highways represent a smaller percentage of fatalities, that doesn't mean you can let down your guard.

We all know that increased speed also increases stopping distances and can result in insufficient time to react to immediate hazards. But riding significantly slower than surrounding traffic is not the solution and can actually put you at more risk if cars feel the need to make abrupt maneuvers to avoid you. A rule of thumb to avoid vast differences in speed is to ride within 10% of the traffic speed. If you aren't comfortable riding at the pace set by the average driver, then consider avoiding the highway.

Lane Position

To be safe on the highway you must also think about where you should be within your lane. Just as on a secondary road, you have the left, center, and right portions of your lane available to avoid obstacles and increase visibility. Pick a lane position that allows you to look far ahead for sudden changes in traffic speed and to see objects in the road. Avoid riding behind large vehicles that obscure vision.

Your lane position needs to change continuously so you can maintain a "space cushion" between you and other drivers in the front and to the side. You may be tempted to move to the center portion of your lane to stay away from other drivers, but remember that this position limits your ability to see and be seen.

Heavy highway traffic doesn't allow a lot of following distance as drivers quickly fill in large gaps in traffic. If a generous following distance is not possible, position yourself so you can see beyond the vehicle ahead and cover your brakes to cut reaction time. Aggressive drivers often tailgate, which can be dangerous. Change lanes to encourage the driver to pass or increase following distance from the car ahead to minimize the need to brake hard in case of an emergency.

It's important to keep an eye out for drivers cutting across lanes in an attempt to find the quickest way to their destination. Position yourself in your lane so you are visible to these drivers, yet far enough away to allow time and space to move out of their way if they decide to cut across your path. This happens most near exit and entrance ramps.

Lane splitting is another special situation where motorcycles thread between slow lines of traffic. This is illegal in most states in the United States. If lane splitting is legal in your state, and you choose to try it, do so carefully. Limit lane splitting to situations where traffic is moving very slowly and stay within 5 mph (8 kph) of the surrounding vehicles for minimum risk.

Highway Hazard Clues

The best riders develop a sixth sense about potential hazards. Keep a lookout for warnings that may require either a change of lane position or a complete lane change, such as brake lights ahead. Even if nothing is obviously amiss, small clues are still present. For instance, multiple head turns or a quick arm movement may indicate a sudden decision to change lanes or even a flash of light from a reflection that can indicate unusual activity.

Distracted drivers are everywhere—reading a text, eating lunch, fiddling with the radio, or talking on the phone. Studies have shown that cell phone users are as hazardous as drunk drivers. Unfortunately, cell phone use while driving has become pandemic. Hands-free devices help, but they do little to eliminate the mental distraction.

It's also important to be aware of others entering or exiting the highway. Avoid riding in the right-hand lane of a multilane highway when approaching exit or entrance ramps because you may become "pinched" by a vehicle exiting or entering the highway. Also, an inattentive driver may try to make his exit at the last second and could unintentionally force you off the road.

Highway Fatigue

Spending multiple hours droning along on the highway can be exhausting. You can't perform well when you're tired or mentally distracted. Avoid highway fatigue by taking frequent breaks to get blood flowing into your brain and limbs and to give your mind a break from the mesmerizing effect of featureless miles passing by.

Certain devices can be very helpful for alleviating fatigue, such as a cruise control or throttle lock that can lessen throttle hand cramping, windscreens that deflect

Riding for hours on a highway can produce dangerous fatigue.

tiresome windblast, and highway footpegs to stretch tired legs. Earplugs dramatically cut the white noise from windblast that can harm hearing and contribute to fatigue as the miles add up. Wind can also cause dehydration or hypothermia if you aren't dressed for the conditions. No matter what the weather, you will be more comfortable and less fatigued with full coverage protective gear.

Entrance Ramps

Entrance ramps serve to merge traffic onto the highway. But some ramps are more challenging than others. Some ramps have ample room to merge, while others empty onto the freeway without allowing much space to filter into traffic or get up to speed. Also, many entry ramps are made up of big, sweeping, decreasing radius curves, requiring more and more lean angle as the corner progresses. If you enter a decreasing radius turn too fast, you may need to adjust your speed or lean angle significantly to stay on the road.

To avoid this, enter at a reduced speed and stay to the outside of the turn for better sight distance until you can determine the radius of the ramp; then accelerate *gently* to avoid going too fast to complete the turn. Entering slowly will help you be better prepared if the ramp turns out to be a decreased radius. Wait until you are well past the middle of the corner before turning tighter toward the apex. This *delayed apex* will point you around the turn. (We discussed cornering lines in detail earlier.)

Once the turn straightens, use the onramp as an acceleration lane to get up to full highway speed before merging into traffic. It's important not to ride too closely to

drivers ahead of you on the ramp because you don't want to be on the gas and on their bumper if the driver ahead hesitates or hits the brakes instead of accelerates. It's usually a good idea to signal several seconds before you merge and check your mirror and blind spot by glancing over your left shoulder for a safe gap. Be careful about looking behind you if you are following a driver in case they slow unexpectedly.

Exit Ramps

When it's time to exit, signal and move into the right lane well before your exit appears. Maintain full speed until you must slow for the exit ramp and make your intentions clear to avoid getting rear-ended. Like entrance ramps, exit ramps can surprise you with a decreasing radius. Slow down more, keep your eyes looking through the turn, and be prepared to lean further. Also, keep your eyes peeled for lubricants that drip in the center of the ramp from other vehicles, such as diesel spills that are often found on exit and entrance ramps.

Some riders use ramps to practice cornering; however, more than a few of these riders have slid into guardrails, concrete walls, and ditches while pushing their limits on entrance and exit ramps. Understand that highway ramps can be quite challenging and deserve respect.

Tollbooths

Traffic slows and converges at tollbooths, and it's not unusual for drivers to frantically jockey for a place in the shortest line. This creates a situation that can be unnerving and downright dangerous. To avoid last-second maneuvers and potential conflicts with other vehicles, it's important to pick your intended lane early and clearly signal your intent. Once stopped, keep an eye on your mirrors for potential rear-enders. Avoid lanes that combine "Fast Lane" booths and regular "stop-and-pay" booths. An impatient commuter with a Fast Lane transponder expects to fly through these booths and could easily pulverize you while you fumble with your change.

Other vehicles aren't the only tollbooth hazard. Oil, transmission fluid, and coolant accumulate between the tire tracks left by waiting cars. This slippery residue can cause a skid or cause a rider to lose footing when trying to balance the bike, especially when it's wet. Slow early to avoid hard braking and plan to stop where your boots can obtain good traction.

Taking tickets and paying tolls can be frustrating for motorcyclists. If it's available

To avoid last-second maneuvers and potential conflicts with other vehicles, it's important to pick your intended tollbooth lane early and clearly signal your intent.

in your area, it's really best to have an EZ-Pass mounted on your bike, but if you don't have an electronic toll taker, you'll have to think ahead. Gloves make it difficult to extract coins and toll tickets. It's not uncommon for ill-prepared riders to drop change while they fumble under the pressure of impatient car drivers waiting for them to give the correct change and move on. This stressful situation can be minimized with a little forethought. For short rides, stash a few coins inside your glove in the palm of your hand. For longer rides, have money ready in a jacket pocket or tank bag compartment.

Blind Spots

We talked earlier about blind spots and how motorcycles can easily get lost in driver's blind spots. This is quite common when droning down the highway. One

LESSON LEARNED

Blind Spot Blunder

You decide to take advantage of the warm evening to show off your new bike to all the motorheads at the weekly car and bike night. The festivities are a few miles away, so you decide to take the highway. You accelerate fast onto the freeway and move into the left-hand lane. Up ahead, you see a slower car traveling in the left lane. You see the sign for your exit, so you decide to move to the middle lane alongside the slower car in preparation to exit.

As you approach your exit, you notice the car on your left begin to move to the right, across your lane. It becomes shockingly apparent that the driver doesn't see you. You lay on the horn, but the driver does not respond, so you quickly move to the right-hand lane and accelerate hard to get ahead of the car. You see in your mirror the headlights of the vehicle cross only a few feet behind your rear wheel.

You both exit and stop at the end of the ramp. Your adrenaline and anger has built to a point where you feel the need to educate the driver about his careless driving. You dismount and walk toward the driver-side door. The elderly man in the driver's seat looks terrified. You signal for him to roll down his window and after a few apprehensive moments he cracks the window and inch or so.

You begin to scold the driver for almost hitting you. He says sorry, but that he did not see you. He says he checked his mirrors and even glanced over his shoulder but that you must have been hidden behind his rear roof pillar. You ask him to please be more careful as you walk back to your bike and head on your way.

WHAT'S THE LESSON?

Close calls can easily cause anger. Before you lose your head, it's smart to take a moment and evaluate your own actions. The truth is that you contributed to this mishap by placing your bike in the driver's blind spot. You also didn't recognize the possibility that the driver might move over to take the same exit ramp as you.

Highway riding is relatively safe, but it has its share of hazards. Keep your wits sharp and adopt effective highway strategies to manage the risks.

of the most important strategies for conspicuity on the highway is to avoid lingering in this area where drivers cannot see you. That's the area just behind a car's front doors and out of range of the mirrors. Remember, if you can't see the face of the driver in his mirror, he can't see you. Large trucks have very large blind spots, so be extra careful to pass trucks as quickly as possible. Continually monitor your position to avoid riding in this blind spot. Remind yourself to ride *through* blind spots. Avoid changing lanes into a car driver's blind spot. Instead, change lanes gradually, allowing time for others to easily predict your intentions.

Anyone can be seduced into riding too fast, so, no matter what bike you ride, keep your wits about you and your speed in check.

And remember that motorcyclists have blind spots too. Typical motorcycle mirrors do a rather poor job of revealing what's behind and to the sides, so be sure to glance over your shoulder to be sure it's safe to change lanes.

Riding Fast

Riding fast is inherently attractive to motorcyclists, especially those interested in sport riding. Although many sport riders push the envelope on the street, most realize that knee-dragging speeds are foolish in that environment. I'm lucky enough to have survived my less enlightened years when the quest for speed was ever-present. I wised up and have come to accept that the street offers very limited opportunities to exercise my desire for speed.

The personality of a motorcycle can encourage fast riding. Modern sport bikes are so good that they could have won professional races just 10 years ago. Yes, these bikes are engineered to be well-behaved, but aggressive, seductive styling and a high-performance attitude can easily coax a rider into riding beyond his skill limits and the limits of the road. Anyone can be seduced into riding too fast, so, no matter what bike you ride, keep your wits about you and your speed in check.

Keeping Up

I talked earlier about how peer pressure can seduce people into riding faster than they should. Normally easygoing folks become influenced by pack behavior as they disappear into the false protection of the collective whole, where inhibitions relax and bravado flourishes.

I've noticed that this is especially evident with male sport riders, whose testosterone can flow like water over Niagara. It's easy to get swept over the edge by this fervor—after all, few want to be seen as a rider who lacks the skill or guts to stay with the pack. Many riders also feel the urge to show off their superior riding skills to those who might notice. This is often a recipe for disaster.

LESSON LEARNED

Busted

You love to ride fast. Ever since you bought your liter-sized sport bike, you've had a hard time keeping within the posted speed limit. Friends warned you about how hypersport bikes can tempt even the most disciplined person to ride faster than he should. But you couldn't resist the allure of the aggressive stance and the racy lines of the sport bike, so you made the deal.

You weren't too worried when you put money down on the machine, thinking that you would be able to resist the temptation and keep the throttle under control. However, soon it became apparent that your friends were right. The personality of the new machine taunted you constantly to stretch its legs, and you often found yourself glancing at the speedometer in disbelief as the needle regularly edged well beyond reason.

You know that this behavior is not sustainable and that one day you will either get in trouble with the law or find yourself in a situation where you aren't able to slow in time to avoid a collision. You make a pact with yourself to chill out and to limit your shenanigans to deserted rural roads.

One day after work, you decide to take the long way home where the roads twist and turn and where there is little chance of being caught by the police. At the edge of town, the road opens up, and so does your throttle. The thrust of the mighty engine makes your heart pound.

Rounding the corner, your euphoria turns to panic as you see a police car parked on the side of the road and the officer pointing a radar gun directly at you. The officer signals for you to pull over. You move to the shoulder and shut off your bike and take off your helmet. The officer gives you a hefty ticket and a lecture about the risks of riding fast. You head home frustrated that you aren't able to enjoy your bike the way you want.

WHAT'S THE LESSON?

Some people give up riding race-oriented bikes because they can't control the urge. This may be the way to go if you can't keep your sporting machine under control. Another option is to take your bike to the racetrack for a track day. Many riders are relieved of the temptation to ride fast on the street once they have the opportunity to enjoy their sport bike to its full potential—legally. Whatever you choose, it is imperative that you get this impulsive behavior under control. Your wallet and your loved ones will thank you.

More often than not, groups consist of riders with diverse skill levels. One big problem is that the least experienced riders often attempt to keep up with the leaders for fear of losing face. By doing so, they also risk losing sight of their mortality by riding beyond the limits of their skill, the road, or their bike.

Reasonable Speeds

How fast you ride directly affects whether you can handle a curve or stop in time for a hazard. The higher the speed, the less time and space you have to react to hazards. Emergency stopping from 30 mph (48 kph) takes about 35 feet (10 m) on a clean and dry surface, and stopping at 60 mph (96 kph) can take more than 140 feet

Sometimes riding in groups creates peer pressure to ride faster.

(43 m). Look at those numbers again, and you'll see that stopping distances are *four times longer* when speed is doubled. Also consider that a single second of reaction time equates to 44 feet (13 m) at 30 mph (48 kph) and 88 feet (27 m) at 60 mph (96 kph). These numbers should convince you that choosing a reasonable speed is important.

We talked earlier about how difficult it is for other road users to accurately judge your approach speed and distance. You make it even tougher for drivers to judge whether it is safe to proceed into your path if you travel at a rate of speed that is significantly different from what is expected. Don't be surprised if vehicles pull out in front of you if you exceed expected speeds.

LESSON LEARNED

Intervention

You arrive at the spot where a few friends are meeting for a day ride through the mountains. You know two of the riders, but you don't know the other guy. After a half-hour of chit-chat, you gear up and head out. The planned route includes some very challenging roads. You decide to ride in the middle of the group.

From this vantage point, you notice the unfamiliar rider directly ahead of you struggling to maintain the group's pace. You decide to back off to give him some room and to give you the time and space to avoid him in case he crashes. Thankfully, he keeps the motorcycle on the road before the first rest break.

At the stop, you approach your two friends to relay what you witnessed and ask what they should do. They respond with blank faces. It becomes apparent that nobody wants the responsibility of talking to this rider, including you. As a way to deal with the situation, they agree to slow down the pace.

Unfortunately, the slowed pace still isn't slow enough, and only 10 minutes into the second leg of the ride, the shaky rider goes off the road. He is mostly unhurt, but his bike is a mess and needs to be towed. This ruins the rest of the afternoon, but it could have been worse, especially if the crashing rider involved another member of the group.

WHAT'S THE LESSON?

Taking responsibility for safety on group rides is a drag for most people. However, it makes sense to minimize the risk to you and others. You were on the right track by soliciting advice from your friends, but when they did not respond, you should have taken the lead. (See the group riding section to read about all options to manage this situation.)

Slow In, Fast Out

"Charging" into blind corners is a bad idea. Depending on the region you ride, many, or even most corners you encounter do not provide a clear view of the corner exit. Hillsides, vegetation, and roadside structures all conspire to block your vision. This means that a hazard may be present around the bend that you cannot see until you are already committed to your corner entry speed. That's why you should adopt the "Slow in, fast out" strategy in which you enter turns at conservative speeds and accelerate out once you are sure the coast is clear, with no drama.

Passing

Passing is a maneuver that can be performed with relative safety. But before you twist the throttle, carefully evaluate the risk versus the benefit. The most obvious reason to pass a slower vehicle is so you can ride at your own pace. But there are other worthwhile reasons to make a pass, including keeping yourself from being sandwiched between a slowpoke and

LESSON LEARNED

Blind Bend

Cornering is one of your most favorite things to do on a motorcycle. You often seek out the most challenging roads so you can exercise your cornering abilities. You are smart enough to know that riding fast on the street is not a good idea, but you make exceptions when twist roads beckon.

Today is the second day of a solo weeklong trip to the mountains of Virginia where the curves and scenery are endless. Your bike is loaded with camping gear and provisions to last the week. Even with all the extra weight, your motorcycle manages it well with confidence-inspiring handling and sufficient power.

You and your bike are working together flawlessly as you carve one sumptuous corner after another and, as a result, find yourself riding faster than you should. Many of the curves you encounter have been cut into the mountainside, which means that most corner exits are obscured by earth and vegetation. There is often dirt at the apex of right-hand turns where cars cut the inside of the corner and drag debris onto the pavement. You grow accustomed to these issues and maintain your sporting pace.

As you round yet another blind right-hand turn, you are shocked to see a large black bear lumbering across the road directly in front of you. Your training kicks in and you immediately straighten your bike before you apply the brakes. Unfortunately, you are going too fast to avoid crossing into the opposite lane. Not only that, but you soon realize that you're about to run out of pavement.

You remain hard on the brakes as you attempt to stay on the road. Suddenly, you feel the handlebars get light as the front tire begins to slide. You release the front brake just in time to regain grip and manage to stay on two wheels.

WHAT'S THE LESSON?

It can be tough to remain mindful of the limits of the environment when we are in the groove, but, as you discovered, unexpected things can happen at any time. If you had entered the blind turn a bit slower, you would have had more time and space to respond. Using the "slow in, faster out" cornering strategy allows you to experience the thrill of skillful cornering with less risk.

If you want to ride fast, do like so many riders do these days and sign up for a track day where you can ride your street bike on a racetrack that is free of typical street hazards and police ready to take away your license. It's fun, and it's a smart thing to do. I talk more about track days in the last chapter.

an impatient tailgater crowding you from behind. An aggressive driver behind you may initiate an unwise pass only to come up short and then wedge between you and the slow car. It may also be smart to make a pass if the driver behind you is erratic or other vehicles hinder visibility.

When it comes to riding behind a slowpoke, it may be tempting to unleash the horsepower stabled inside your machine, but often you must be patient for a legal and safe place to make your move. Instead of making an aggressive or potentially risky pass, consider adopting the technique of pulling over and waiting a minute or so to allow the slower vehicles to get well ahead and then proceed to ride at your preferred pace until you catch up to the slowpokes once again. This technique limits the amount of risky passing.

Passing Procedure

To avoid surprises during passing, it might be helpful to think through the passing sequence:

- **Check oncoming traffic**. Identifying whether it is safe to pass is the first and most important action. Look far down the road for any oncoming cars and scan carefully for vehicles approaching from side streets and driveways.
- **Check your mirror**. Make sure the coast is clear behind you before initiating the pass. Someone may already be in the process of passing you and the slow driver ahead.
- **Downshift if necessary**.
- **Signal**. It's smart to signal your intention to pass well before making any moves. Don't make a sudden decision to pass and flick on the blinkers just as you lean the bike. Leaving your left turn signal on during the pass also adds some conspicuity.

Be patient for a legal and safe place to pass slower vehicles.

- **Passing position**. Move into the oncoming lane.
- **Accelerate**. Get on the gas to limit your exposure to oncoming dangers. But remember that it's illegal to exceed the speed limit even when passing.
- **Signal again**. Activate your turn signal to indicate that you're moving back to the right lane.
- **Check your mirror**. Before you move back into the right lane, take a look in your mirror or over your shoulder to make sure you're far enough ahead of the slow vehicle to move back into your lane. You may be passing someone who was awakened by your move or is upset by your pass and decided to speed up to teach you a lesson.
- **Lane return**. Return to your lane and maintain enough speed to avoid holding up the driver you just passed.
- **Cancel your signal**.
- **Reduce your speed**.

Legal Maneuvering

It seems that there are fewer legal passing areas than there were in the past. Some stretches of road are marked as "no

LESSON LEARNED

Bad Pass

Andy finally found time in his busy schedule to get away from the suburban congestion where he lives to ride the challenging rural roads that exist a couple of hours from his home. Andy is especially excited about riding a particular stretch of smooth, insanely twisty piece of tarmac where he can let loose and experience his sport bike's cornering prowess.

Andy starts to enjoy the road, but, unfortunately, just as he is approaching the best part, he comes up behind a line of three cars, creeping as if in slow motion. Andy reluctantly slows behind the caravan of vehicles. He knows that the only legal passing area is miles ahead, far beyond the most entertaining section of road. Andy can't bear to waste this great road at such a piddling speed, so he decides to make a pass as soon as he can.

Planning ahead, Andy considers passing each vehicle individually, but discounts that option because of the limited space between cars. He'll try and pass all three vehicles at once. Andy's gut wrenches with impatience. His throttle hand is tense and poised to act at the next opportunity. Finally, Andy sees an opening in the trees where the road straightens for a short distance. He downshifts in anticipation. Is there enough space to pass? He determines that there is. Andy waits just long enough to see that the oncoming lane is clear and rolls the throttle open. His adrenaline level is pegged as he propels his bike forward to make the pass.

His bike lunges forward past the first car, then the second. One more to go. But suddenly he sees an oncoming a car around the approaching bend. This is gonna be close! Andy pins the throttle and just manages to dive back into his lane, with inches to spare. He is relieved that he missed becoming a hood ornament, but he quickly realizes that he is going way too fast for the approaching corner. He gets on the brakes, and then leans the bike as much as he dares, but it's not enough. Andy's front wheel touches the soft shoulder and his bike lowsides and slides off the road and into a ditch.

Andy fell into a common trap of frustration that led to poor judgment and a grim outcome. He knew that passing increased risk, but he allowed himself to become fixated on the task of getting by the slower cars so he could fulfill his expectations of an enjoyably brisk ride on his dream road. Andy made a snap decision about passing, only to find himself in a desperate situation when his calculations proved too optimistic.

WHAT'S THE LESSON?

Even though a stretch of road may provide ample space to make a pass, it is important to make sure that there is enough sight distance to ensure that a car will not appear in the oncoming lane from around a corner or from a side street. Andy would have been smart to recognize that his sight distance was too short and that it would become even shorter when he accelerated to pass the cars. Highway departments provide some useful road markings and signs that tell us when passing zones begin and end to help us determine whether it's safe (and legal) to pass. I suggest you heed their warnings.

passing" zones for mile after mile. This can be frustrating when motorcyclists are often capable of passing safely in "no passing" zones where an auto or truck wouldn't have adequate acceleration. Because of this advantage, motorcyclists are more likely to be tempted to make an illegal or excessively risky pass. But remember, the police know exactly where to hide to catch errant motorcyclists who try to capitalize on their power advantage.

In the past, some US states showed leniency when it came to passing speeds, recognizing that it is necessary to exceed the speed limit in order to pass safely. But these days, you won't get much sympathy for twisting the throttle in an attempt to get by quickly. Also, passing in a no passing zone will very likely get you a ticket. Keep in mind that many drivers are quick to dial the police from their cell phone to report any behavior they consider dangerous or that merely ticks them off.

In a perfect world, there would be ample legal passing zones and laws tolerant to realistic passing speeds and even lane splitting (riding between lines of cars). Unfortunately, this isn't the case. So, what's a law-abiding motorcyclist to do? Most of us suck it up and wait for a legal place to pass, and then keep overtaking speeds at a rate that balances risk exposure and legality.

LANE SPLITTING

Lane splitting is a unique form of passing that involves riding between lanes of slow-moving vehicles traveling in the same direction. Riders split lanes on the highway when traffic slows. But they are also known to split lanes as they filter to the front of stopped traffic at a stop light. Lane splitting benefits all road users by reducing the number of vehicles adding to traffic congestion and can even be safer for motorcyclists...if done correctly.

Lane splitting is practiced in many parts of the world, but is presently illegal in all US states, except California. Permissible or not, it is important to weigh the risks associated with lane splitting. One argument in favor of splitting is that it is safer to be riding between lanes than be sandwiched between cars in stop-and-go traffic. A recent study by the California Office of Traffic Safety reports that lane splitting can be less prone to serious injury than sitting in stopped traffic.

This may have some truth, but lane splitting itself is risky. If it's legal where you live, and you choose to split lanes, it is important to keep your speeds down to within 5 mph (8 kph) or so of the slower traffic. And keep your eyes peeled for resentful drivers who may squeeze you into stopping your forward progress.

Chapter 10

Mastering Everyday Situations

Dealing with hills, obstacles, hazards from the rear, and other challenging situations are all in a day's work of a motorcycle rider.

Surface Hazards

One of the most significant hazards a motorcycle rider must manage is the road surface. All it takes is a misplaced tire or a failure to recognize when traction is limited for you to end up in big trouble.

Gravel and Other Loose Surfaces

Managing traction is one of the highest priorities for any motorcycle rider. Gravel and other loose surfaces can cause a serious traction problem if you don't know how to manage them. Most street riders find riding over loose surfaces disconcerting, but as long as you maintain a steady, reasonable speed and refrain from using abrupt throttle, brake, or steering inputs, you will most likely be okay. If braking is necessary over loose surfaces, it's better to use mostly the rear brake. This is especially important when braking on downhill dirt roads. This is because front brakes are often very powerful and sensitive and can easily cause a front tire skid.

Gravel can cause a serious traction problem if you don't know how to manage it.

Riding off-road is one of the best ways to master loose surfaces and make you a better overall street rider by improving balance, visual acuity, throttle and clutch control, and traction sense. I talk in detail about off-road riding later in the book.

Construction Zones

Construction zones are a common site on our nation's highways and include some serious safety concerns, especially for motorcyclists. Construction signage often precedes these hazardous zones alerting you to possible lane changes, construction debris, and surface irregularities such as raised pavement edges.

During construction, traffic is often diverted onto a temporary detour or lane shift. Expect an abrupt transition between the original pavement and the bypass. Plan a line that allows you to cross the transition as perpendicularly as possible. Watch for metal plates or other temporary surfaces. Keep your speed down and the bike vertical when crossing these slippery surfaces. Concrete barriers are commonly used in work zones to define lanes and separate

oncoming traffic. These lanes can be narrow, reducing your lane options. Also, these barriers can trap debris as well as water and mud in wet weather, which can reduce traction.

Ground-away pavement surfaces (*scarified* or *milled*) cause the motorcycle to weave back and forth as the tires hunt for a single track on the uneven grooves. These surfaces can feel scary, but control will be maintained if you relax and avoid braking or changing lanes abruptly.

Edge Traps

Certain road hazards have the potential for trapping the front tire and preventing you from turning the handlebars. Without the ability of the front wheel to steer, it is likely that the bike will fall as you attempt to keep the bike in balance. Railroad tracks are an obvious example of a potential edge trap. Another example of an edge trap is uneven lanes that occur when a road is being paved and one lane has a thick layer of new pavement, but the other lane is at the original level (or has been milled below the original surface level). Construction standards allow pavement ridges to be 1 ½ inches (4 cm) high without tapering. This may not sound like much, but crossing this ridge can cause balance problems and can even snatch the handlebars from your hands.

Problems occur when changing lanes from the "lower" lane to the lane with the thick layer of new pavement. If you were to simply ease over to change lanes, the front tire will be forced to follow the edge of the new pavement, thus preventing you from adjusting the angle of the front wheel to maintain balance. Also, the front tire must climb the edge to get into the other lane, which requires the center of the tire to lose contact as the side of the tire tries to grip the "wall" of the new pavement. Avoid crossing any steep pavement edges if possible. If you must cross a raised edge, attack it at as close to a 90-degree angle as possible to prevent your tires from sliding along the ridge.

Achieving a 90-degree approach is not easy at highway speeds. To move from the lower lane to the upper lane with the new pavement, swing wide so you can cross the transition at an angle that is at least 45 degrees. Then rise slightly off the seat and shift your weight rearward before hitting the pavement edge. If the edge is very high, then an approach angle that is closer to 90 degrees may be necessary, but understand that some edge traps may be too high to safely cross, in which case you should avoid making the lane change altogether because the consequences of a botched attempt may be high.

Flying Debris

Some drivers aren't terribly concerned or aren't aware of the consequences of improperly secured loads and don't seem to consider how seemingly benign objects in the road can cause serious injury to a motorcyclist. All sorts of objects come flying from other vehicles, including construction

Railroad tracks are an example of a potential edge trap.

materials, furniture, and garbage bags. Beware of shredded truck tires because many have steel wire imbedded in the tread that reveal sharp, jagged edges when they come apart. Avoid having an obstacle appear suddenly from underneath a car in front of you by keeping a 2- or 3-second following distance to give yourself time to take evasive action. Look for clues about possible obstacles in the road by watching for brake lights or adjustments in lane position of cars ahead. If you do come upon an obstacle you cannot avoid, rise off the seat, lean rearward, and accelerate just before hitting the obstacle to help the motorcycle surmount the object.

Dips

I remember hearing about a woman who crashed her motorcycle when she hit a dip in the road at a fairly high speed. This caused her bike's suspension to compress enough for the frame to lever her tires off the pavement. She would have been smart to reduce speed before the dip and then weight the footpegs or rise off the seat so that her legs could act as a second set of shock absorbers. With weight off the seat, the bike probably wouldn't have compressed the suspension so much that the frame made contact with the pavement.

Weather and Environment

Motorcycle riders are not protected by metal and glass and are balanced on two relatively small tire contact patches. For us to remain safe and comfortable, we must be keenly aware of weather and other environmental factors.

Wind

Riding a motorcycle means you must deal with drag and crosswinds. The wind you

RIDING TERM
AERODYNAMIC DRAG

The wind you feel as you ride through the atmosphere.

feel as you ride through the atmosphere is referred to as *aerodynamic drag*. You encounter drag as soon as your motorcycle begins to roll; the faster you go, the more the wind increases. You overcome drag with engine power.

Windscreens are designed to reduce windblast. But, sometimes, windscreen design can cause an annoying buffeting. The amount of buffeting depends on the shape and angle of the windscreen and where the wind strikes the rider's torso. Adjustable original equipment windshields, aftermarket windscreens, and attachable spoilers can provide relief from buffeting. A windscreen that is shorter, taller, or angled differently may help, but this often requires trial and error to get right. Wearing earplugs and snug-fitting riding gear can increase comfort and decrease fatigue caused by buffeting and wind.

Crosswinds

Many riders have stories of being blown around or even forced off the road by a mighty wind. I remember a trip many years ago where my two riding companions and I were crossing the open landscape of New Brunswick, Canada, on our way to Newfoundland. We were about 50 miles (80 km) away from our overnight destination when some mean-looking clouds appeared on the horizon. We forged on, assuming the worst we'd encounter would be some rain. What we didn't count on was the nasty winds that preceded the storm.

Our motorcycles veered violently in response to the gusting crosswinds. Thankfully, the road was wide enough for the motorcycles to swerve sideways and stay on the pavement. It became even more challenging when the rain finally fell. Sheets of water sliced across our path, diminishing our visibility and causing our tires to struggle to grip the wet pavement. Eventually, we arrived at our cabin, exhausted. Depending on where you live and ride, extreme winds may be common.

Crosswinds can be a big or small problem depending on how hard the wind blows, the shape of the bike's bodywork, the combined weight of bike and rider, the length of the motorcycle's wheelbase, and the speed at which the motorcycle is traveling.

Generally speaking, the greater the mass, the less effect a given side force will have on the motorcyclist's ability to maintain a straight-line trajectory. Anyone who has ridden a lightweight motorcycle will attest to how dramatic the deflection can be when encountering crosswinds. In contrast, a heavyweight tourer will be less affected. Many large motorcycles resist directional change caused by side winds because of their weight and longer wheelbase.

Speed also affects how much crosswinds divert the path of travel. Gyroscopic forces from the spinning wheels, as well as inertia, contribute to motorcycle stability and lessen the relative deflection from the straight-line path of travel. This doesn't

Depending on where you live and ride, extreme winds may be common.

mean that you should go faster to deal with crosswinds. As a matter of fact, it is safer to slow down. You may be blown around more, but you will have more time and space in which to react.

The size and shape of the motorcycle's fairing, fenders, and luggage also influence how much crosswinds affect the bike. The taller the motorcycle and the broader the side area, the more the machine will be affected by crosswinds. Heavyweight tourers may have an advantage because of their significant mass, but often these motorcycles also have large, broadsided fairings that act as sails in a crosswind. Passengers and large top boxes will also contribute to this sail affect. In contrast, motorcycles with small fairings and a more "open" profile act less like sails.

Another factor that dictates whether a particular motorcycle is affected by crosswinds is where the force contacts the motorcycle. There is less effect if the wind pushes on the motorcycle on a point located behind the center of mass, but more effect if it contacts nearer the front. Think of an airplane with its tail sticking up vertically above the fuselage. Side forces pressing on the tail pushes the rear of the plane away from the side wind. This automatically causes the front of the aircraft to steer into the wind to help maintain direction of travel. Compare an airplane to a motorcycle, and you see that the largest vertical feature is the rider and the fairing, both of which are located mostly *in front* of the center of mass. This causes the front of the motorcycle to move away in a crosswind, which requires significant input from the rider to steer the bike back on track.

Side wind also affects directional divergence by pressing on the front wheel to cause it to turn. A smaller front wheel and less trail reduces the effect side winds have on steering the front wheel. In contrast, the broad-sided fenders and solid "disc" wheels found on some cruiser models are more apt to suffer from this effect. Handlebar-mounted fairings and windshields can increase this wind-induced steering effect as well.

Handling Crosswinds

To counteract the effect of a side wind and to maintain balance and direction of travel, lean the motorcycle against the wind using handlebar pressure—press on the right handlebar to lean right and vice versa (countersteering). The stronger the crosswind, the more you must lean, which means pressing harder on the handlebar on the side from where the wind is coming. Leaning the upper torso into the wind can also help, but handlebar pressure is the most effective way to initiate and maintain lean.

Fortunately, your motorcycle is designed to do some of this work on its own. Let's say you encounter a wind gust from the left. This causes the front wheel to steer to the right for a brief moment. What happens next is a self-correcting effect that countersteers and leans the motorcycle into the wind. Tire profile and the out-tracking of the front tire contact patch, as well as gyroscopic forces from the spinning wheels, help keep the motorcycle leaned. Only a portion of the correction occurs through motorcycle dynamics, which is why it is necessary for the rider to use handlebar pressure to ensure that the motorcycle tracks straight.

Crosswinds can cause serious problems while leaned in a curve. Maintaining a consistent path through a corner depends on the relationship between speed and lean angle; the faster you go, the more lean angle is needed. Wind can upset both of these things, causing you to adjust lean angle mid-corner. Wind can also lift the motorcycle enough to reduce traction. To minimize problems, slow down, especially if the road surface is bumpy, dirty, or wet.

A passing RV could produce a wind gust.

Gusts

Wind is rarely steady and often comes in gusts. This means that you must act quickly to counteract constantly changing side forces and be extra attentive. Gusts may occur because of passing trucks and RVs, or because of windblocks, such as buildings, tunnels, or stands of vegetation. When the wind eases, release handlebar pressure on the windward side and be ready to lean into the wind once the wind resumes. Identify windbreaks before you get to them and be ready with the appropriate handlebar inputs.

Wind and Body Position

One way to minimize the effect of both drag and crosswind is to make the area above the center of gravity smaller. You can't change the motorcycle's shape, but you can change the combined shape of bike and rider by crouching low to minimize how much your upper torso catches the wind.

Racers bend forward into a tuck beneath the windscreen on very high-speed sections of the racetrack to get out of the windblast. Street riders can also crouch forward to reduce the effect of a strong headwind at highway speeds and to avoid being wind-blasted by an RV or oncoming truck. But, don't get carried away. An extreme tucked-in position is not recommended for street riders because it may restrict the ability to scan the environment and mirrors.

Also, it is important that you choose a position that allows your arms to remain loose so you can quickly and accurately adjust handlebar pressure. Maintain a firm grip on the handlebars, but not so firm that you cannot respond quickly and fluidly to changes in wind pressure. Do not fight the bike; instead, let it move beneath you. Obviously, there is a point at which you must intervene, but you will preserve energy and traction if you allow the bike to wander a bit.

Wind and Traction

Racers use their body as an air brake to increase stopping power by popping up from behind the fairing. Racers learn to delay sitting up until their speed is reduced to minimize the shock of the windblast. Waiting a second or so is enough to reduce speed by 20 or 25 mph (32 to 40 kph), and the difference between being hit in the head and chest with a 120 mph (193 kph) windblast and a 100 mph (160 kph) windblast is significant.

Few motorcyclists consider the influence that drag has on traction. As speed and aerodynamic drag increases, front tire grip is reduced. Many riders think that the force of a motorcycle rocketing through the air will result in a downward force on the front tire. But the opposite is more typical, with the front of the bike lifting as the air hits the "point" of the motorcycle.

Upward lift unweights the front tire and reduces front tire traction, which can increase the likelihood of skidding the front tire when slowing from a very fast speed. The solution is to first squeeze the brake lever to load the front tire. Once weight has shifted forward, squeeze the brake harder. Better yet, apply the rear brake a moment before the front brake to help transfer weight before applying front brake force.

Wind becomes more of a hazard when accompanied by rain. Strong winds and rain increase the possibility of losing traction as the front tire struggles to maintain grip on a wet surface. A strong enough gust can lead to a sliding tire. One way to manage this situation is to slow down so you have traction in reserve. Another way to minimize the chance of losing traction is having as light a grip as possible on the handlebars. Stiff arms cause handlebar inputs to be abrupt, leading to sudden spikes in traction demand.

Blow Me Down

Wind can cause problems even when you're not moving, as when a motorcycle is blown off its sidestand by a strong wind. To prevent this, try parking with the motorcycle's nose facing into the wind. You can point the tail into the wind, but it might be possible for a gust to roll the bike forward and fold the sidestand. Parking with the motorcycle in gear will prevent this from happening. Another option is to park the bike so the wind pushes on the side of the machine opposite the sidestand, or better yet, park near a building or other solid object that can be used as a windbreak. Just be sure the object can't be blown over onto your pride and joy.

A much more common problem is wind knocking your helmet onto the pavement because you placed it on the seat. Rest your helmet on the ground in a location where insects are not likely to crawl inside or, better yet, attach it to a helmet lock hook or secure it inside luggage. Some riders rest their helmet on a mirror. But a helmet perched on a mirror can be blown onto the ground, and you risk poking and compressing the EPS protective liner so that its ability to protect you in a crash is diminished over time.

You cannot completely avoid the effects of wind, but most windy conditions can be dealt with successfully. However, if winds become too severe, then you may have to wait for the blustery weather to subside or abort your ride completely.

Rain

Riding a motorcycle in the rain is not a situation that most people find enjoyable. This is understandable since rain riding can be uncomfortable, stressful, and dangerous. However, you certainly can enjoy inclement weather with a bit of preparation.

Staying Dry

It's been said that there is no bad weather... only inappropriate preparation. Wearing effective rain gear is the first step in

Riding in the rain can be uncomfortable, stressful, and dangerous.

minimizing discomfort. Many manufacturers of motorcycle gear claim that their jackets, pants, gloves or boots are "waterproof" without the need for additional rain gear. However, the level of protection from these garments varies widely.

Better quality garments have breathable fabric liners with Gore-tex®-type material that allows body moisture to pass through from the inside while stopping larger water droplets from coming through from the outside. The outside of the garment will get wet, but the liner will block water from reaching your undergarments. Waterproof liners are good, but the best way to get maximum protection is to wear dedicated rain gear over your riding jacket or pants.

Rain pants are just as important as a jacket for staying comfortable. Be sure that the pants fit snuggly at the ankles so as not to get caught in the chain or on a foot peg. The bottom cuffs should zip or secure outside your boots to prevent water from running down into your boots.

When buying a rain suit, consider the benefits of two-piece and one-piece designs. Two-piece suits allow you to use the jacket and pants separately and are easy to put on and take off. However, two-piece suits give water the opportunity to infiltrate at the waist. One-piece suits eliminate this ingress point, but are more difficult to put on, which can be a significant factor if you must get into the suit quickly as a storm rapidly approaches. Also, two-piece suits make bathroom breaks more convenient.

The benefits of motorcycle-specific rain gear ensure that the garment will withstand the rigors of riding, but it is possible to find sturdy raincoats, rain pants, and boots from outdoor outfitters or sporting goods stores. When selecting non-motorcycle-specific rain gear, you must make sure that it can withstand highway speeds without shredding to pieces and have the ability to seal tightly to prevent wind-driven rain from soaking you around the wrists, collar, waist, crotch, and ankles. Also, consider that reflective material is usually scarce on non-motorcycle-specific rain gear.

Speaking of footwear, most motorcycle boot manufacturers offer the choice of a waterproof boot with a breathable liner. The outside of the boot will likely get soaked, but the liner will prevent the majority of the wetness from reaching your socks. For added protection, waterproof leather treatments can be applied to the outside surface. Over-boots are a good solution for those who prefer to keep both their boots and feet completely dry.

Several glove manufacturers offer waterproof gloves, but gloves are tough to make completely waterproof and may offer inferior crash protection compared to dry-weather gloves. Some people wear surgical gloves or rubber kitchen gloves as over-gloves, but these are difficult to put on. Motorcycle-specific over-gloves work pretty well, but the added bulk is unwelcome. Instead, I usually carry a second pair of regular gloves that I use in the rain. This way I have good dexterity and protection while keeping my primary gloves dry for when the rain stops.

I wear a full-faced helmet, so keeping my eyes and face protected from pelting rain is not an issue. For those who use an open-faced helmet, eye and face protection is more challenging. Regular eyeglasses usually provide poor protection, but safety glasses that wrap around may seal well enough to handle light rain. Tight-fitting goggles provide better eye protection.

Open-faced helmet wearers can protect their face from pelting raindrops with a bandana or some other wrap that fits around the cheeks and chin. A better solution is an open-faced helmet with a shield system. Large windscreens can provide a decent level of rain protection, but most sport and sport-touring screens are too low to be beneficial.

Cargo also needs protecting. Soft luggage requires separate rain covers. Be sure you secure these covers so that they do not cause a crash from distraction or from coming loose and getting caught in the drivetrain. For the best weather protection, hard luggage cannot be beat. Hard saddlebags and top boxes provide peace of mind that your stuff is safe and dry.

Warm and Safe

Staying dry is important for both comfort and safety. Discomfort from cold increases the risk of distraction, reduces muscle control, impairs judgment, and slows reaction time. Extreme chilling can lead to hypothermia, which occurs when body heat dissipates

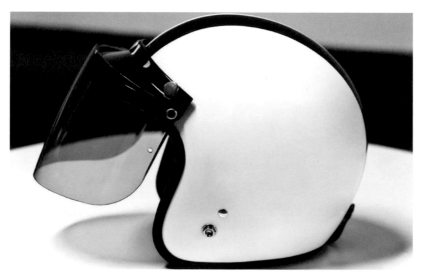

If you ride with an open faced helmet, consider a shield system to help with the elements.

faster than the body can burn energy to replace it. Body temperature that falls below 95°F (35°C) will produce symptoms of hypothermia, which include confusion, shivering, and bluing of the lips and skin. Even moderately cold air temperatures can lead to hypothermia if exposure occurs over a long enough period of time. If you suspect hypothermia, get to a warm place and remove wet garments.

Waterproof outer garments not only repel water, but also block wind, which slows convective heat loss. However, it's not enough to only block wind and rain if you want to stay warm. A base layer of snug-fitting wicking material, such as polypropylene, pulls moisture away from the skin to prevent sweat from causing evaporative cooling.

Breathable, insulating layers between the wicking layer and rain gear help trap body heat. Fleece is a good choice because it resists moisture and has many nooks and crannies to effectively lock in heat. For very chilly rides, consider upgrading to an electric vest to avoid the bulk of many layers.

See and Be Seen in Rainy Weather

Dim light and rain droplets obscure visibility, thus increasing the likelihood that you will miss seeing hazards and drivers will have a harder time seeing you. Riding in the rain at night is especially hazardous because the glare of lights reflects off windshields and the wet road surface.

Because conspicuity is a serious concern, be sure your rain gear has plenty of reflective material, and choose a rain jacket with bright colors. For added visibility, buy some reflective tape to add to your helmet and saddlebags. Knowing that it is more difficult for drivers to see you in rainy conditions should prompt you to be extra vigilant about being seen.

Being seen is critical for safety, but so is the ability to see hazards. Unfortunately, motorcycle riders don't have windshield wipers to clear away water and road spray. Turning your head left and right at speed can shed water from helmet shields, but for more thorough cleaning you may consider purchasing a squeegee from Aerostitch that slips over a glove's thumb or forefinger. Some glove manufacturers include a small squeegee built into the index finger of their gloves for clearing rainwater from goggles or faceshield.

To see hazards early, it is important that your eye protection is clear and scratch free. Be prepared by carrying a clear shield inside a tank bag, top box, or saddlebag, wrapped in a protective sleeve to prevent scratches. A repurposed helmet bag or tube sock can work, or buy a specially made shield sleeve. Some goggles and glasses come with both tinted and clear replacement lenses, as well as amber-tinted lenses that are helpful by increasing contrast in low light conditions.

Traction

Being comfortable and protected is important for reducing distraction and injury. But surviving rainy rides also means maintaining control when traction is sketchy. Wet surfaces are much less forgiving compared to dry surfaces. A dry surface with a bit of road grime usually causes few problems; however, that same surface coated with water can become quite slick.

Oil drippings and other contaminants accumulate in the middle of the lane where cars idle, such as at intersections and tollbooths. To avoid sliding your tires, aim for the wheel tracks. When stopped, place your foot away from the slick part of your lane to avoid having your boot slide out from under you.

Road grime eventually gets washed away; however, this can take time, which means that you must be particularly careful at the beginning of a rainstorm. A hard rainfall will wash away these contaminants rather quickly, but a light mist can prolong the hazard for a longer period of time.

Surfaces that are especially hazardous when wet include painted road markings, metal gratings, manhole covers and construction plates, railroad tracks, brick, cobblestones, wooden bridge decking, and crack filler. Avoid these hazards if possible, but if you must cross them do so

as upright as possible and avoid braking or accelerating. When cornering, slow early so you can avoid the need for last-second speed adjustments. Also, minimize lean angle and be gentle with the throttle to prevent traction loss.

Scan aggressively to spot areas with less traction. Be wary of standing water and large puddles that can lead to traction loss and can obscure potholes or other obstacles. Also, be careful when the road surface itself changes from one material to another, such as asphalt to concrete, because traction levels vary between different surfaces. To identify surface quality, look for changes in texture and color.

Tires

It's important to have good-quality tires that are kept properly inflated and monitored for condition. Tires for general street use have plenty of grooves (*sipes*) to shed water from between the tire and the road surface and have silica embedded in the rubber compound to enhance wet-weather grip. But sometimes there is too much water for the tire to evacuate. This leads to *hydroplaning*, which is what happens when water gets trapped between the tires and the pavement, causing the motorcycle to skate above the road surface. Riding fast increases the likelihood of hydroplaning, as can riding on worn tires. We talked earlier about how you can use the tread wear indicators molded into the bottom of tire treads to monitor tire wear.

Tires should be inflated to the manufacturer's recommended pressures to help them perform at their best. Some riders think it's smart to reduce tire pressures when riding in the rain as a way to increase

Painted road markings can be especially hazardous in the rain.

contact area. But a larger contact patch can actually increase the likelihood of hydroplaning because water is more easily trapped beneath the larger contact area. Also, less inflation pressure allows the sipes to close, which reduces their effectiveness at dispersing water.

Some tires perform better in wet conditions than others. Touring and sport-touring tires have ample grooves for managing rainwater, but sport tires have fewer grooves, which can cause them to hydroplane more easily than a touring tire. You may have noticed that supersport tires have practically no grooves near the edge of the tire. The logic is that no one is likely to lean that far over in the rain.

Having the right tire for the conditions leads to a sense of security and encourages rain-riding enjoyment. An extreme example is rain tires that are used exclusively for riding on the racetrack in wet conditions. I have ridden many rainy track day laps on regular street tires with mixed results as the limits of the tire are quickly reached. However, the fun factor increases significantly when riding with dedicated race rain tires. Not only was I able to ride at near knee-dragging speeds in pouring rain, but I also did so with confidence.

It's not practical to have super-soft, dedicated rain tires on a street bike, but thankfully, modern tires are excellent at handling both wet and dry conditions.

Rain Riding Techniques

It's important to brake, accelerate, and corner smoothly whenever traction is reduced. Slow down and look well ahead to spot hazards early so you can avoid abrupt braking and steering inputs. Allow generous following distances so you have plenty of space and time to slow if a vehicle ahead stops quickly. When the road becomes curvy, enter turns at a slower speed to keep lean angles moderate. This helps you handle a misjudged turn radius or an obstacle that appears suddenly, both of which can lead to abrupt mid-corner steering inputs. Plan to approach turns at slower speeds and turn in a bit earlier using gentler handlebar inputs.

One way to allow the motorcycle to remain more upright is to position your body to the inside of the curve. To reduce the risk of a front tire slide, it's important to relax your arms because tense arms transmit bumps from the road surface to the handlebars. It can be difficult to relax when you feel anxious, which is why it is important to enter turns at a speed that is well within your comfort zone.

Throttle control is an important aspect of traction management. Anxious riders often keep the throttle shut when cornering. This isn't a good idea because decelerating while leaned can overload the front tire. Instead, use a gentle amount of neutral-to-positive throttle to help balance the load between the front and rear tires for better traction and direction control.

Be careful when accelerating out of corners because too much drive force can cause the rear tire to spin. A useful technique for controlling wheelspin that was described earlier is the throttle ratchet technique in which you imagine a series of small "clicks" as you gradually roll on the gas. If the rear wheel spins, stop "clicking" to let the tire regain grip. You can "unclick" a little bit, but it's best to avoid chopping the throttle off completely, which can lead to a highside fall.

To become more comfortable with rain riding, you have to get some experience riding in the rain. You can plan a ride in the rain, head to a parking lot to practice, or sign up for a track day and hope for rain. The experience will increase confidence next time the skies open up unexpectedly.

Few people seek out rain riding—myself included. However, you can never predict when a rainstorm will appear. With a bit of knowledge and experience, it is possible to not only endure the challenges of rain riding, but even enjoy it.

Nighttime Riding

As much as I like the feeling of hurdling through the darkness on a cool night behind my headlight beam, I am very aware that one of my most effective crash-avoidance skills–spotting hazards early—is greatly diminished. It takes slower travel speeds and excellent diligence to reduce risk to an acceptable level.

Be Seen at Night

The most obvious challenge of navigating in the dark is seeing where you're going. But when you're out on the public streets, it's equally important to be seen. And we know that drivers have a hard time seeing motorcycles even in daylight.

Nighttime crashes often occur when the intruding driver does not recognize a rider's presence. Perhaps the bike's single headlight became lost in the glare of other vehicle headlights, streetlights, and lit signs surrounding the roadway. This certainly makes it difficult for drivers to see motorcycles and also judge their speed and distance.

To help drivers recognize motorcycles, some manufacturers wire the front turn signals with dual-filament bulbs that illuminate constantly. Dual headlights and auxiliary lights mounted near the headlight can also help drivers distinguish motorcycles.

Another serious hazard when riding at night comes from the rear. It's easy for drivers to lose track of your bike and misjudge following distance if all they can see is a small red taillight. Some motorcycles have taillight designs that provide a widely lit area. But many motorcycles have only one small taillight unit with nothing more than a single bulb. Touring riders have been adorning their rigs with rear-facing auxiliary lights for many years. Sport tourers who may not want the added weight and glitz of auxiliary rear lights will often place reflective material on the backside of their saddlebags. Many luggage manufacturers provide reflectors on the back and sides of their bags. Be sure that any side-mounted reflectors are not obstructed and can be easily seen.

Aftermarket light emitting diode (LED) lights offer a bright light source that turns on faster, lasts longer, and is more reliable than incandescent bulbs. The University of Michigan did a study that concluded that motorists respond more quickly to the early warning of LED lights. Small diode brake light units are available that can be mounted near your stock brake light. There are also electronic units that can be programmed to flash the brake lights when the brakes are applied to alert drivers behind. The

High-visibility gear helps you be seen at night.

advantage these lights offer can be tremendous, especially when riding at night.

I said it before, and I'll say it again: it's smart to wear light-colored riding gear with reflective material rather than the typical black helmet and black leather jacket. This is especially true at night. But we all know that the most popular color for motorcycle jackets and helmets is black, and many riders wouldn't dare risk ruining the image by riding in reflective clothing or a reflective vest over the black jacket. Okay, so how about applying additional reflective tape onto all sides of your helmet? In fact, many US states actually require reflective material on helmets.

Seeing at Night

Human beings have limited nighttime vision. But there are some other things we can do to improve our nighttime vision. First, it's important to realize that we simply cannot see as well at night as we can in the daytime. This means that many hazards go by unnoticed, including hazards that rob traction, induce instability, or cause a tire puncture. A pothole may appear to be a benign dark splotch on the road with no definition to tell us how deep it is. Warning signs may be posted near construction sites, but at night it may be impossible to see just how hazardous the surface is until you're upon it.

The obvious strategy for night riding is to slow down and scan aggressively for hazards. Unfortunately, not many headlights illuminate very far ahead, making it easy to travel faster than the distance your headlight can illuminate. To increase nighttime vision, use your high beam when possible. If you're following another vehicle, you need to dim your headlight, but you can often see what's ahead of the next vehicle, illuminated by that vehicle's headlights. You may consider installing auxiliary lights to illuminate more of the roadway. There are many low-wattage LED auxiliary lights available from the aftermarket.

Motorcycle headlights may do a pretty good job of illuminating the road directly ahead, but offer very little light off to the sides. This makes it tough to spot roadside hazards and makes cornering a challenge. Good cornering technique includes looking far into the turn to spot hazards and to keep your bike going where you want it to go. This is difficult to do when the exit of the corner is out of reach of your headlight. Add to that the fact that the angle of the headlight dips as lean angle increases, and the likelihood of a hazard suddenly appearing mid-corner grows. Aftermarket auxiliary lights can help in this regard. Look for advanced headlight technologies that actively point the beam into the corner.

It's important to change a tinted faceshield to a clear one for night riding and to make sure your eye protection is clean with no significant scratches that will increase glare. Bugs fly in great numbers at night, and most of them seem to find their way onto our face shield. Keep a damp rag or some other cleaning device handy, and pull over if necessary to keep your shield or goggles clean. The lights of oncoming vehicles can cause temporary blindness if you look directly at the lights. The trick is to keep your eyes on the white fog line on the side of the road to help keep you in your lane.

Stay Warm

When the temperature drops, it is important to keep your body warm to prevent muscle cramping, which leads to discomfort and loss of fine motor control. Layers are effective in retaining body heat for moderately cool temperatures and shorter rides, but electric vests and gloves may be called for if the temperature falls below 50°F (10°C) and the ride is long. Riding pants and a neck warmer also makes a tremendous difference in keeping the body warm.

Stay Awake

Whether returning home from a late work shift or trying to get some miles behind you during the cool, traffic-free nighttime hours, we must be aware that these late night rides may involve potentially dangerous sleepiness. The effects of sleepiness can be compared to alcohol intoxication in which judgment, vision, and reaction time are negatively affected. And we all know how dangerous riding with dulled senses can be.

Some riders rely on caffeine to sustain their alertness, but caffeine wears off, leaving the rider often groggier than before. It may be better to catch some sleep a few hours before embarking on a night ride. And if you begin to feel the signs of tiredness—inability to keep your eyes open,

NOCTURNAL MENACES

Drunk drivers are a real hazard to motorcyclists at any time of day or night. Knowing the difficulty *sober* drivers have seeing and identifying motorcycles, it is particularly scary to think of an inebriated driver heading toward you or approaching from behind at a stoplight. You should be especially wary when riding near bars and nightspots.

LESSON LEARNED

Night Moves

It's midnight when Nocturnal Nick puts on his helmet and black leather jacket to make his way home from his second-shift job. He's tired from working a full shift, but he knows to ride carefully through the darkened streets that lead home.

Nick makes his way through a series of stoplights that control traffic entering from various shopping centers and popular nightspots. Suddenly, Nick sees the headlights of a car weaving across his path. He applies the brakes smoothly but forcefully, confident that there is just enough space to stop short of the offending driver. But as his bike pitches forward, the front tire loses traction and immediately slides sideways, causing Nick and his bike to slam to the ground. Nick tumbles as his bike slides into the side of the car he was trying to avoid.

The driver and his passengers look out the window at Nick, but don't seem to comprehend that they have been involved in an accident. After a moment, they tear off into the darkness, leaving Nick stranded in the middle of the intersection with a trashed bike and a sore shoulder. After a bit of investigation, Nick notices a large patch of sand with a skid mark from his front tire cutting straight through it.

WHAT'S THE LESSON?

The risk of being involved in an incident rises significantly when riding at night. Nick became a victim of more than one nighttime riding hazard, including low visibility, a surface hazard, and a driver's questionable sobriety.

Nighttime riding can be very rewarding. Some of my most memorable rides were nighttime rides through quiet back roads and bright city streets. But it is critical to keep in mind the dangers specific to night riding and act to reduce the risk so you can enjoy many more day and nighttime adventures.

daydreaming, forgetting where you are for a moment—act quickly by pulling off for a stretch and a brisk walk or even a nap if necessary.

Animals

Whether riding during the day or at night, animals are one of the most significant dangers motorcycle riders face. There are many animals, such as dogs, deer, bear, and moose, that cause roadway crashes. Even though animal collisions are much less common than collisions with vehicles at intersections, the number of animal-induced crashes is still significant. According to the National Highway Traffic Safety Administration (NHTSA), there were about 275,000 animal collisions per year, or about 4% of all motor vehicle crashes. Needless to say, motorcyclists are more at risk of injury and death from animal collisions. According to the Wisconsin DOT, 83% of collisions between motorcycles and deer resulted in human injury or death, compared to only 3% of collisions between cars and deer.

Predictably Unpredictable

No matter what type of hazard you encounter, you must first predict its presence so you can act to avoid becoming another statistic. It's easy to predict that problems might occur at intersections, construction sites, and blind corners, and we know that it's smart to approach these areas with extra caution. Unfortunately, animal hazards are much less predictable. Animals are more likely to appear when we least expect and without any overt warning. With this lack of predictability, it may appear that avoiding animals is a matter of luck or fate. But there are ways to minimize the risk.

It's helpful to know that your chances of being involved in an animal collision increase significantly depending on when and where you ride. For instance, you're at greater risk of a canine collision if you ride through neighborhoods with a large dog population and where pet owners tend to let their dogs run free. You run a greater risk of a deer encounter if you ride through wooded areas during dusk or dawn and during autumn and early winter.

Most of us aren't willing or able to limit our riding to avoid these locations and times. So what can we do to avoid a collision? Let's take a look at the characteristics and behaviors of common animal hazards and discuss some ways to reduce the likelihood of a collision.

Dogs

Dogs come in many sizes, shapes, and temperaments. Some are fun loving, others are aggressive. Some are docile, submissive, and indifferent, while others are active, domineering, and ready to take on any challenge.

Dogs are naturally territorial and, if they're not restrained, will roam the neighborhood actively enforcing ownership of their "turf." Many of these canines have no fear of vehicles, especially a relatively small motorcycle. They may hide behind rocks, brush, or parked cars, waiting to dart into the road, giving chase whenever the opportunity allows. These dogs may be rather stupid when it comes to the danger vehicles pose to their health, but their keen sense of hearing and sight make them quite sharp when it comes to timing their actions for "the kill." They'll calculate the point of interception then wait for the precise moment to dart out from their hiding place, usually aiming for your front wheel in an effort to trip up their prey.

Thankfully, not all dogs are interested in attacking vehicles. But that doesn't mean they are any less of a threat. A dog can easily dart across the street completely unaware of a nearby motorcycle. The moral of the story is that any dog needs to be treated as a real threat, whether aggressive or docile. Scan the roadside for any signs of man's best friend and act immediately by slowing down and creating space between you and the dog.

The trick to thwarting an aggressive attack is to outsmart the dog by forcing a last minute recalculation. Do this by slowing unexpectedly (don't forget to downshift), then accelerate hard to leave Fido in the dust. This technique will only work if you can see the dog early enough, so keep your eyes open. A word of caution:

if you frequently ride the same route and perform the same evasive maneuver on the same dog, eventually the dog will catch on to your technique. Also, if you're following a rider who is involved in a dog chase, it is important to know that you will have a different type of hazard to deal with when the chase ends—a dog stopping directly in front of you as your friend speeds off. Or the dog may give up on your buddy and come after you thinking you'd be an easier target.

If a particular dog continually causes problems, it may be worth approaching the dog's owner. Tell him or her that you are anxious about the possibility of a collision with their pet who would very likely be seriously hurt or killed. And that if a collision were to occur, you could be injured and your motorcycle could suffer significant damage that they may be liable for. If this person-to-person discussion gets you nowhere, you may want to get the animal control people involved. Most towns have leash laws these days, although many aren't aggressively enforced. But a call to the dog officer might get some results.

Avoiding a collision with a loose dog requires a special technique.

Deer

Deer cause thousands of collisions each year throughout many parts of North America, and their numbers are on the rise. In 1980, there were an estimated 10 million wild deer. Today, that population has swelled to an estimated 25 million. Michigan has the most deer strikes, with almost 67,000. Other states of note are Georgia with 51,000 and Wisconsin with about 45,000. But these numbers are probably

Animal Magnetism

Karen decides to take advantage of the beautiful weather by taking the long way home from work. She exits the freeway onto a quiet road winding through a wooded neighborhood. Ranch houses line both sides of the road and are set back behind a row of tall trees and stone walls. Karen notices a woman and dog walking along the side of the road a couple hundred feet ahead on the left. She relaxes a bit when she sees that the dog is leashed. Karen keeps a close eye on the dog and maintains her speed, but keeps her fingers curled around the front brake lever in case the dog gets loose.

Suddenly, an object appears in Karen's right peripheral vision. A second dog has dashed out from behind a rock wall, running at full speed and on a collision course with Karen's front wheel.

The next couple of seconds are a blur. Karen remembers her handlebars being wrenched from her hands and the pavement rushing toward her. Now she is lying face down in the middle of the road, a searing pain radiating from her hip and chest. She glances over to see her bike on its side, gas seeping from its tank. She also sees the dog stretched out motionless a dozen feet away.

WHAT'S THE LESSON?

Never take animals for granted.

low because there are surely many more collisions that go unreported.

Most deer collisions occur during autumn and the early winter months when deer become most active. This increased activity is largely due to mating and hunting season when deer are establishing their territory or are on the move to avoid hunters. Deer are most active between dusk and dawn when they come out of their hiding places to graze on the tender grass found along roadways. Deer are social beings that congregate in groups. So if you come across one deer, expect more to be nearby, usually following close behind the leader. Deer tend to cross roadways in the same locations, using familiar routes to navigate through

their territory. Highway departments attempt to warn motorists of these areas by posting deer signs in locations where an exceptionally high number of collisions occur. It should also be obvious that you are riding in an area with heavy deer collisions when you see a carcass lying on the side of the road or telltale bloodstains on the roadway.

So, what can we do to prevent a deer collision? Some avoid riding when deer are most active, but that isn't always feasible. Some people tout the effectiveness of deer whistles saying that the ultrasonic sound waves will alert the deer and scare them away, but pessimists suggest that since deer have a hearing range similar to humans they

The best solution to avoiding a deer collision is to slow down when traveling through rural areas in the late afternoon and the early morning hours.

probably can't hear the ultrasonic whistles any better than the rider can hear them. So, deer whistles may give a false sense of security that can make riders less vigilant.

The best solution to avoiding a deer collision is to slow down when traveling through rural areas in the late afternoon and the early morning hours. Pay attention to road signs warning of deer in the area. Use your high beam to help light up the landscape, actively scan the roadsides for any suspicious shapes or movement, and keep a lookout for the reflections from deer eyes.

Evasive Action

It's also smart to keep your fingers curled around the front brake lever when riding in deer country to reduce reaction time. When you spot a deer or any other animal near the roadway, it's best to slow immediately, even if the animal doesn't appear to be startled. Deer seem to ignore threats until you get very close, and then they suddenly take flight. A slower speed will allow more time for the animal to escape, a shorter braking

distance, and reduced impact force if you guess wrong.

Is swerving a good evasive tactic for avoiding a deer? Maybe. But, the problem is that swerving to avoid a collision requires knowing which way the animal is going to jump, and, as we suggested earlier, deer leap unpredictably when spooked. Experts recommend that motorists avoid swerving because colliding with a tree or some other roadside object may be worse than a deer strike. Consider swerving only if you feel control can be maintained.

Other Critters

Dogs and deer are probably the most common animals we encounter, but North America is the home of many other creatures that can cause problems. Moose are formidable creatures who lumber through the northern regions hardly noticing vehicles passing only a few yards away. These creatures are often twice the weight of a Gold Wing and can reach 7 feet tall at the shoulders.

In some areas of the southern US, you may even encounter alligators.

you roll over small critters. If a chipmunk or squirrel appears in front of you, darting about indecisively, it's usually best to keep your eyes ahead and stay the course instead of attempting evasive action to avoid the critter.

Of all the hazards that we encounter on our two-wheeled travels, animal hazards may be the scariest due to the relative unpredictability and serious injury they can cause. The limited number of avoidance measures can also make us feel helpless. But, as we have learned, we can reduce our risk through awareness and being prepared for maximum effort braking.

The Other Guy

Remember, you are not the only rider on the road. You must take into consideration how other drivers increase risk and affect your well-being.

Watch Your Back

Collisions from behind are statistically less frequent than collisions from ahead. However, I have firsthand experience that rear end collisions do indeed occur. To avoid being creamed from behind, you cannot let your guard down when stopped at a traffic light, tollbooth, or intersection.

Like most crashes, rear-end collisions occur when drivers fail to see the motorcycle or misjudge the actual location of a motorcycle stopped in traffic. Our small size and few lights contribute to why drivers fail to see stopped bikes. To increase your visibility, use

Moose are close relatives to deer, and, like deer, moose are active between dusk and dawn and find the roadside an inviting place to graze. They are also known to lick residual road salt from last winter's deicing efforts. Also, like deer, moose fur doesn't reflect light very well. Unfortunately, the eyes of these towering beasts may be well above your high beam—too high for your headlight to create a reflection. You will find moose signs posted in collision hot spots to warn you of their presence. And if the highway department goes to all the trouble to erect a warning sign, you ought to take advantage of it. Other animals are known to cause crashes, such as bears, raccoons, fox, beavers, horses, and cows. In the West and Midwest, herds of open range animals, such as antelope and bison, regularly ignore roadways as they move across the landscape. In southern regions, you may see armadillos or even alligators.

Smaller animals usually pose less risk due to their size. You will likely maintain control if you are upright and not on the brakes as

LESSON LEARNED

Close Stop

Over the years, you've developed strategies for managing traffic and impatient commuters, including keeping a broad view of your surroundings. One strategy you put high on your list is to scan your mirrors as you slow for a stoplight and continue to monitor your mirrors to ensure that vehicles approaching from behind don't rear end you. You once had a distracted driver bump you from behind, and you swear it will never happen again.

Today is another typical ride to work. You approach yet another red light on the busy multilane boulevard. You stop well behind the car in front of you and then scan your mirrors. You immediately notice a white SUV closing a little too fast. You flash your brake light and ready your clutch hand for a quick escape if necessary. The SUV driver doesn't respond quickly enough, so you squeeze to the left of the car ahead. You hear the crunch of two bumpers making contact and look back to see the SUV and the car to your right resting against each other.

WHAT'S THE LESSON?

Your habit of scanning your mirrors when slowing and while stopped is excellent, as is your strategy of flashing your brake light to alert approaching drivers. Equally important is your strategy of stopping far enough behind the car in front to allow space to move forward or slip by one side of the car ahead in case a vehicle approaching from behind fails to stop in time. Being alert and ready to utilize this escape route allowed you to avoid a nasty crash from behind.

turn signals and brake lights and wear brightly colored riding gear. Reflective material on a vest, on the back of your helmet, or stitched onto your jacket can make you much more visible when it gets dark.

A more active way to alert drivers behind you is to flash your brake light when coming to a stop and after you're already stopped. Your brake light switches should trigger the light without applying any brake force.

To enhance rear end visibility, install aftermarket auxiliary lights that automatically flash for a few seconds when

the brake lever or pedal is used and then stay on continuously until you release the brakes. Another way to increase nighttime conspicuity is to add reflective tape or reflective sheets to the rear of the bike.

Be Prepared
Lane position can affect whether you are involved in a rear-end collision or a near miss. Be prepared for the possibility of a driver colliding with you by positioning yourself so you have an escape route. This means stopping well behind the car in front and in the right- or left-hand portion of your lane to allow a quick escape in case a driver

behind you cannot stop. This position also gives the driver an escape route to your side if he can't stop in time. Remember to keep an eye on your mirrors and stay in first gear if you need a quick getaway.

Hindsight

We don't have eyes in the back of our head to spot potential rear-enders, so we must rely on mirrors. Unfortunately, some mirrors are better at reflecting a shoulder or an elbow than rearward hazards.

You can improve rearward view by installing mirrors with longer stalks. Bar-end mirrors are an option. They give a cafe racer look while providing a better view of where you've been—at the cost of a much wider handlebar span that can make tight maneuvering a bit dicey.

Most motorcycle mirrors have convex optics, providing a wider view of what's behind. A minor drawback is the image distortion that makes objects appear farther away than they actually are. Some riders add small fisheye mirrors in the corner of their stock items to get a wider angle of view.

Mirrors cannot detect vehicles in your blind spots. That's why it's important to glance over your shoulder before moving into another lane. Head checks need to be executed efficiently to get enough visual information without diverting attention away from what's in front of you. Perform head checks as quickly as you can but not so fast you can't distinguish what's there.

Tailgaters

Tailgaters are rude, inconsiderate, and annoying and can make the hair on the back of your neck rise. But, your main concern should be the effect a tailgater has on your safety because they may be unable to stop in time if you need to stop quickly. If you're concerned about an obnoxious tailgater, don't simply ride along hoping the bully will back off.

Your first response may be to speed up under the pressure or to get angry and slow down to show your displeasure. But that will just increase the risk. Flashing your brake light might get the driver to back off. It may be tempting to gesture for a tailgater to back off. But be aware that this can infuriate a tailgater and escalate the situation. If the brake light doesn't work, pull over to let him by. Yes, he "wins," but it's better to not let him ruin your ride or increase the risks.

If you can't (or won't) pull over, then give yourself more following distance behind the vehicle in front of you. This increases the time and distance you have to slow if the car ahead suddenly stops, allowing the car behind time to avoid rear-ending you.

Road Rage

The decision to confront a driver in traffic is foolish, especially when you

Avoid confrontations with road ragers.

are on a motorcycle. It's critical to avoid confrontations with potential road ragers because we are so vulnerable to their wrath. There have been stories about riders being rear-ended and run over by drivers enraged by what they perceive as a motorcyclist's aggressive and inconsiderate behavior. Even if you don't mean anything by your gesture, you risk being misunderstood.

Be extra careful if you suspect a driver to be drunk. For example, many years ago, I was on my way home, sitting at a stoplight late at night, when a beat-up sedan stopped behind me. The car didn't have its lights on, so I kindly signaled to the driver about the problem. He retorted with an incomprehensible statement that was obviously fueled by alcohol. I pointed to his lights once again to clarify my intent. This time, the passenger of the car opened his door and began walking toward me with a baseball bat in one hand! Uh-oh. I looked

to see that the intersection was clear and quickly got myself outta there. That incident taught me just how vulnerable I am and that irrational individuals too easily see motorcyclists as an easy target

The risk of other drivers feeling threatened is also quite real, especially since the well-publicized confrontation between motorcycle riders and an SUV driver in New York City. This can mean a driver overreacting to what you thought was a minor altercation.

The message is that we must keep our own rage in check and do not engage drivers even if they are at fault. Resist any temptation to "teach him a lesson," swallow your anger, and remove yourself from any situation. Take a moment to cool down and then consider how your role could have contributed to the near miss. You just might learn something about your own behavior in traffic.

Chapter 11

Group Riding

There is a lot to be said for sharing your motorcycling passion with others, whether simply hanging out at a rally talking about bikes or firing up your engine and joining in on a group ride. Group rides can be small or large, relaxed, or spirited. No matter what type of ride you're on, there are certain issues you must consider if you are to have a good time and remain safe.

Rules

Group rides can be safe and fun or chaotic. What makes one ride better than another is leadership and some well-thought-out rules. This includes the use of hand signals, clear communication about route, behavior, and particulars like who leads and who follows and group formation.

Formation

When riding alone, you are free to continually adjust your lane position and speed, but riding with two or more other motorcycles limits your options significantly. When riding in a group, you will likely ride in a staggered formation with the lead rider in the left-hand portion of the lane and the second rider positioned in the right-hand portion of the lane. The third rider is directly behind the leader in the left-hand lane position, and the staggered formation continues

down the line. Where you end up in the lane is determined simply by whether you are an odd- or even-numbered rider in line. Many groups expect there to be no passing between group riders so that everyone remains in his or her same position.

The general rule of thumb is that each rider should maintain at least a 2-second following distance from the bike *directly* ahead in case that rider must stop quickly. This means that you will be about 1 second behind the rider to your immediate left or right. The 1-second gap allows you to move laterally to avoid a surface hazard, but only if this distance is maintained.

The staggered formation should be abandoned when the road is narrow or riddled with surface hazards. Riding single-file allows each rider to use the full width of the lane to dodge these obstacles. Each rider must slow down so that the group can spread out and maintain a minimum 2-second following distance between him- or herself and the rider ahead.

The same goes for riding in curves. It's okay to maintain the staggered formation for gentle curves, but when the corners become tighter, it is best to form a single line. That way, each rider can use the full width of the lane to use cornering lines or to avoid mid-corner hazards that may be difficult to detect around a bend. Exit ramps should be ridden single-file. The staggered formation can be reestablished as individuals merge into the highway.

The only time riders should be side-by-side in the lane is when the group comes to a stop or when entering traffic.

Three-wheelers in the group should follow a single-file formation and be given a minimum 2-second following distance.

Riding two abreast should be avoided because it does not allow side-to-side lane positioning. The only time riders should be side-by-side in the lane is when the group comes to a stop or when entering traffic. When stopping at an intersection, the leader should come to a complete stop so the whole group may regroup. When it's time to leave, the leader should be in the left portion of the lane and be the first to leave when the light turns green or when it is safe to proceed from a stop sign.

Individual Skill and Attitude

One challenging aspect of group riding is the variation in rider ability, attitude, and riding style. An obvious indicator of potential problems is when someone shows up for a ride in a t-shirt and shorts when everyone else is in full gear. In this situation, you can bet that this person is either unaware of the real risks of riding or has a less serious attitude toward risk than the rest of the group.

Many times, mismatches in individual style or attitude aren't immediately obvious. A group of mild-mannered motorcyclists will not appreciate a rider who is erratic, passes indiscriminately, or pulls wheelies. Another significant problem is the issue of alcohol. It should be stated clearly before the ride begins that there will be no alcohol consumption at any time before or during the ride.

Of course, there will always be "problem riders" who cannot check their egos or adhere to the rules. Having the group's ride policy clearly posted on social media or the Internet forum will help weed out those who might otherwise spoil the group's fun. In the end, the group will be happier and stronger with well-established rules and procedures.

Mixing experienced riders and newbies can be dangerous. For new riders to safely join experienced riders on group rides requires care. Some groups insist that new or less skilled riders be located in front, where they can be monitored and where they will feel less pressure to keep up. This may serve the new rider in some ways, but he could easily feel pressured to ride faster than he should so he doesn't hold up the group or appear to be incompetent by riding too slowly. Most new riders who join groups elect to ride in the back. To prevent new riders from getting into trouble, it is important for ride leaders to maintain a moderate pace and have at least one rider keep an eye on these individuals.

Group Attitude

Right from the beginning, it's important for you to evaluate the participants. If

It's best to form a single line for tighter curves.

LESSON LEARNED

Second Group Ride: Necessary Changes

With the new rules in place, Randy decides to give the group another chance. This time, the leaders brief the riders about the route and where planned gas stops will be. They also explain that the lead riders will stop at turn-offs to make sure nobody gets left behind. Their words seem to put the group at ease, which results in a much more relaxed start to the ride.

Soon after the ride begins, it becomes apparent that these procedures did not solve all of the problems. Two guys ahead of Randy are riding too fast for their ability and endangering those around them. Both struggle to stay in their lane in the corners and then blast ahead on the straights.

At the first break, Randy approaches one of the group leaders to discuss the two riders. He explains that they appear to be anxious about holding up the group and are going to crash if they continue riding at this pace. The leader is reluctant to take responsibility and brushes off Randy's concern.

Convinced that nothing will be done, Randy decides to introduce himself to the two riders to see if he can get them to slow down. Randy invites the two men to ride with him at the back of the pack where the pace is more relaxed. Roy thinks this is a good idea. However, Steve—seemingly driven by ego—wants to ride in front with the fast guys. Randy risks angering him by asking that he take it easy. Steve scoffs and turns away.

Back on the road, Randy and Roy enjoy a brisk, yet comfortable pace near the back. Up ahead, Steve is not having such a good time as he struggles to keep up and save face. Steve's ride ends a few corners later when he drifts wide exiting a left-hand turn. His front tire slides on the roadside sand, and he is down with a broken collarbone and a severely battered ego.

Steve is like many riders who allow their "Mr. Hyde" personality to overtake their usually well-mannered "Dr. Jekyll" when exposed to the pressures of group riding. He succumbed to his desire to appear competent, which caused him to ride faster than his abilities would allow.

WHAT'S THE LESSON?

Randy was smart to voice his concern about the two erratic riders to the group leader who, unfortunately, was unwilling to do anything about it. The leader would have been smart to assure Roy and Steve that they would not be thought of poorly if they rode more slowly. He could have also suggested that they ride near the back or assigned a willing, experienced rider to keep an eye on them. As it turned out, Randy took on this role and saved at least one of the two riders from harm.

After the ride, Randy writes privately to the forum administrators encouraging them to implement a few more rules that may prevent future mishaps. Again, the response is cool, but, with Randy's help, they come up with a plan they can all agree on. They decide to post a written policy on the website designed to discourage unsafe or reckless riding and have sweep riders monitor activities. Things were looking up.

Sometimes group riding will encourage novice riders to go faster than they should.

Good communication is essential for pulling off a group ride.

can either not ride with them or ask that they wait at intersections so you can regroup.

The "Lesson Learned" boxes in this chapter follow our imaginary friend, Randy, as he joins a few different group rides, each with its share of rewards and potentially dangerous challenges.

Benefit Rides

Another type of group ride is a benefit run. These events can vary in their level of organization. A major challenge with very large group rides is the difficulty for the organizers to coordinate the ride's logistics and communicate them to the participants. As you can see from the "Lesson Learned" box on the following page, What Randy encountered was a ride that began without any instructions, relying instead on the majority of attendees knowing the protocol and the masses simply following suit.

LESSON LEARNED

Third Group Ride: Leadership

The next ride has the group leaders taking an active role in organization. This results in a more relaxed atmosphere. The ride turns out to be extremely enjoyable, with a lot of smooth, well-controlled riding and plenty of smiles to go around—and no unfortunate incidents. What Randy reads online the next day confirms how much fun everyone had.

WHAT'S THE LESSON?

Most "Sunday" rides are informal events with five or six riders in attendance and little in the way of preparation or meaningful leadership. Things become more complicated when the number of riders increases. Larger groups are harder to keep together, and it's not uncommon for some to ride aggressively and make unsafe passes in an attempt to keep up. To prevent these problems, smart leaders break large groups into several smaller groups of riders with similar ability and attitude.

Seasoned organizers of larger group rides use well-honed organizational techniques that ensure safety. These groups often stick to the posted speed limits and stop frequently to keep the group members together. Hand signals, sweep riders with communicators, and strict policies about rider behavior are typical. To ensure that everything runs smoothly, formal groups select individuals who are willing to accept responsibility for organizing and executing rides. These "Road Captains" are often required to have advanced riding skills training and some sort of organizational experience to help carry out their responsibilities so that everyone has a safe and fun time.

A written policy of rules for group rides can make the experience safer.

LESSON LEARNED

Benefit Ride

The following week, Randy joins a fellow forum member, Chris, on a benefit ride. Randy arrives at the meeting spot along with 300 other motorcyclists. Volunteers hand out route maps while someone with a bullhorn announces a 15-minute departure time but, much to Randy's dismay, there is no riders' meeting describing the logistics.

Randy and Chris roll forward into the crowd, but they become separated, which means Randy will be riding next to someone whose skill level and attitude toward safety are unknown.

Once under way, Randy falls into a side-by-side, two-abreast formation along with the rest of the riders. This seriously limits lateral maneuverability and at one point Randy is almost hit by the rider to his left when he swerves to avoid a pothole.

Another concern is that some riders are erratic, and their following distances are rather close. Randy cringes when he looks in his rearview mirror to see a rider on his tail. To prevent being rear-ended, Randy increases his following distance from the rider ahead in case he stops quickly.

The ride continues for more than an hour and a half without a stop, which is okay with Randy but he can imagine some of the riders becoming dangerously fatigued. Riding a motorcycle requires a lot of concentration, especially when riding at close quarters; minds wander and riding skills become dulled to a point where mistakes occur more frequently.

The ride ends with the group filing into a high school parking lot where there is a barbeque and soft drinks. While munching on a hot dog, Randy hears a rumor that two riders collided and another who went off the road. Randy isn't surprised to hear this, thinking that only two mishaps probably isn't bad considering how many riders were in attendance.

In the end, Randy's experience with the benefit ride is mixed. He was happy to donate money and ride for a good cause, but the potential for a mishap is a bit high for his tastes.

WHAT'S THE LESSON?

Running a large group ride can be like herding kittens. It takes good leadership, scheduling, and coordination to pull off a big ride. One way that leaders try to corral all the participants and help minimize miscommunication is to institute standardized hand signals.

Chapter 12

Carrying Passengers

One of the joys of riding a motorcycle is to share the experience with friends and loved ones. Sometimes that means riding on separate bikes, but, for many, sharing the ride means riding two-up. Riding with a passenger is a responsibility that requires you to be diligent about not only your own safety, but also the safety of your passenger.

Are You Passenger Worthy?

When carrying a passenger, consider that a mistake on your part can cause significant injury to the person who trusts you with his or her life. This responsibility cannot be taken lightly. Think about how you would feel if your failure to manage the risks resulted in the injury or death of a friend or family member.

Before you consider taking a passenger on board, look in the mirror and assess your ability to avoid a mishap. You probably wouldn't jump on the back of a bike operated by a new rider, with someone who tends to show off, or a rider who is not particularly skillful at controlling his or her machine. So, why would you even ask someone you care about to jump on the back of your bike if you are not a very

Before you consider taking a passenger on board, look in the mirror and assess your ability to avoid a mishap.

good rider? I know what you're saying, "I am a good rider!" Perhaps you are, but are you good enough to risk the life of another person? If not, then you must get your skills to a point where the odds of a tipover or an incident in traffic are as low as possible.

Realistically, you don't have to be a professional-level motorcyclist to qualify to carry a passenger. The odds of an average rider making it home safely with both rider and passenger intact are usually pretty good. My point is that before you consider asking another person to trust you to keep them safe, you must first make sure you can operate your bike with complete control and in a safe manner.

Preparation

Okay, so you asked yourself the tough questions and are satisfied that your

abilities are sufficient to take a passenger for a ride. What's next? Before you tell your partner to mount up, there are several things you need to do to ensure a good experience.

Gear Up!

You've heard me talk about All the Gear All the Time (ATGATT) as it pertains to the rider and how wearing protective gear can significantly reduce injury in the event of a fall. So, it should not be a surprise that I am telling you to insist on having your passenger wear the best protective gear you can muster.

What? You don't have a second full-faced helmet, riding jacket and pants, motorcycle gloves, and boots? Not many people do. But you would be a fool to not protect your passenger. Don't be tempted to give him or her your helmet and you go lidless. A better idea is to borrow a good-quality helmet that fits. If you plan on taking this person on more than one ride, then it may be time to go shopping for her own helmet and riding gear, including eye protection.

It may seem like an okay solution to dust off an old helmet, but remember that helmets lose their protective qualities over time, so think twice about what you ask your passenger to put on her head. Don't forget to show her how to secure the helmet strap.

For those of you who rarely ride with a passenger, it's not likely that you'll have a dedicated jacket, boots, gloves, or riding pants for a would-be passenger. So, it is likely that you will have to make sure your passenger does the very best she can to wear protective clothing. A pair of sturdy jeans, jacket, work gloves, and hiking boots may be the best she can do. It's not ideal, but the real world dictates that you must balance idyllic protection with practicality.

Be sure to tell your passenger to wear layers. Non-motorcyclists don't often realize how much wind chill affects comfort. For example, riding at 65 mph (105 kph) when the air temperature is 60°F (15°C) will feel like 53°F (12°C). At the other end of the spectrum is the need to remain cool in hot weather. Ask your passenger to wear clothes that allow air to flow and that can be easily shed when you stop for breaks. Don't be tempted to ride with bare skin. Not only are you unprotected from possible road rash, but uncovered skin will also burn in the sun and lose moisture when exposed to hot wind.

Your passenger must wear the appropriate gear.

A passenger should sit still with his or her feet on the pegs.

If there is a threat of rain, pack sturdy rain gear so you and your passenger remain comfortable.

Educate Your Passenger

Being a passenger means participating in the demands of riding a motorcycle, which includes the risks as well as the rewards. A passenger needs to understand that her role as a "co-rider" is very important and that she must take this responsibility seriously.

Part of your job is to ensure that your passenger knows how to be a partner on a motorcycle. Do not assume anything! You must remember that you are the motorcycle expert compared to your passenger who may have never straddled a two-wheeler before. You must take the time to educate her about being on the back of a motorcycle. Start by walking around the bike to point out areas that will become hot and can burn. Point out areas that pose a risk if a finger, toe, or garment were to get caught, such as the chain and sprocket area.

Hang On

I recently heard about a woman who relaxed her grip around the waist of her then boyfriend at a stoplight. He then took off hard enough to launch her backward onto her head. It's easy to assume that the passenger would have the common sense to hang on at all times and that there is a possibility that the rider might accelerate at any time. But, perhaps the rider did not emphasize the importance of this fact. Even so, the rider should have made sure to accelerate smoothly and gradually. To prevent a possible calamity, show your passenger where and how to hang on and to be ready at all times.

Some riders like their passenger to hold onto their waist, while others prefer the passenger to hold onto a grab rail or other secure part of the bike. Some motorcycles have a strap between the passenger and the rider, but these straps do not provide a very secure way to brace for braking or acceleration.

Brace for Braking and Acceleration

Ask the passenger to pay attention to what is happening and what is about to occur. Warn about the effects of acceleration and braking and to brace by holding onto the grab bars or your waist. To prevent your passenger from piling into your back and knocking helmets, ask her to brace herself and to squeeze her legs against your hips as you brake.

When it comes to acceleration, remind your passenger that it's important to hang on firmly and to lean slightly forward under acceleration. Remember that it is your responsibility to minimize abrupt or extreme braking or acceleration that can cause your passenger to be unbalanced.

Sit Still, Feet on the Pegs

It's natural for new passengers to want to help you support the bike at stops, because of their fear of falling over. But passengers will certainly upset balance if they attempt to reach the ground when you stop. Instead, coach her to keep her feet on the pegs at all times, even at stops.

Sitting still is another important coaching tip to help you maintain balance at stops and when maneuvering at slower speeds. A passenger who shifts body weight can cause you to struggle with stability and direction control. Tell your passenger that a good passenger is one who seems like she isn't even there.

Lean with Me

You may be completely comfortable leaning your motorcycle. However, people who are not used to being on a bike can freak out at what may seem like moderate lean angles. This should be expected with any new passenger. A passenger who does not lean with the motorcycle will require you to lean further as you respond to the counterleaning passenger.

One way to avoid this problem is to ask the passenger to not only lean with you, but to also look over your inside shoulder. If she does this, it will force her to lean with the bike. Having your passenger look in the direction where you are going will also help

Ask the passenger to not only lean with you, but to also look over your inside shoulder.

LESSON LEARNED

Passenger Pressures

Chris doesn't get out on his bike much anymore since he started renovating his house. But he is between projects and the forecast for today is great, so he talks his wife Jenny into going for a ride to one of their favorite lunch spots.

Chris's bike has been sitting for a few months, but it starts right up. He dusts off the helmets and climbs on board. Jenny has never been totally comfortable on the back of a motorcycle, but enjoys the experience nonetheless. As Chris rolls out of the driveway, he gets a disturbing sensation that the bike is floating. Chalking it up to not being in the saddle for so long, Chris continues to accelerate down the road.

On the curvy roads on the outskirts of town, Chris is alarmed by the way the bike feels in the corners, so he pulls over to ask Jenny to sit still, thinking she is the cause. She rebuts with a declaration of innocence, so Chris continues the ride.

Chris and Jenny reach the lunch destination, but wonder what is causing the unstable feeling when cornering. A fellow rider and his passenger pull up and park next to them at the restaurant. The rider strikes up a conversation about Chris's motorcycle and the quality of the nearby roads.

He seems knowledgeable enough so Chris asks his opinion about his concerns. The rider immediately suspects the tires and asks whether they have the proper amount of air pressure to support both Chris and his wife. Chris tells him that he hasn't ridden the bike in several weeks, but assumed the tires were fine. After all, they looked okay in the garage. Chris's new friend pulls out his tire pressure gauge and hands it to him. Chris presses the gauge onto the stem of the rear tire and it reads 21 pounds (1.4 kg)! He scans the area for a gas station and sees one down the street, so he and Jenny ride over and fill both tires to the proper level for a rider and passenger.

After a nice lunch, he and Jenny say goodbye to the rider with the tire gauge and get back on the road. Chris immediately notices how much better the bike feels.

WHAT'S THE LESSON?

By failing to check the tire pressures before the ride, Chris put himself and his wife in a dangerous situation.

her feel more comfortable while leaning. You can also ask her to hold onto your waist as an added measure to help her feel connected to you and lean with you.

These tips will help newer passengers feel comfortable with their first two-up rides, but it is unrealistic to think that they will feel comfortable at more extreme lean angles. Attempting to carve a corner fast with a nervous passenger can lead to an angry partner or even a mishap.

A nervous passenger's tension and likely counterweighting will require you to force the bike to lean further, which can potentially stress the tires enough to cause a slide. It can even cause reluctance for your bike to hold a tight enough line in a corner. Save your spirited cornering for another time when you are alone or when the passenger has gained the necessary comfort to allow sporty cornering.

Communication

It can be difficult to hear each other speak when riding at speed, so hand signals are often used to communicate important information. A double-tap of the shoulder can mean "I need to stop" or that the passenger is about to mount.

A very effective way to enhance communication is to install rider-to-passenger communicators that mount inside your helmets. These not only allow rider and passenger to communicate about important issues, but to also comment on interesting sights during the trip. These devices can add a great deal of convenience and enjoyment to your two-up rides. Just be sure to limit unnecessary chatter if distraction is an issue.

Passenger Practice

Before you head into traffic with your first passenger, it's a good idea to run through

A headset is a good way to communicate with your passenger.

some riding exercises in a parking lot with your passenger on board.

Start with how to mount and dismount the bike. First, make sure the passenger footpegs are in the down position and mount the machine. Place both feet firmly on the ground with your legs splayed wide for support and your butt firmly in the saddle. Squeeze the front brake firmly and then ask you passenger to get on board. Tell your passenger to wait until you give the signal to mount; otherwise, you may find yourself crashing down as your passenger steps onto the peg.

How your passenger mounts depends largely on the type of bike you own. A low-slung cruiser (without a backrest) may allow your passenger to swing her leg over the seat with the other foot still on the ground and then place both feet on the pegs. However, if the passenger has short legs or your bike is tall, then she will likely have to use the nearest footpeg as a step. This will throw the bike off balance, so you must be ready.

It may be possible for your partner to slide her leg over the saddle, scoot onto the seat, and then place her feet on the pegs. Another method is to have the passenger mount the bike first (with the sidestand down) and then scoot from the rider's seat backward onto the passenger pillion. Be sure that the bike is in first gear and hold the front brake to prevent the bike from rolling. Try various methods to find the one that suits you both. Dismounting should also be done carefully with a signal and careful shifts in weight.

Once your partner is seated, instruct her to remain as still as possible, especially when stationary or riding slowly. Remind her to keep her feet on the pegs and hold onto your waist or a grab rail. Instruct her to look over your inside shoulder when cornering. Go ahead and have her practice this as you pretend to corner left and then right. Mention how she must brace for braking and acceleration.

Once you have run through the basic steps, ride around the parking lot slowly to familiarize yourself and your co-rider with what it feels like to lean, swerve, and brake. Progress up to some harder braking and cornering, but don't go crazy and scare your passenger. If you and your partner plan to ride a lot together, it is smart to eventually be able to perform very advanced riding maneuvers with her on board. If you want formal training, some advanced safety courses encourage passengers to participate.

Effects on Handling

One thing you will notice in your practice session is how different your bike feels with a passenger. Some bikes manage the extra weight of a passenger better than others, but adding 120 or more pounds (54 kg) to the back of a bike will affect any bike's balance and handling, as well as its ability to stop and accelerate.

Before you consider riding with a passenger, be sure your bike is rated for the extra weight. Check your owner's manual for weight limits, which will include rider, passenger, and any luggage.

One way to help your bike manage the extra weight is to adjust the suspension. At the very least, you should increase the rear spring preload, which allows the spring to remain in the middle of its range of travel so the shock can absorb bumps without bottoming. Weak springs will still bottom if the weight is too great, so a stiffer spring rate will be in order. Fortunately, most modern motorcycles come with suspension that can handle average-weight passengers with a little adjustment.

With an educated passenger and suspension adjusted, you may be tempted to ride fast, the way you would if you were solo. Even if your passenger is willing and able to be on the back of your bike while you rip through the corners, think twice about riding fast with any passenger. The extra weight of a passenger affects stability and cornering in a way that can cause you and your bike to be stressed beyond your limits. You won't be able to stop or accelerate as quickly either, so it's best to give extra time and space to slow and go.

Riding with Children

Many parents want to share motorcycling with their kids. If you plan to ride with a child on board, be sure to follow all laws that may limit how young the child can be. Even if the child is old enough, you must follow a few guidelines to ensure his or her safety.

The most significant problems with riding with children are finding good protective gear and a helmet that fits properly and making sure they don't fall off! Understand that many children will fall asleep on the back of a bike, which is a very dangerous situation.

Be sure they can securely reach the footpegs and can hold on tight enough to resist the forces of swerving, braking, or acceleration. Some people use various aftermarket seats and straps to help keep their kids on board, but I cannot vouch for any of these products. It is up to the parent to evaluate whether the child is ready to be a passenger or if it's best to wait a few more years.

Whether you ride regularly with a passenger, or only occasionally, it is important that you take this responsibility very seriously. The consequences of a mishap are too great not to.

Chapter 13

Returning Riders and Aging

A large proportion of the riding population is made up of older riders. Some have been riding nonstop since they were kids, but most have had interruptions in their riding career and are returning to the sport they once knew. Let's take a look at some of the issues that returning riders and older riders face.

Returning Riders

Returning riders are made up of mostly middle-aged men who rode during a previous life before a mortgage and kids and are now eager to relive the experience of riding on two wheels. Unfortunately, returning riders represent a significant number of fatalities and injuries.

Many of these born-again riders are smart and mature enough to know that they should get some training. But many are not easily convinced that basic rider training is worth their time and money. They fall into the trap of thinking that their skills have survived intact so they can pick up where they left off, only to discover that riding is more complicated than they remember. Even though the basics of riding haven't changed much, motorcycles are more complex, and managing traffic has become more challenging than in years past.

Old Dogs

Returning riders surely need help tuning their rusty skills, but they also need help erasing outdated and inaccurate viewpoints about how to ride. Some returning riders hold onto antiquated notions about riding that are based on old myths. The concepts of "laying it down" or "never use the front brake" are two common myths that come to mind. These ineffective techniques survive from the bad old days when tires and brake technology made this form of "controlled crashing" a viable option. Today, only riders who are uneducated in the ways of proper braking consider using these techniques. Let's take a look at some of the issues that returning riders encounter and follow along as our imaginary friend, Kevin, returns to motorcycling.

The Process Begins

Kevin's coworker, Chris, is a longtime motorcycling enthusiast. Over the years, Kevin has enjoyed talking with Chris about motorcycles. Now that Kevin is ready to get back in the saddle, he decides to ask Chris' opinion on what motorcycle to buy. Chris is happy to help and offers to accompany Kevin to the motorcycle dealership.

Kevin is excited and suggests that they make a date for the following weekend. But Chris hesitates, explaining to Kevin that he should take a motorcycle safety course before buying a new motorcycle. That way, he can brush up on his skills and get a good feel for which motorcycle will best match his ability. Kevin is reluctant. After all, he didn't think he needed any training because he already knows how to ride.

False Confidence

Kevin is like many returning riders who assume that they can pick up where they left off years ago. It's great that Kevin has a working knowledge of motorcycle operation; however, this knowledge of basic operation is hardly enough for Kevin to hit the road safely.

Kevin will have little trouble with the most basic lessons of operating a motorcycle, but he will learn that there is a lot more to riding than simply making the motorcycle go, stop, shift gears, and go around simple corners. He'll learn that executing slow-speed maneuvers, mastering higher speed corners, and performing effective swerves and emergency stops are all necessary for staying safe. But even more critical is learning about effective strategies to survive on today's busy streets, such as efficient information gathering and the ability to predict likely outcomes and make good decisions.

If Kevin is like most returning riders, he will be surprised by how little confidence he feels after so many years away from two-wheelers. This is to be expected because motorcycle skills are a perishable commodity, and even experienced riders must work to keep their skills sharp. This is why Chris suggested that Kevin enroll in a rider-training course.

Rider Training

Kevin decides to take Chris's advice and sign up for a basic rider course. He arrives at the classroom skeptical that he will learn much but is willing to do all he can to make sure he is as safe as possible. The class starts with student introductions, which reveal that Kevin is not the only returning rider in the class.

The instructors explain the schedule and the curriculum before diving into a discussion about risk. This topic is a sobering reminder that motorcycling is a hazardous activity. The instructors make sure that everyone understands the gravity of their decision to ride and then promise to discuss methods to help manage the risks.

Out on the riding area, Kevin is soon challenged. One thing he has trouble with is trusting the front brake. When he rode years ago, he avoided using the front brake because he was told that it would cause him to flip over the handlebars. The instructors assure Kevin that proper use of the front brake is safe and that it is the best way to get a motorcycle to stop in the shortest possible distance. He's told that squeezing the lever progressively ensures adequate traction for maximum stopping maneuvers. After several practice runs, Kevin realizes just how effective the front brake is.

The rest of the weekend involves more classroom time talking about ways to manage traffic and roadway conditions. The second on-bike session allows students to practice more complex cornering situations and evasive maneuvers. In the end, Kevin is convinced that taking the course was a smart move.

Bike Shopping

Kevin thanks Chris for recommending the rider course and makes a date to have Chris help him choose his new bike. At the

Taking a course will help returning riders brush up on their skills, including how to manage traffic and roadway conditions.

dealership, Kevin and Chris immediately eye the newest performance machines. Dennis, the salesman, is happy to show Kevin the latest and greatest in sporting hardware. Chris notices that Dennis keeps pointing Kevin to the larger supersport motorcycles. Chris intervenes, reminding Dennis that Kevin is a returning rider and that a smaller bike is probably a better choice. Dennis seems to ignore this information, suggesting that because Kevin has ridden before, he should be able to handle the liter-sized motorcycles just fine. Chris pulls Kevin aside for a pow-wow.

Chris explains to Kevin that owning a less powerful motorcycle will minimize the chance that he will become overwhelmed and intimidated. At the other end of the spectrum, it is also possible that Kevin will try to use the massive power and ride faster than his skills can manage. Kevin wisely takes Chris's advice and decides to

Returning or aging riders should consider purchasing a less powerful bike.

purchase a more subdued middleweight sporting machine that Chris says will have all the performance he will need for the foreseeable future.

New Gear

Now that the motorcycle is chosen, it's time to select a helmet and jacket. At the accessories department, Kevin picks a helmet that matches his new bike. Back in the day, most people wore a simple open-faced helmet, but Kevin knows that a full-faced lid offers better protection. Besides, it complements the sporting style he is looking for.

Kevin tries on several different models and thinks he has found the helmet he wants. But before making a final decision, Chris checks the fit. After securing the strap, Chris asks Kevin to grab the helmet chin bar and move it around on his head. The amount of free movement demonstrates that the helmet is a bit too large. Kevin tries the next smaller size, which fits tighter around the head and makes good contact with his cheeks. Kevin is concerned that the smaller-sized helmet will be a bit too tight, but Chris explains that a properly fitted helmet should feel snug and that the liner will break in and the fit will loosen up a bit over time. After wearing the helmet for several minutes, Kevin decides that it will work out fine.

Shopping for jackets proves to be equally time-consuming. There are many styles and colors to choose from, but after trying on several brands, Kevin picks a nice leather jacket with trim that matches his new helmet and bike. Chris is fine with Kevin's choice, but points out that he might want to consider a nylon jacket that provides very good protection while offering many comfort and convenience features not found on most leather jackets. Kevin likes the look and feel of leather, so he decides to stick with his decision.

Kevin starts to walk away from the clothing department when Chris stops him. Chris points to a pair of leather pants that go with the jacket. Chris explains that the legs often suffer significant injury in a crash and strongly recommends that he consider buying some sort of leg protection. Kevin assumed that he would ride in jeans the way he did in the past. He isn't ready to commit to a full leather suit, but is convinced to purchase a pair of riding jeans embedded with Kevlar and lightweight armor. Chris approves.

Next on the list are gloves and boots. A nice pair of motorcycle boots with armor and Gore-Tex is selected, as are a pair of gauntlet gloves with knuckle armor and sturdy stitching. The bill for the riding gear is more than Kevin expected, but figures that the protection is worth the price. Chris wholeheartedly agrees.

The First Ride

It's a comfortably warm day when Kevin and his wife arrive at the dealership to take delivery of Kevin's new bike. Chris shows up a few minutes later on his own motorcycle to accompany Kevin on his first ride. Dennis wheels the shiny new bike out of the service bay and performs a quick briefing. After a few handshakes, Kevin straps on his new helmet and mounts his pride and joy.

Returning riders must invest in the latest safety gear.

Chris suggests that Kevin take a moment to get used to the new bike's brakes, clutch, and throttle before heading into traffic. Kevin agrees and proceeds to perform the clutch drill taught in the rider course. It takes a few tries for Kevin to become familiar with the clutch and to control the sensitive throttle.

Once he is satisfied with his performance, Kevin makes an effort to engage the clutch fully and ride across the parking lot. This goes smoothly, but when it comes time to turn, Kevin becomes anxious and abruptly grabs the powerful brakes, almost dropping the bike. Embarrassed, he quickly straightens the machine and makes a second attempt. This time, things go much better, but it is clear that this motorcycle is much different from the one he used in the training course and will take some time to get used to.

A few turning maneuvers later and Chris is satisfied that Kevin will be okay to proceed on their ride. After kissing his nervous wife goodbye, Kevin points his new ride toward the street and eases out the clutch. Chris follows, keeping an eye on his friend.

Chris knows that he cannot assume responsibility for Kevin's safety, but he can help reduce the risks by selecting a route with little traffic. Chris lets Kevin set the pace by having him lead and makes sure to follow at a distance that will not pressure Kevin to ride faster than he feels comfortable.

Things are going well. However, there are a couple of tense moments when Kevin barely avoids some sand in a corner and then almost loses balance while stopping at an intersection. He also notices that Kevin is positioning himself improperly in his lane so that oncoming cars cannot easily see him. There is work to be done.

They reach Kevin's house and his relieved wife greets them as they pull into the driveway. Kevin's smile is broad, and his excitement is intoxicating. After Kevin settles down, Chris decides to give Kevin some advice. He explains to Kevin that he needs to keep his eyes scanning further ahead to spot hazards and to predict problems and that keeping his eyes up also helps maintain balance.

Chris also stresses the importance of maximizing conspicuity and that lane positioning is an important tool for achieving that goal. Kevin remembers a discussion in his rider course about lane positioning and how it should be continually changing.

Kevin begins to realize that the transition from car driver to motorcycle rider will require a much higher level of hazard awareness, including being seen and avoiding road surface hazards that can rob traction—all things he rarely thought of when driving his car.

It is good news that Kevin understands that motorcycle skills are different from "car skills." Fortunately, information is readily available to help increase knowledge of survival strategies and motorcycle handling. And, if you're lucky, you have a friend like Chris to help you out.

Aging Riders

The average age of motorcyclists in the United States is rising, increasing from 40 in 2001 to 49 in 2010. The number of riders over the age of 50 is nearly 25%, compared to 10% back in 1990. One reason for this is that older riders continue to ride, but not as many young people are entering the sport.

With this increase in the average age of motorcycle riders, we can expect statistics to show more fatalities and injuries among older riders. And so it has. According to the National Highway Safety Administration (NHTSA), riders 40 and older made up 44% of motorcyclists killed in 2002, compared to 56% in 2011. That's a staggering increase over a 10-year period. In 2011, the average age of riders who were killed was 42.

Even if an older rider doesn't die in a crash, he or she is much more likely to be seriously injured compared to a younger rider. The numbers are backed up by a recent study from the peer-reviewed journal *Injury Prevention* stating that older bikers are three times as likely to be severely injured in a crash as younger riders. This means that an older rider is much more likely to suffer injuries that will affect the rest of his or her life; their aging bodies just cannot withstand trauma or heal as easily as when they were younger. Injuries that result in minimal damage to a youngster can become fatal to an aged body, and it takes a fewer number of cumulative injuries to cause a fatality.

Even if injuries are not fatal, older people experience much longer hospital stays compared to someone younger suffering the same injuries. Normal aging conditions can increase the risk of a severe injury—bones break and soft tissue tears more easily. Things get even riskier for older people who have preexisting medical conditions. Diabetes, heart conditions, and other ailments complicate treatment.

The message is that we must be aware that we aren't able to tolerate injury the way we used to and that the consequences of a seemingly simple misstep can add up to significant problems.

New Limits

We can't stop our facilities from diminishing, but we can slow the decline by staying healthy. Staying healthy means watching your diet and blood pressure, but also staying safe. First thing to do is recognize how your limits are changing and adjust your expectations to match the "new normal." This isn't easy because limits decline slowly, so it may be difficult to recognize that your reactions have slowed or your eyesight isn't as sharp as it once was.

Tissues in older adults contain less water, causing joints to become less elastic, which leads to stiffness, decreased mobility, and possibly arthritis. The discs between vertebrae in the spinal column become less

As we age, our eyesight diminishes.

flexible and more compressed, which can pinch nerves.

It's no secret that senses also diminish over time, including eyesight and hearing. While hearing is an important sense for identifying possible hazards, diminishing eyesight is of particular concern because our eyes are the primary tool used for gathering information about how to manage challenging traffic situations and roadway features. Focusing your eyes from closer objects to those far away takes more time. Nighttime vision also becomes more difficult, especially when adjusting to oncoming headlights and glare. As eyesight diminishes, we need to adjust our expectations by slowing down, especially when gathering complex visual information.

Some aging riders trade in their two-wheeled machines for three-wheelers.

Physical abilities, such as balance, flexibility, and strength, also diminish as we age, partially due to the slowing of nerve response and reflexes. Nerves are responsible for delivering information to our brain (or directly to the muscles via the spinal cord) to keep us in balance or to allow us to react to a hazard.

Keeping tabs on your physical condition is critical if you want to ride late in life. Mental condition is even more important. If judgment becomes impaired or response times increase because of cognitive decline, then the risk of being in a crash increases significantly.

Brain function is an area where the effects of aging vary depending on the lifestyle and health of the individual. In most people, the number of brain cells decrease as we age.

What to Do?

So, what's an aging rider to do? Well, you can try your best to delay the aging process by doing all the usual stuff … eat right, exercise,

all the things your doctor tells you. Too many of us ignore this advice. Maybe you'll take it more seriously if you knew that a poor diet and sedentary lifestyle might mean you have to stop riding before your time.

Staying healthy means more than low cholesterol and healthy blood pressure; it also means staying safe. There are many other ways to reduce the risk of getting hurt. One is to always wear high-quality protective gear that is brightly colored so you are as conspicuous as possible. Another is to make sure that your skills are up-to-date and sharp. This requires purposeful practice, either on your own in a parking lot or by attending a training course. I discussed earlier how track days are an excellent way to explore the limits of your bike and to improve your cornering skill.

Many older riders adopt a more relaxed attitude toward riding and choose to ride at a slower pace. This is a good thing for reducing stress and risk. In many cases, our senses *require* a slower pace, otherwise we risk riding beyond our ability or skill level. But riding slower is not a guarantee that we won't become involved in a crash. It's still important to develop and maintain excellent mental skills to avoid mishaps. If your ability to concentrate is diminished through fatigue or other age-related reasons, then it's smart to reconsider getting on your bike until your mind is up to the task. Be sure to take frequent breaks to help ensure that fatigue doesn't become a problem during a ride.

A Mature Machine

At some point, you may need to determine whether you need to consider a different bike for your capabilities. Once agile bodies may find the cramped ergonomics of sport

JUST TOO OLD?

At some point, all motorcycle riders will be forced to give up riding two-wheelers due to deteriorated abilities. Diminished coordination, eyesight, muscle strength, and cognitive abilities can each increase risk to a point when it is time to hang up the helmet. I do not look forward to the day when I must call it quits due to old age. Until that time, I plan to stay healthy and safe and take opportunities to enjoy riding like tomorrow may be my last.

bikes or the reclined posture of a cruiser no longer acceptable. Bad backs, poor circulation, and other weaknesses begin to dictate which motorcycle makes most sense.

Bar risers, lower footpegs, and taller windscreens can improve the comfort of an existing machine, while some older riders choose to purchase a new motorcycle with creature comforts and a more neutral riding position. Others choose to trade their two-wheeled machines for three-wheelers, such as a CanAm Spyder, a sidecar outfit, or a three-wheeled conversion to minimize the risk associated with balancing a motorcycle. There are various aftermarket contraptions available that are designed to stabilize a motorcycle, such as bolt-on retractable wheels, although I cannot vouch for their safety or effectiveness. Whatever bike you end up with, it is important that the motorcycle you ride is appropriate for your needs and abilities.

Chapter 14

Off-Road Riding

I recommend that every street rider experience off-road riding to help develop motorcycle control and traction management techniques. Encountering unpredictable surfaces when dirt riding trains the street rider to manage instability and minimize anxiety when his street motorcycle gets a little unstable. For example, in wet conditions, the rear tire may slip a little under acceleration. This can be scary, but if you have previous experience with instability, then you'll likely remain relaxed and manage the situation without much drama. However, a rider who has never felt this unstable sensation is more likely to panic and make matters worse.

Let's take a look at different off-road riding styles, discuss the benefits of off-road riding, and touch on considerations and techniques that are special to off-road riding.

Adventure, Trail, or Dual-Sport

There is a rather wide range of disciplines that fall under the off-road riding umbrella, including dual-sporting, trail riding, and adventure touring. A whole different category of off-road riding is enduro or motocross, which are usually competition and performance-based. We will discuss dual-sport, adventure, and trail riding, which are the most likely off-road riding styles that street riders might consider.

What is the difference between these three genres?

- **Dual-sport riding** combines both street and off-road riding using a street-legal machine that is designed to have some level of off-road capabilities.
- **Adventure touring** is a form of dual-sport riding done on larger machines that are at home doing long miles with the capability to explore relatively easy dirt roads along the way.
- **Trail riding** is done on terrain ranging from smooth fire roads to narrow, rocky, single-track trails with steep ascents and descents, as well as water and log crossings. Trail bikes are either smaller street-legal dual-sport motorcycles or enduro bikes that are not legal to ride on the street.

Types of Dual-Sport Machines

Some dual sport machines are capable of handling rugged single-track trails, while other machines are best kept on smooth gravel roads and pavement. Most off-road motorcycles feature large-diameter spoke wheels that allow the bike to more easily roll over rough terrain. The tires used may have knobby tread for the roughest off-road terrain or less aggressive dual-sport tread for a smoother ride on the road, but with marginal off-road capability.

Adventure bikes are designed to perform well on pavement and moderate off-road environments. Examples of big adventure bikes include the BMW R1200GS, Yamaha Super Tenere, Triumph Explorer, and KTM Adventure. The Suzuki V-Strom, Triumph

Dual-sport riding combines both street and off-road riding.

For riders who are interested in riding rougher terrain, a lighter machine is preferable.

Tiger 800, and Kawasaki Versys may appear to be off-road capable, but are best kept on the pavement. Middleweight adventure bikes like the BMW F800GS are also available for those wanting decent on-road comfort but less off-road heft.

Unfortunately, most adventure bikes are quite large and heavy for anything more than relatively flat, smooth off-road terrain. Yes, there are those who mount knobby tires on their 500+ pound (227 kg) adventure bikes and can negotiate gnarly sections of trail, but the average rider is better off limiting his or her adventures to easier topography.

For riders who are interested in riding rougher terrain, a lighter machine is preferable. Within this category is a range of machines with varying levels of on- and off-road capability. The venerable Kawasaki KLR650 can't be beat for its competence both on- and off-road. The Suzuki DR-z400 and DR650 are good choices for off-road ability, but at the expense of some road comfort. Going one step further toward more off-road capability is the Yamaha WR250R and KTM EXC dual-sport models. Smaller and less intimidating trail bikes, such as the Kawasaki KLX250s, Honda CRF250L, Yamaha XT250, and Suzuki DR-200S are great for newer off-road riders and those looking for causal off-road outings.

When choosing a bike, you must consider what percentage of your riding will be on-road and how much will be off-road. Yes, you can ride a lightweight dual sport on the highway, but you won't have much fun doing

it. Likewise, you will struggle and become quickly fatigued trying to manage a big bike on tight, technical trails. The best option is to have a dedicated off-road bike sharing the garage with your road machine.

If owning two motorcycles isn't possible, then find a motorcycle that offers the least compromises based on your specific needs. You may be able to modify or accessorize your motorcycle to perform better either as a trail bike or as a street bike. Aftermarket handlebars, levers, and footpegs can enhance off-road capabilities. And don't forget bike protection. Skid plates, crash bars, and radiator guards can help reduce engine and frame damage, and hand guards can minimize lever destruction and hand injuries.

Seat Height and Fit

One common problem a lot of people have with off-road motorcycles is the tall seat height. Some change suspension components to lower their motorcycle in an attempt to touch the ground with both feet. Unfortunately, this means reduced ground clearance that limits your ability to surmount larger obstacles.

A better solution is to learn to deal with the tall seat height. Putting your full body weight on the seat will compress the suspension somewhat to help you reach the ground. If it is still difficult for both feet to touch, you can shift your butt to the seat edge to allow one foot to support the bike. When parking, pick an area where there is a slight uphill slope and position your bike so one foot can extend to more easily reach to the ground.

To help the bike fit you better, adjust the handlebars, pedals, and levers. Because much of off-road riding includes both seated and standing positions, you must adjust the handlebars to accommodate an "elbow out" posture in both positions. Angle the bars and levers so that your reach feels natural when braking and using the clutch while standing. This usually means rotating the handlebars up and forward.

Getting Dirty

Riding off-road is physically demanding and requires agility, coordination, flexibility, and excellent balance to manage the rugged terrain. You will need to have enough coordination and agility to counterweight as the motorcycle slides and bounces beneath you and have the strength to stand on the pegs for minutes at a time. You also need to be fit enough to remain focused after hours

of bounding over rocks, plodding through sand, climbing steep hills, and raising a fallen bike.

Off-road riding will also challenge your ability to control a motorcycle in extreme conditions. You must learn to ascend or descend a rock-strewn hillside at less than 10 mph (16 kph) while standing on the footpegs. You may also need to be able to corner at higher speeds on a gravel road with your front tire hunting for grip and your rear tire spinning as you round the bend.

Before you dismiss off-road riding as too challenging, understand that most reasonably healthy people can endure the rigors of light to medium off-road riding. However, more severe riding venues will

Off-road motorcycling means getting wet and dirty.

indeed require greater fitness and skill to ensure maximum safety and enjoyment. Until then, stick to the easy stuff.

Falling Down

Off-road motorcycling means getting wet and dirty ... and you should expect to fall every once in a while. Even though off-road crashes are usually less serious that street crashes, the frequency of tipovers tends to be higher. Typical injuries usually consist of bumps, bruises, and perhaps a torn ligament or broken bone if you're unlucky. Because of these challenges, you should not ride alone without the help of someone to come to the rescue if necessary.

Having good skills can minimize falling. But for many, tipovers are a reality. Don't take your safety for granted. One way to do that is to protect your body with proper riding gear.

Dirt Riding Gear

Whether riding on the street or off-road, it's important to reduce the likelihood of injury by wearing protection. For casual off-road riding, you can use nylon street-riding gear. But for more challenging terrain and more aggressive riding, consider upgrading to sturdier off-road-oriented gear.

A full-faced helmet is the only way to go when riding off-road to protect your face and jaw from flying rocks and low-hanging branches. You can use a street helmet, a dirt-riding helmet, or a hybrid, which features the full-face shield with an extended chin bar and sun visor typically found on a dirt-riding helmet. Goggles are necessary when wearing a traditional dirt-riding helmet that does not have a built in shield. Sunglasses and eyeglasses do not offer enough protection from rocks, dust, dirt, and branches.

For trail riding, you can wear a lightweight motocross jersey and off-road pants with elbow and knee armor. For adventure riding, medium-weight street-based nylon jackets and pants, such as an Aerostitch suit, are acceptable. Protecting your torso from protruding sticks, flying rocks, and other hard objects means wearing some kind of armor. Armor at the shins, knees, elbows, forearms, back, and shoulders is critical. Armor can be built into the garments or strapped on. A chest/back protector can protect your upper torso from flying rocks, sharp objects, or a handlebar end. You can use a street-based armor vest underneath or a hard plastic motocross-style "roost" guard worn over a jersey.

Boots are one of the most important pieces of protective gear for off-road riding. Sturdy boots protect your feet, ankles, and shins from inevitable impacts with rocks and stumps and from injury when the bike lands on your leg. Heavy-duty motocross type boots offer the best protection, but are stiff. A hybrid dual-sport boot offers the right balance of protection and comfort if you plan to ride in rough terrain, but also need to do some walking.

Just because you can ride a street bike does not mean that you can swing a leg over a dual-purpose bike and safely hit the trails.

Gloves protect from debris and abrasion, as well as provide grip and comfort. Street riding gloves can be used when dual sport riding, but true off-road or motocross gloves offer better grip and lever feel and provide more durability than typical summer street gloves.

Off-road riding is athletic, so be sure to wear clothing that is appropriate. It's a good idea to wear layers that you can shed as the day becomes warmer. You may think that very lightweight gear is the way to go to prevent becoming overheated, but don't go so light that you compromise protection.

Off-road Techniques

Aspects of dual-sport riding are similar to street riding, but certain specialized riding techniques need to be learned. For example, riding a lightweight dirt bike means that much more of the steering is done with the footpegs and body. By positioning your body forward, rearward, and side to side, you influence direction control. Generally, you sit forward on the seat when riding an off-road bike to increase front tire traction and allow quick maneuverability.

You'll need to learn to ride while standing on the footpegs so your legs can act as shock absorbers. This can be tiring at first, until you learn the proper "neutral" position that keeps your body weight over the front of the fuel tank with knees slightly bent and elbows out.

The technique for maneuvering any motorcycle at slow speeds is to be loose so that the motorcycle can lean independently of your upper body for quick maneuvering. *Counterweighting* is when you let the bike lean beneath you, but you remain more or less upright. This keeps the center of gravity vertically over the tire contact area to maintain grip when traction is low. Unlike street riding, where your body is in line or inside the centerline of the motorcycle, when riding off-road, you will use counterweighting on almost every off-road corner. Push the bike down into corners, keeping your body on top of the upper edge of the seat. When riding on surfaces with good traction, such as pavement, it is fine to lean with the motorcycle, as you would on a full-sized street bike.

You will also learn to use the throttle and rear brake to change direction by breaking the rear tire loose under acceleration or when braking. It's scary at first, but once you learn these techniques, your confidence will grow quickly.

Off-road riding is athletic, so be sure you are reasonably fit.

The front brake offers the most braking power whether riding on or off road; however, the rear brake becomes more important when riding in the dirt. When traction is low, the amount of brake force is minimized, and forward load transfer is reduced. This means that the rear of the bike remains planted for more effective rear brake power. Another reason to favor the rear brake is to avoid a front tire skid, which must be avoided if you want to avoid a fall. Loose surfaces are unpredictable, so it's best to apply more rear brake pressure and modulate the front brake to avoid a skid.

There is a lot more to learn about off-road riding. Understand that just because you can ride a street bike does not mean that you can swing a leg over a dual-purpose bike and safely hit the trails.

Drills

A good way to get comfortable riding an off-road bike is to do some simple drills. First, get all of your protective gear and find a clean, paved parking lot where you can do some tight U-turns. Counterweight so that the bike leans beneath you, and your upper body remains upright. Weight the outside footpeg and the outside edge of your seat as you push the inside handlebar forward and down. Look through the turn and control the speed using your rear brake and clutch, keeping the throttle in a fixed position. Repeat in both directions until you can make tight U-turns while remaining in balance.

Next, repeat the U-turn exercise while standing up. The neutral standing position has your arms slightly bent, with elbows out and your knees against the tank. Your body weight should feel balanced over the steering stem. When performing U-turns,

let the bike lean independently of your upper torso by bending sideways at the knees and hips.

Repeat both U-turn drills in a dirt or grassy area. The bike will feel more unbalanced as it rolls over surface irregularities. Relax and use smooth, steady drive to balance the motorcycle.

More advanced drills are practiced on dirt and are designed to acclimate you to breaking the rear tire loose by twisting the throttle or applying the rear brake to help turn the bike. Ride an oval slowly while sitting. As you round the corner, lean the bike beneath you and quickly twist the throttle enough to cause the rear tire to spin. Be sure to counterweight, relax your arms, and let the rear of the bike drift outward. Gradually increase throttle intensity until you can drift the rear tire out a foot or two. Next, do the same while standing up.

Then, find a hill that you can ascend and descend. Ascending a steep hill is usually done by standing on the pegs and leaning forward over the handlebars. Descending can be done sitting or standing, but be sure to pivot yourself backward over the rear part of the seat to keep your weight over the rear wheel. Gently apply both front and rear brakes, but favor the rear brake to avoid a front tire skid. For more drills, I recommend you look at Shane Watts' DVD, *DirtWise*.

As you can see, off-road riding is fun and challenging. It is demanding on the mind and body, and it tests your physical and mental fortitude. In other words, it's just the thing for people who love to try new things and enjoy new challenges.

Chapter 15

Track Days:
The Best Way to
Advance Your Riding

Imagine a place where there are no speed limits so you can go as fast as you want without the risk of getting an expensive speeding ticket and insurance points. Not only that, but the place you get to ride resembles the most perfect twisty road with no sand, gravel, guardrails, old folks in big sedans, or texting teens. Sounds fun, doesn't it? That's what awaits you if you attend a track day.

You may think that attending a track day is not a good fit for your interests or riding style. I contend, however, that any rider, regardless of the bike ridden or the preferred riding style, will benefit greatly by attending a well-run track day that caters to street riders. I'd like to clear up a few myths about track days and then paint a picture of what a typical track day is like so you will seriously consider participating in a track day.

RIDING TERM
TRACK DAY

A motorcycle event where riders pay to ride their motorcycle on a racetrack. Track days provide an opportunity for street riders to improve control skills in a noncompetitive environment free of typical street riding hazards.

Riders seem to fall into a few different camps when it comes to track days:

- Those who don't know that track days exist.
- Those who will never be convinced of the benefits of riding on a racetrack because they assume it's only for hooligans or racer wannabes.
- Those who ride fast on the street and think this is okay because they have yet to feel the pain of the inevitable consequences.
- Those who know better than to rip up the streets but think that track days are competitive race events, so they stay away.
- Those who try a track day and discover that there is no better place to improve cornering and braking and return a couple times a season to keep their skills sharp.
- Those who try a track day and are hooked for life.

Common Excuses

Here are some common excuses why riders don't do track days:

- *I don't have proper riding gear.* Yes, you need to protect your body in the event of a crash, but that's a good investment whether you ride on the track or the street. Most track day organizations allow standard armored street gear in the novice group. However, a rigid back protector may be required.
- *I am worried about crashing my bike.* As I mentioned earlier, it can happen. But if you ride within your ability and your bike's capabilities, you'll likely be fine.
- *I'll be the slowest rider out there.* You just might be, but so what if you are? Some egos can't handle being the "slow guy," but you'll get faster as the day goes on and will likely be passing people before you know it. It's important not to base your speed on trying not to look slow. This will only lead to a crash. Be comfortable at the level you're at and ride within that level. You'll gain more respect than if you try to show you're better that you are and end up tossing your bike down the track. Remember: Slow first, Fast second!
- *I don't have a way to get to the track.* Many organizations have a forum or Facebook page where you can ask for help getting your bike and yourself to the track. If it comes down to it, just ride your bike there. Bike prep is usually minimal, and much of it can be performed at the track. The downside is that you are risking crashing the vehicle you expect to get you home. You'll also be tired after a day on the racetrack, but many people do it.
- *I don't ride a sport bike.* You don't need the latest rocket sport bike to attend a track day. All types of bikes show up at track days ... sport tourers, adventure bikes, standards, vintage bikes, even the occasional Gold Wing and cruiser. Check with the organization to make sure they

don't have restrictions about what motorcycles they allow, but, in many cases, if you can ride it on the street, you can ride it on a racetrack. No matter what you choose to ride, make sure it is in good condition.

● *Track days are too expensive. Why should I pay to ride someplace?* It makes little sense to risk serious injury, a speeding ticket, and insurance points by pushing the limits on the street rather than pay to ride on the track. The cost of a track day varies from region to region and from track to track, but you can expect to pay anywhere from $150 to more than $300 per day. This often includes some instruction.

● *I'm not comfortable doing a track day yet.* Maybe you're just nervous. If so, then rest assured that you're not alone. A good guideline is to have a season of street miles under your belt, but if you're comfortable riding around corners at brisk street speeds, then you're probably ready to do a track day. Many organizations allow spectators to come check out an event. This is a great way to see if it might be right for you.

Any rider will benefit greatly by attending a well-run track day that caters to street riders.

Safety

One of the most common reasons people are afraid to do a track day is because they are afraid to crash. Although it is true that crashes happen, the chances of crashing are no greater on a racetrack than on the street, as long as you ride within your limits. And if you do crash, you're much better off doing it on the track. With no surface hazards, oncoming vehicles, or roadside obstacles to hit, serious injuries are rare. If a mishap does occur, an ambulance is just seconds away, making the track the safest place to ride, especially if you want to ride fast.

The reason why most track day crashes happen is because the person was riding beyond his or her ability to manage the limits of the higher speed and available traction. Traction is as good as it gets when the track is dry and the tires are warm. What gets riders into trouble is their inexperience with high-speed cornering. But, you'll likely be okay if you don't rush things and learn how to go fast *before* you go fast.

Track days allow you to go fast without the pressure of competition.

It's Not Racing

When I suggest to riders that they could benefit from a track day, they often reply "but I don't want to race." I understand that most people automatically think "racing" when they hear "racetrack," however, a track day is not a race event.

Track days and racing share one thing in common—you can go as fast as you safely dare. Racing is inherently risky because your goal is to try to beat the next guy. But track days are different because they allow you to go fast without the pressure of competition.

Track Days are Fun

I don't know too many motorcycle riders who don't like to "open 'er up" from time to time, and the racetrack allows you to do that all day long, and you won't get a ticket for breaking a speed limit. Yes, you are free to let it rip on the straights, but the real fun is in the corners. There is no better way to find the illusive "Zone" than to seamlessly string a series of corners together without the dangers and distractions typical on the street.

Another great benefit of attending track days is the camaraderie that comes from socializing with other motorcyclists who are there to have fun and thrive on the challenges of mastering the track. Most new track day riders show up for their first day nervous and afraid, only to find a friendly group of fellow riders eager to help them learn the ropes.

Concentrated Learning

Track days are fun, but it is also the best place to develop your braking, cornering, shifting, and accelerating skills and to explore the limits of your bike and tires. Many track days offer instruction, including classroom time and perhaps a garage seminar on body positioning. On-track coaching may be available if you ask for it.

Circulating around the track allows you to visit the same corners over and over so you can practice what you learned in the classroom and perfect the challenges that each corner offers. Compare that to riding on the street, where it's impractical to try to revisit the same corner until you get it right.

My daughter Jeannine and I both enjoy track days!

Track days are not all about speed. Yes, we are talking about riding on a racetrack, but that doesn't mean you have to go flat out. Many track day organizations accommodate people who want to go only a little faster than they already do on the street (the novice group).

No matter what group you ride in, it's best to ride at no more than about 80% of your ability. Once you become more familiar with the track and the higher lean angles, then your pace can be increased. This may take all day, or it may not be until a second or third visit to the track when that level of comfort allows you to safely ride faster. How do you measure whether you're riding within your limits? Basically, if you are tense, then you are going too fast. Slow down, gather up your thoughts and emotions, and work on being smooth. The speed will come in time.

Shop Around

There are many different track day organizations to choose from, each with a different philosophy about how a track day should be run and whom they market to. Many track day organizations cater to the aggressive sport bike rider or wannabe racer with few rules to keep the intensity at bay. Passing can happen anywhere and everywhere. Track day events like this are not what I recommend for a first-time track day rider or street rider who has a less aggressive attitude toward motorcycle riding.

Instead, look for track day organizations that discourage aggressive riding and cater to the average street rider who just wants to have fun and learn how to ride better without the stress of sharing the track with aggressive riders. The organization I work for, Tony's Track Days, is one of these friendlier track day organizations that focus less on speed and ego and more on education and safety. One way to accomplish this is the three-group format that keeps slower and faster riders in different time slots and provides a new rider's program that allows new track riders to learn the ropes with less stress.

Conclusion

Before we part, I would like to leave you with some advice that I hope will help you on your journey to become the most proficient motorcyclist possible.

Be a Thinker

Being a thinking motorcyclist means making conscious decisions about risk management. This is one of the biggest reasons why I've survived all these years on two wheels.

Thinking riders consider what they wear, where they ride, and the consequences of their behavior. These riders are also able to accurately measure their strengths and weaknesses. They can evaluate whether their habits and behaviors are in line with their values and goals. They can pinpoint areas where a tune-up is needed and are not prone to blaming others for mishaps that could have been avoided with a little forethought.

Thinking about your choices and actions is critical for safety, but don't overthink things to the point where you become disconnected from why you began riding in the first place—enjoyment. The trick is to balance thinking with the ability to tune in to the often quiet, visceral sensations that transform motorcycle riding into an almost spiritual experience.

Accept Risk

Asking you to accept risk may sound like I'm telling you to *take risks*. It is not. It is a call for you to understand what amount of risk you are willing to accept and then live and ride within that level of risk acceptance. The goal is to align your values with your actions.

We all know that riding a motorcycle is risky. But are your choices based on this reality? The simple, but difficult act of admitting to yourself that straddling a two-wheeler increases the likelihood of harm should prompt you to do all you can to minimize the risk as best you can.

And, for goodness sake, don't make riding more risky than it already is by drinking and riding! You owe it to yourself and your loved ones to learn survival strategies, practice your skills, and keep your behavior in check. Are you willing to do what it takes to make this happen?

Resist Complacency

Complacency can compromise safety by lulling you into thinking your skills are adequate. This can lead to an inaccurate and dangerous sense of self-confidence and ability. Keep a close eye on whether you are slipping into a complacent state of awareness and wake yourself up ASAP.

Complacency can also erode enjoyment if it causes you to fall into a rut. This is common among veteran riders who identify with a single type of bike or riding style. To combat complacency, seek new riding venues and genres. This may mean trying off-road riding or long-distance touring, or perhaps racetrack riding or city cruising. You may also try riding a different type of motorcycle.

Rent a cruiser if all you know is sport bikes. You just may find it refreshing to ride in a different way. Renew your relationship with motorcycling by shaking things up, and you'll rediscover that spark that may have dulled over time.

Keep Learning

One sure-fire way to fend off complacency is to keep learning. Unfortunately, many motorcycle riders think it is unnecessary to develop their mental and physical skills beyond what they consider to be adequate and go no further to improve the skills they have.

It often takes a close call to realize that their skills may not be sufficient to handle complex braking or cornering situations. This wake-up call can go two ways: it can either scare you enough to cause you to stop riding, or it can jumpstart your skill development. Motorcyclists who are motivated to develop their skills after a mishap soon discover that being prepared for hazards not only makes them safer, but also increases confidence and fun.

It may be difficult to realize, but even very experienced and proficient riders have more to learn. You must remember that riding skills are perishable if neglected. Yes, keeping your skills current and sharp can seem like work, but the rewards are well worth it…for you and the ones who love you. Keep learning how to be safer and more skillful, and you'll enjoy riding more and increase the odds of living a long and fruitful life.

Inspire and Mentor Others

Consider sharing your knowledge with fellow riders by being a mentor. Being a mentor does not have to be a big deal. It can mean taking a newbie under your wing for a ride or to help him or her learn the ropes at a track day. Small gestures can make a big difference in helping a new rider have a positive experience and possibly avert disaster.

Patience, consideration, and knowledge are keys to good mentoring. Even if you possess these traits, it doesn't mean you're the best person for the job. If you don't feel qualified to mentor, point them in the direction of someone who may be better at the task. You can also suggest other venues for learning, such as training courses or track days that offer instruction. There are also a myriad of books on the market meant to help riders improve their skills, including my book *Riding in the Zone* and the *Riding in the Zone* blog.

If you decide to mentor someone, consider these mentoring basics. First, recognize whether or not your efforts are welcome. Not all riders are open to guidance, and forcing your advice on someone is usually unproductive. Once you're reasonably sure the rider is open to your advice, put your ego aside. Remember that the goal is to help riders improve their skills, which means tuning into their needs, not indulging yours.

Avoid forcing your opinions too strongly. Share your experience and wisdom in a way that is easily understood and tolerated. Sometimes being a mentor simply means listening to stories and sharing your own experiences. If a rider tells about how he had to "lay his bike down" to avoid a crash, you may be tempted to come out and say "you're wrong." Instead, share your own story that illustrates the correct way to handle the situation.

Advice is best absorbed if the motivation comes from the receiver, so wait for an opening if possible. But, sometimes you must intervene to avert catastrophe. If that becomes necessary, be gentle yet firm as you try to enlighten the rider. This tough love could just save a life.

There is no doubt that mentoring can benefit individual riders. But, mentoring can also contribute to improving safety and enjoyment of all motorcycle riders as more people become enlightened by the wisdom shared by experienced riders like you. It will change the life of both you and the person or people you mentor.

Be an Example

Even if you don't think you're up to the responsibility of mentoring, you can still encourage and inspire other riders simply by being an example. New riders are easily influenced by more experienced riders, so ride in a way that reflects positively on motorcyclists. Demonstrate respect for the public by riding quietly and in a responsible manner and wear full protective gear to demonstrate sensible decisions and respect for the risks of riding.

These are probably things you already do, but when you think about how your choices and behavior influence others, then it takes on new meaning. No need to preach about ATGATT or the problems with loud pipes; just behave the way you see fit and perhaps this will influence a new rider to reject the more unsavory behaviors of others.

Being a lifelong learner is another way to not only improve your survival strategies and control skills, but also encourage others to do the same. Talk about how riding courses or track days helped you become a more confident and better rider.

Support Motorcyclist Safety's Future

In the coming years, you will likely hear about new and controversial proposals about how to revamp rider education in the United States. Many motorcyclists will be thankful for these proposed changes, thinking that this is long overdue. But many more will resist changes to the status quo, especially if it hints at making it more difficult to obtain a full motorcycle license. I understand the resistance. However, current methods of training aren't reducing fatalities and injuries the way the motorcycle safety experts hoped, which means that new ways must be considered.

I've been a Motorcycle Safety Foundation (MSF) Instructor/RiderCoach for 20 years and have been an advocate for the MSF's efforts during that time. But, it's time to reassess training underpinnings and methods. I have no delusions that motorcycling will ever be "safe," but there are too many tragic mishaps that might have been prevented with a more stringent training process.

Tougher standards may deter less-committed people from buying and riding a motorcycle, which will surely reduce fatalities. But, fewer butts in seats will also be a blow to the motorcycle industry that will fight hard to maintain sales numbers by keeping the current model of easy licensing intact. State governments will also put up a fight as politicians try to placate constituents who demand easy access to a motorcycle license. Law enforcement may also complain as they imagine dealing with an increase in the number of people willing to ride unlicensed. Even state motorcycle safety programs will resist because they've invested heavily in the current model.

Coming up with a more effective training solution will not be easy or instantaneous. But, over time, there will be a higher quality of riders, which means that fewer people will die and fewer families will suffer. Politicians will brag about the positive outcomes and the motorcycle manufacturers will spend less time fighting litigation. Motorcycling will then become more attractive, and I'll bet the number of licensed riders will eventually rebound.

What I'm asking of you is to keep an open mind about new rider training proposals. But, before you choose to support a particular program, look carefully at the motivations of the involved people and organizations. Not every player will have motorcycle riders' best interests in mind. Educate yourself about proposals, and write your state legislators in support of programs you feel are on the right track.

That's a Wrap

Well, I guess that's it. Please take your riding seriously. It's easy to put skill development and maintenance on the back burner, but these skills are perishable and need to be kept fresh. So make a point to take a quick trip to the local high school parking lot to practice from time to time.

Thank you all for giving me your ear. I hope I was able to help you to ride safer and have more fun. See you on the road!

Index

bold denotes photo; *f* denotes figure

Photo Credits

Shutterstock: Mindscape studio, 1, 71; Dudarev Mikhail, 3; Anna Omelchenko, 9; phadventure, 11; BestPhotoStudio, 14; Orientaly, 17, 27 (bottom); wawritto, 20; ChameleonsEye, 21; 1000 Words, 40; Evikka, 43; Christian Mueller, 47, 146; Alexander Erdbeer, 61; Yelena Panyukova, 64; Art Konovalov, 53; Dasha Petrenko, 69; Carlos Caetano, 73; tezzstock, 75; Dasha Petrenko, 83; pudiq, 93; Andrey Armyagov, 101, 155; stockphoto mania, 126; vtwinpixel, 131; roibu, 137; Milos Muller, 142; Liz Van Steenburgh, 144; ToskanaINC, 148; Johnny Adolphson, 159; BoydzPhotoz, 164; Panuwat Phengkhumphu, 173; fastfun23, 175; Laurie L. Snidow, 176; Kaspri, 178; NikoNomad, 179; ToskanaINC, 181; Denis Kuvaev, 188; Marques, 191 (top right); auremar, 191 (bottom); Lindsay Basson, 192; Bocos Benedict, 193; Steiner Wolfgang, 197; Alexey Losevich, 199; Ljupco Smokovski, 201 (bottom); i4lcocl2, 204; Merkushev Vasilly, 211 (bottom); PhotoStock10, 214; Yarygin, 218; David Acosta Allely, 221 (top left)

Annalisa Boucher: 7

Ken Condon: 5, 13, 18, 19, 22, 25, 27 (top right and left), 28, 29, 32, 34, 36, 39, 41, 42, 43 (bottom), 44, 48, 50, 52, 56, 59, 66, 71 (top left), 72, 77, 79, 81, 83 (top left and right), 85, 87, 88, 89, 91, 93 (top left) 94, 96, 100, 102, 104, 106, 108, 110, 113 (top right, bottom), 114, 116, 117, 119, 120, 122, 123, 124, 125, 129, 131 (top left), 132, 133, 134, 138, 139, 140, 151, 156, 157, 163, 161, 166, 169, 182, 183, 187, 194, 195, 201 (top left and top right), 203, 205, 207, 208, 211 (top left and right), 212, 213, 215, 216, 217, 221, (top right), 223, 224, 225, 227, 231, 240

Jenni Eiswerth: 221 (bottom)

OwensTrackDayPhotos.com: 221 (bottom), 227

Kevin Wing Photography: 113

Front cover: Andrey Armyagov/Shutterstock

Back cover: OwensTrackDayPhotos.com

About the Author

Ken Condon has been riding for over 40 years. He has 20 years of experience as a certified Motorcycle Safety Foundation instructor/ coach, 15 years as a track day instructor, and 3 years as owner of Riding in the Zone Motorcyclist Training. He is the author of the book *Riding in the Zone: Advanced Techniques for Skillful Motorcycling* and has written more than 250 skills and safety articles for *Motorcycle Consumer News*, including the "Proficient Motorcycling" and "Street Strategies" monthly columns. Ken currently writes the "Street Savvy" column for *Motorcyclist Magazine*.